LANGUAGE OF SPACE AND FORM

LANGUAGE OF SPACE AND FORM:

GENERATIVE TERMS FOR ARCHITECTURE

James Eckler

John Wiley and Sons

Library of Congress Cataloging-in-Publication Data:
Eckler, James, 1982–
  Language of space and form : generative terms for architecture / James Eckler.
    p. cm.
  Includes bibliographical references and index.
  ISBN 978-0-470-61844-8 (cloth) ; ISBN 978-1-118-10342-5 (ebk); ISBN 978-1-118-10343-2 (ebk); ISBN 978-1-118-10532-0 (ebk); ISBN 978-1-118-10533-7 (ebk); ISBN 978-1-118-10534-4 (ebk)
  1. Architectural design—Terminology. I. Title. II. Title: Generative terms for architecture.
  NA2750.E34 2012
  720.1′4—dc22
                        2011010955

978-0-470-61844-8

Printed in the United States of America

10 9 8 7 6 5 4 3 2 1

CONTENTS

ACKNOWLEDGMENTS

I would like to personally thank all of my colleagues at Marywood University and the University of Cincinnati, friends, and family that have helped and supported this effort. I would especially like to thank the institutions, faculty, and students that have contributed images to this project. It is through their talent and commitment to the discipline that such exemplary work has been produced to fill the pages of this text. Wherever possible, authors of works have been identified. Every reasonable attempt has been taken to identify and credit the owners of copyright. Any errors or omissions will be corrected in future editions.

Institutions and faculty whose students have produced work contributing to this text:

Arizona State University
Milagros Zingoni, Lecturer

Louisiana State University
Michael Hamilton, Assistant Professor
Jim Sullivan, Associate Professor

Louisiana Tech University
Tim Hayes, Associate Professor

Marywood University
James Eckler, Assistant Professor
Stephen Garrison, Assistant Professor
Reagan King, Adjunct Professor
Matthew Mindrup, Assistant Professor
Kate O'Connor, Adjunct Professor

Miami University
John Humphries, Assistant Professor

University of Cincinnati
James Eckler, Visiting Assistant Professor
John Humphries, Adjunct Professor
Karl Wallick, Assistant Professor

University of Florida
John Maze, Associate Professor

University of North Carolina, Charlotte
Peter Wong, Associate Professor

University of Southern California
Valery Augustin, Adjunct Assistant Professor
Lauren Matchison, Lecturer

Valencia Community College
Jason Towers, Adjunct Professor
Allen Watters, Professor

INTRODUCTION: ON THE ROLE OF WORDS IN THE DESIGN PROCESS

What is a generative term? And what role does it play in the process of design?

Words are tools for architectural design. They engage each step of the design process—at the conception of intent, the generation of spatial conditions, the representation of elements, and the communication of ideas in a resolved project. In this way, they have the capacity not only to illustrate what has been done but also to generate the ideas that direct what is to be done.

The language of design is not one of identification, but of intention: what something *does* can be more important than what it *is*. This language has the ability to do more than just identify the components that make up our environment; it has the ability to challenge designers to consider the role those components play in the operation of space.

The words presented in this book are used frequently in the architectural design discipline. These words are intended to be a point of departure for two things: discussion and conception. Discussion is an avenue toward realizing the possibilities of design, and conception is a process of thought derived from that realization. It is through discussion (either the exchange of ideas among peers, or the introspective questioning of one's own ideas) that the possibilities presented by various techniques, elements, or positions in architecture can be considered in the development of space. This is the foundation of architectural conception. These possibilities define a framework for study and testing. They also provide a trajectory for advancement through an iterative process of making. A word can define an intention for spatial operation or experience, a strategy for the development of spatial systems, or a technique for testing spatial qualities. The language of space and form is a language for architectural thinking.

How can a term be used as a design tool?

The terminology of design acts as a tool for the development of design intent or strategy. The language of space and form is a language that allows a designer to read and understand space, as well as to construct the ideas that drive its creation. The language of space and form is generative in that it does more than describe architectural gestures: it has the potential to be a foundation for their invention. A generative term is a catalyst for thought and inquiry, for exploration and discovery. A generative term is one that opens up possibilities for design and frames an intention for making space and crafting form. A generative term is a starting point—a position on what the architecture should be.

This book divides terms into five facets of architectural thinking: process and generation, organization and ordering, operation and experience, objects and assemblies, and representation and communication. These categories are not ordered to describe a sequence for the design process. Instead, they are to be considered, more often than not, as overlapping or interdependent. For instance, generative strategies can rarely be used independently of an ordering system to define limits. These categories become useful as a means of codifying design intent—for defining a role that a particular word might play in your own way of thinking about design. They speak to the various ways architects think of space and its creation, from the acts of thinking and making to the reading and interpreting of existing spaces. They are codified this way to act as guide for the development of the design process. Each word is a starting point for imagining and developing ideas for creating form and space.

The **process and generation** terms outline modes of thought or ways of making in the creation of form and space. For a designer, thinking and making go hand in hand. With that in mind, many of these terms will describe techniques for making that might be used to frame a process

1

of thought. Others may refer to an intellectual strategy as a guide for the making of space. Use these terms to articulate a goal or intent for the space that is to be designed, or to formulate a strategy by which that goal can be achieved.

The **organization and ordering** terms refer to strategies for inventing relationships between forms and spaces. This could be a system for deciding which elements are more important than others in a design. Or it could be a system for arranging spaces, functions, or form to achieve a desired outcome. Terms that define techniques for organizing elements of a design can also bring clarity or resolution to an idea. Use these terms to define the ways in which different elements of a design might interact with one another—physically, spatially, or functionally.

The **operation and experience** terms describe ways that an occupant might perceive or interact with form and space, as well as design intention for creating spaces that facilitate that perception or interaction. These are the descriptors of architecture's ability to engage the senses. They define the influence that sensory experience can have over design process and intent. Operation and experience represent specific aspirations of architecture. They have the potential to be catalysts for both thinking and making. They can direct the design process by establishing a set of conditions to be created in space and form. Utilize these terms as descriptors to generate the intent of a project, or even a single space. Use them as a way of directing conception of space as well as a means to evaluate results.

Objects and assemblies terms refer to strategies for the use of physical elements to construct or define space. These terms define formal typologies and form-based strategies for design. Additionally, they address joint-making and object relationships as components of the design process. Use these terms to describe the influence of formal qualities on the creation of space. They may also be used to explore the many possible roles that a joint might play in the creation of space, possibilities that move beyond the act of connecting one object to another.

The **representation and communication** terms present possible ways in which ideas of space and form are communicated through the act of making. These terms address the communication of ideas as a connection between the ways that form and space is understood and the ways that it is made. Use these terms to guide production of design so that in making space, you might better understand that space.

Process goes hand in hand with speculation. Questions test the possibilities of space, experience, operation, and construction. Questions lead the designer to discover what something *can be* instead of identifying what it *is*. A generative term is not a static definition, but a starting point for that speculation. Preconceptions in the reading of the built environment are undone through critical speculation. In keeping with this spirit of exploration and discovery, the words and categories presented here are by no means canonical or absolute. In many cases words may fit into multiple categories, as there may be multiple potential roles for them in a design process. In those instances other possibilities for the term are suggested.

There may also be (and should be) possibilities for a term that are not addressed here. There may be other categories, or subdivisions within a category, that evolve as students better understand their own way of thinking. To this end students should add their own notes, sketches, or additional entries to this text. This document, as well as the techniques and thoughts described within, should evolve with the student. New applications of a word to the process of making or conceiving of space should be recalled in later design efforts. As discoveries are made that relate to a word, they should be recorded for later use. This expansion in the understanding of a word's ability to be applied to the generation of architecture is important to the advancement of a designer's architectural process. Generative terminology is a guide for exploration as opposed to a reference to static preconceptions. Language is malleable.

This book is a guide for the development of design process and intended to follow students as they advance. It is a studio companion through the foundation levels and beyond. Every entry has multiple stages of information regarding the word at hand in order to engage students at multiple points in their academic careers. The entries will contain the definition of the word in the strictest sense in order to link the term to the common, conversational use that a foundation student might reference. Additionally, each entry will present a short narrative, and many are supported by images of student work to begin the process of exploring possibilities for that word in design. The images presented are those from design students in their first or second year of design studio education. They are meant to illustrate the use of the term as a design that other students can readily understand and access. Each entry will also have a text that will guide students in more advanced investigations of the term as they move beyond the foundation levels of design.

It is intended to provide additional inspiration for continuing to test ideas related to the term, its connotations, or its previous manifestations. Principally, this is a field guide for architecture students, allowing them to explore new avenues for their creativity. These generative terms will become tools, among many others, that students will develop for conceiving and interpreting architectural space. Those tools will open up many possibilities for creating architecture. Generative terminology will contribute to a more versatile process of design.

1. TERMS OF PROCESS AND GENERATION

Student: Cari Williams—Critic: James Eckler—Institution: Marywood University

ABSTRACT

To represent a subject in a way that is not pictorial or responsible for documenting its actual existence

Abstraction: An interpretation of a subject based upon a study of particular characteristics

Generative Possibilities in Non-Figural Representation

The drawing was an abstraction of a real subject—in this case, the plan of a building. It didn't look like the building; it didn't seem to conform to the image of the building at all. Instead, it revealed how the designer was thinking about the structure. The intention behind its composition seemed to be to study organization or spatial relationships. Abstraction was used to document a process of thought that ultimately led to a new design. Even though a casual observer might not be able to understand it entirely, it was a useful tool for the designer, a tool used to understand the old and to create the new.

The origin of the word *abstract* is the Latin *abstractus*, which means "to draw away." To make something abstract is to represent it in a nonliteral way: to deviate from the actual. Everything that designers produce, from conception to the development of a design, is a form of abstraction. Drawings, models, and diagrams reduce a reality into a representation, and therefore an abstraction.

How can design benefit from representation that moves away from actuality? Since each stage of a design process is an investigation that tests possibilities of space and form against a generating idea, abstraction is a means for defining the scope of the study. For instance, abstraction might be used to focus the study on one particular idea, composition, or set of relationships; it may be used to spotlight typology, configuration, or function, or to define a language for representing any of the above. It is a method that has the potential to exclude superfluous information so that the subject of study is not diluted in the information that is gained. As a method, it is able to frame a process of thought in a way that facilitates iteration. It is a way of simplifying complex information sets, or focusing a study on information of particular relevance.

Through abstraction, a designer might be able to recognize possibilities that were previously not considered. Those discoveries drive subsequent investigations, which is the foundation of an iterative design process. When a representation is not abstract—that is, when it is figural—capturing the reality of the subject becomes a goal unto itself. That finality has the potential to limit discovery and undermine the iterative process.

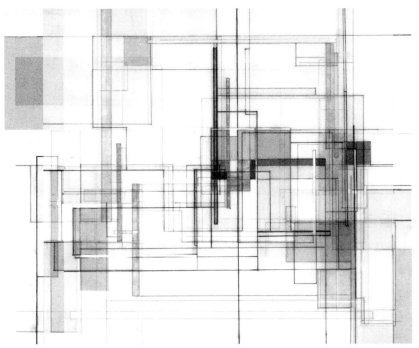

Figure 1.1. In this analytical mapping the student uses abstract graphic language to indicate relationships between elements of a composition. Components of the subject of analysis are reduced to orthogonal figures (an act of abstraction) in order to more easily identify relative position, alignment, overlap, and other instances of compositional relationship. STUDENT: TAYLOR ORSINI—CRITIC: JOHN MAZE—INSTITUTION: UNIVERSITY OF FLORIDA

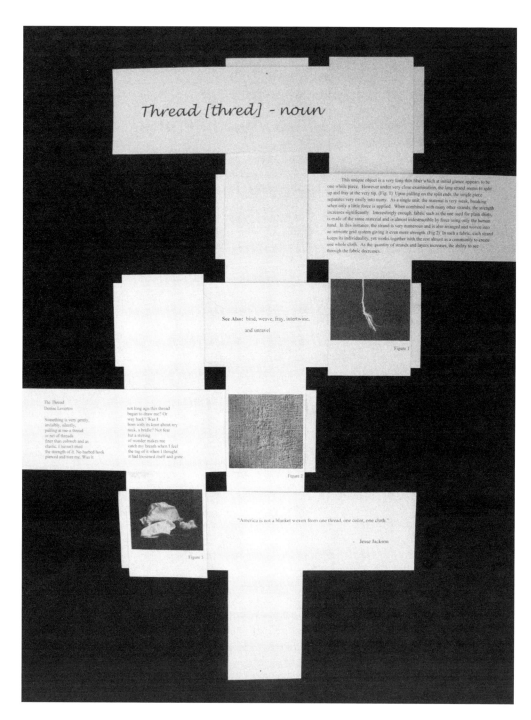

Figure 1.2. *This is a presentation of information gathered through research. The information is composed in a way that reflects its role in the design it is to generate. In this case, information about form and material are abstracted into a method of assembly specific to the topic of research. This frames a point of departure for further design investigations.* Student: Bart Bajda—Critic: Matthew Mindrup—Institution: Marywood University

ADDITIVE

A strategy of making characterized by accumulation

Generative Possibilities in Accumulation

Faced with a challenging and complex integration of spaces, each holding a different event, the student decided to employ an additive strategy for making. She did this in order to definitively articulate each space without changing the tectonic language that she had established earlier in the design. She continued to accumulate elements that defined each space and the joints between them until the density of components became confusing. Spaces began to lose their distinction, and the assembly of parts began to lose its rationale. At that point she began a subtractive process to edit the design. Her goal was to discover that perfect moment when the accumulation of components allowed each space to be distinct but still an integral part of the larger spatial composition.

Addition is a simple process that allows a designer to quickly iterate a design through intuitive decision making. As more and more objects accumulate, it becomes possible for progressively more ideas to be generated. This strategy for iteration fosters discovery; however, using it, the designer may become preoccupied with the forms that define a space, rather than the space itself. In

Figure 1.4. *Additive making can be a strategy for assembly. Crafting intricate joints between many elements can provide opportunities for the design of the spaces they contain. It might be a way of affecting the space by filter light or providing access. It might also be a way of communicating relationships between parts through physical connection.* Student: Dan Mojsa—Critic: Reagan King—Institution: Marywood University

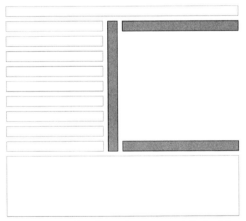

Figure 1.3. *This shows how one might build up a component through an additive way of making. The single component is actually an assembly of much smaller parts. The opening to the right of the assembly is achieved by altering the size and configuration of elements rather than cutting away at the component.*

that instance additive making is gratuitous and possibly a distraction from the primary design objective. It shifts the focus of the design process away from making spaces and toward a preoccupation with craft and objects.

In what ways might this, as a method, propel a design into another level of resolution, or begin the next iterative step? As a preliminary design technique, it could be employed to discern variations in spatial composition as described in the narrative. Or it could be used to develop a tectonic language for the communication of spatial information that can be employed in future iterations of a design. In addition to this strategy for making through accumulation, it can also describe a strategy for making at a smaller scale. Individual components or elements to be layered or built up can be developed through additive techniques. This contrasts with the subtractive carving of large pieces to create individual components. The additive and the subtractive speak to the difference between the tectonic and stereotomic methods for crafting.

» *See also* Subtractive.

Figure 1.5. Additive making can also be a strategy for the configuration of space. Different materials can foster control over inhabitants' perceptions; the intricate assembly of elements can foster precise control over the configuration of spaces they contain. Student: John Levi Weigand—Critic: John Maze— Institution: University of Florida

Figure 1.6. Additive assembly furthers control over the play of light in space. These techniques of assembly also establish a hierarchy through the size and configuration of elements. They help communicate a scale through the relative proportion of elements to the spaces they contain. They also communicate organizational logic by indicating direction, a relationship to other elements, and patterning. Student: Liu Liu—Critic: James Eckler—Institution: University of Cincinnati

ANALYSIS

The process of separating a complex subject into constituent parts so that each part can be studied independently

Generative Possibilities in Investigation and Inquiry

An architect has just received a project about which he is very excited. A couple who purchased an older, historic house has asked him to design an addition that preserves the character of the original structure.

Before design can begin, an extensive study of the existing conditions has to take place. The architect begins by analyzing the site, breaking it up into several categories of study: dimension and topography, existing site features, adjacent buildings, and public access. The addition will have to respond to the existing spatial composition of the house, so he analyzes circulation, program, and degrees of privacy. The new addition also has to respond efficiently to the environment, so he analyzes it in relations to daylight, solar orientation, and climate. All of these studies enable him to conceive of a design strategy through synthesis. The product of that synthesis is a single diagram that incorporates the information gained from each individual study into a spatial composition. He uses that diagram to develop the first set of process drawings and models.

Analysis is a type of abstraction in which a designer is able to isolate pieces of information from a more complex set of issues. Those isolated parts can then be more effectively studied. The primary goal of analysis is to generate information of something particular. How is the process of analysis generative? How does it generate information? How does it generate design?

Documentation is often confused with analysis. One might note the direction of the wind across a site; that is documentation. But studying the impact that wind might have on a design is analysis. Similarly, mapping the program in a building is not in itself an analysis because there is no study or generation of knowledge. But by mapping the programs of a building relative to the number of people inhabiting its spaces, the building's actual primary function might be determined. From this information new ideas for augmenting that building might be conceived. Analysis facilitates learning as a form of research and inquiry. Analysis generates new information as a function of design.

Figure 1.7.   Components of a precedent building are analyzed to discover the ways in which they are related through both formal and spatial connections. In this analysis, the building is reduced to a set of interrelated systems.
STUDENT: ELIZABETH SYDNOR—CRITIC: MILAGROS ZINGONI—INSTITUTION: ARIZONA STATE UNIVERSITY

This is important to the design process, as it is often a vehicle for iteration. Analysis presents new possibilities for design as new information is generated. Discovering how far daylight penetrates into a space might lead to testing other design variations of an edge. An analysis of program as it impacts the arrangement of the new spaces in the previous example will lead to testing new methods for organizing and distributing the functions of the new design. The importance of analysis to a design process—especially when coupled with a synthesis of parts—lies in its ability to define limits for experimentation and measurable criteria for success.

» *See also* Synthesis.

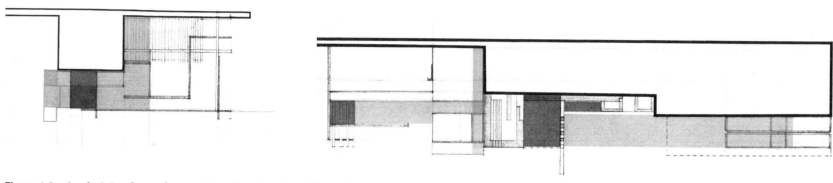

Figure 1.8. Analysis is a form of research and inquiry that relies on the separation of a complex system into its constituent parts. In this case the student investigates multiple spatial functions within her project. This analysis yields compositional information regarding spatial relationships relative to tectonic assembly. STUDENT: MICHELLE MAHONEY—CRITIC: JAMES ECKLER—INSTITUTION: UNIVERSITY OF CINCINNATI

COMPOSE

To arrange the parts of a whole

To physically relate elements

To configure space or form through making

Composition: Any instance of arrangement, relationship, or configuration

Generative Possibilities in Configuring Elements

She made a set of models, each one in accordance with the requirements of a single function within the program. She had resolved the details specific to the various parts of the program, but she realized that she didn't know how the parts should relate to one another.

So she sketched out strategies for positioning the parts relative to one another. From those sketches she started to arrange the parts. She would place one next to, on top of, or interlocked with another. She would continually reposition parts, sliding one a little along the surface of another, or rotating a part in minute intervals. Through the composition of parts she was able to define the relationships between aspects of her project. The act of arranging generated ideas for the way in which parts would be linked together.

Composition consists of a set of principles that direct the positioning or arranging of elements. The compositional act occurs any time two or more components are arranged, and it is fundamental to architectural thinking. It is present in the processes of formal assembly and defining spatial relationships. Compositional principles can also be employed in documentation, analysis, and representation. Composition influences nearly every aspect of the architectural design process. One space cannot be related to another without relying on compositional logic to position them relative to each other. Composition is therefore inherent to design, whether it is a product of design intent or merely an afterthought. Compositional principles can be used as design tools; they inform decision making by providing criteria for relating elements.

If principles of composition are used throughout the process of design, how can they be specifically applied to individual goals? How can compositional principles be used to define particular methods within a process if it is

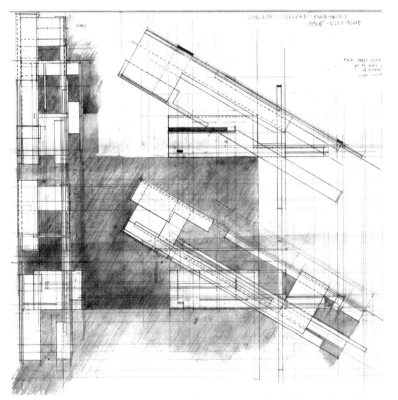

Figure 1.9. *Composition is the adherence to a set of guidelines that allows us to determine relationships among components. Here composition is used to further the communication of spatial and formal configuration. Plan drawings are correlated with section drawings in the way they are composed relative to one another. Registration lines reinforce the correlation and specifically reference individual elements of the project.* Student: Ashley Eldringhoff—Critic: Michael Hamilton—Institution: Louisiana State University

integral to so many aspects of process? All of the various applications of compositional principles to design thinking can be divided into two types. Those types are defined by the intent of the compositional effort and its position within the process of development. Composition can be either exploratory in nature, or it can be communicative.

Exploratory composition seeks to discover that which was previously unobserved. It is generative in that this type of composition is intended to develop design ideas or expand on existing ones. This process tends to be more intuitive than formulaic. It involves arranging components of a design through drawing, modeling, or other means of craft in order to figure out various configurations or relationships. Using composition as a tool for exploration results in a freedom from responsibilities greater than basic compositional principles. It is a method for iterating and testing ideas quickly based upon relationships that pertain to proportion, organization, proximity, and hierarchy. It can be a valuable method for forming a design intent, strategizing the way different elements might interact, or analyzing aspects of an existing condition that are not evident at first glance.

This exploratory intent is usually reliant on the abstraction of a graphic language in order to reduce the amount of information being processed through the act of making. Elements are reduced to basic components and evaluated according to simple ideas of relationship. This sometimes makes the information difficult to understand by those outside the process. Exploratory composition is primarily a tool for conception rather than communication, and as such it should advance the understanding of a project even if those ideas are not explicitly represented.

As opposed to the implicit information of abstraction and exploration, communicative composition relies on the explicit documentation of relationships. That documentation is meant to be clearly legible to a larger audience so that design ideas can be understood without explanation. This type of communicative composition often relies on conventions for representation—on a graphic language that is uniform and commonly accepted. At this stage in the process, composition becomes a tool for resolving more complex ideas. Here more responsibilities can be added to the process. Issues of proportion, organization, proximity, and hierarchy can be used to define issues of program, structure, scale, movement, and environment. Communicative composition is not necessarily relegated to documenting complete design ideas, but it can be used in bringing greater specificity to them. Whereas exploratory composition remains generic, communicative composition becomes specific through process.

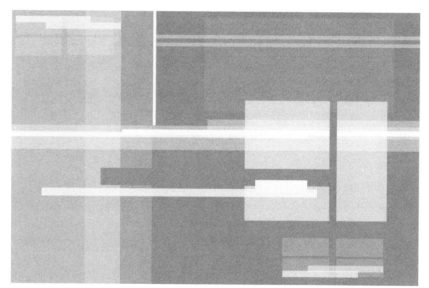

Figure 1.10. Compositional principles can provide a simplified language for documenting and analyzing an existing project. They can also provide a simplified language to begin the design process of a new project, as in this example. In positioning, proportioning, and connecting various elements in a simple composition, decisions and discoveries can be made that help shape future iterations. Student: McKinley Mertz—Critic: John Humphries—Institution: Miami University

Figure 1.11. The same principles that govern graphic language can also be applied to the architectural language of built form. In this instance composition relates the size, shape, and proportion of an aperture to the plane it penetrates. Composition provides a logic for the assembly that defines the aperture within the plane. It also determines the relationship between that plane and other components of the construct. Student: Cari Williams—Critic: James Eckler—Institution: Marywood University

DIAGRAM

An imprecise drawing meant to illustrate a plan or an idea

An abstract representation used as a tool for study or analysis

To create one of the above

Generative Possibilities in Simplified Representation

He wanted to understand his site, a busy street corner. The buildings were tall and often held multiple programs. The sidewalks were crowded with pedestrians, and the streets clogged with vehicles. There were too many variables to account for, and no obvious starting point for the design process.

He began diagramming. He wanted to simplify the information so that it could be more easily understood. He began mapping various aspects of the site: where

people walked, where they paused, where cars would park, and the different programs around the intersection. He also documented physical characteristics of the site: its shape, the size and proportion of buildings around it, and environmental factors. Each of these issues was produced independently. Each was drawn on a separate sheet. When he understood each issue separately, he layered the translucent sheets. Looking through them he began to see relationships and correlations between different issues as they overlapped. The simplified graphic language enabled him to understand more about the site, and it provided a construct to which he could respond architecturally.

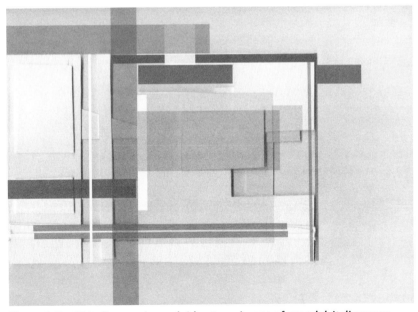

Figure 1.12. *This diagram is overlaid onto an image of a model. It diagrams compositional relationships between parts of the model. The diagram is a tool that can be used for reading and interpreting an existing condition; it can also be used to generate new ideas.* STUDENT: UNKNOWN—CRITIC: JOHN HUMPHRIES—INSTITUTION: MIAMI UNIVERSITY

The diagram plays a crucial role in the architectural design process. It is something that, through crude graphic language, can quickly illustrate rudimentary design ideas as well as formal or spatial patterns. The origins of the word *diagram* lie in the Latin *diagramma* and the Greek *diágramma*, which both refer to something marked by lines. This origin speaks to a simplicity important in current applications. The diagram, as it applies to architectural process, is something that strips away irrelevant content in order to illustrate a specific set of information. The reductive graphic language used to construct it makes the diagram simple to generate and simple to read.

How can simplicity of language contribute to a design process? How can it influence design ideas? Because of the minimalist quality of diagrammatic language, it can be applied in two ways. The diagram can act as a starting point for design or problem solving. Or it can be used to clearly communicate ideas to others.

The generative diagram relies on abstraction to establish a simple graphic language. This abstraction better enables the designer to quickly iterate design ideas or to invent solutions to design problems. The abstract diagrammatic language creates a convention for representation in which only specific elements are included. This quality makes the generative diagram an ideal vehicle for most analytical exercises. Decisions can not only be made through the production of the diagram, but they can be tested through an iterative sequence. There is also the potential for the diagrammatic language to influence a more sophisticated design language developed later in the process. As the diagram is transformed from the first iteration to the next, more explicit information can be layered into its construction. As this occurs, the generic and abstracted language of the original diagram can evolve into the explicit and literal language of a resolved design.

Communicative diagrams establish symbolic conventions that can be used to quickly illustrate simple ideas or functions of a design. They are used less often to test or analyze than to simplify complex information sets. A broader range of people can more easily understand the simplified representation of architectural ideas in communicative diagrams. They reflect decisions that have already been made through process and documented in an easily accessible way. Often these communicative devices isolate one idea or function from others in a design in order to reduce overlapping information that may overwhelm or confuse someone unfamiliar with the project.

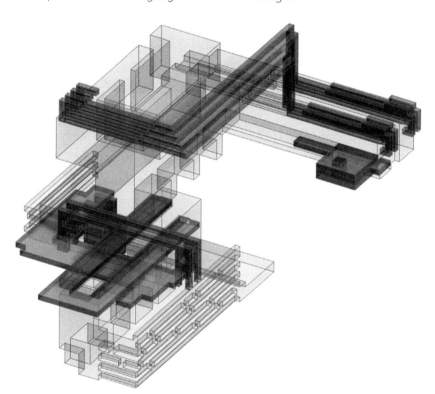

Figure 1.13. This is a generative diagram produced digitally. It studies the composition and joinery of components within an assembly. It is generative because every decision made in its production leads to a new discovery that ultimately motivates the student to change or reconfigure the design. It is a document that evolves; it is continuously reworked as it is produced. Student: George Faber— Critic: James Eckler—Institution: University of Cincinnati

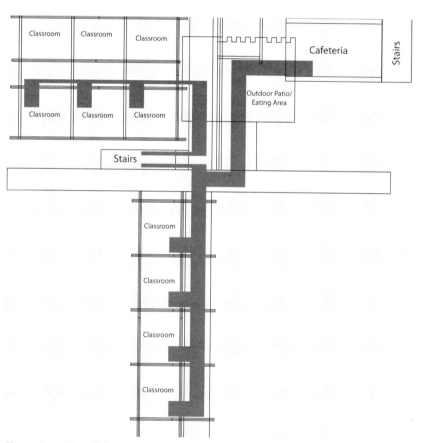

Figure 1.14. Not all diagrams have to be generative in nature. This one is used as a communicative tool. It reduces a complex set of spatial and formal conditions to a simple piece of information. It communicates the location of pathways through a project so that others might more easily understand the intent of the design. Student: Tim Smith—Critic: James Eckler—Institution: University of Cincinnati

GENERATE

To create or invent through process

Generative Possibilities in Found Ideas

He wasn't sure how to proceed. He had some ideas and criteria the design had to satisfy, but not enough to formulate a scheme. He began making a simple, gestural representation of one of his ideas applied to a small fragment of the overall project. As he made the model, crafting techniques and material limitations provided a framework for his thinking, and his ideas began to resolve. In making, the compositional decisions he made provided opportunities for even more development. The more he crafted, the more spatial and formal information existed that he could respond to in later iterations. Each decision generated opportunities for subsequent ones. As ideas became resolved in form and space, new concepts were generated to build upon those ideas.

Process results in the generation of something either physical or conceptual. Consequently, many of the creations of process can be used as

generative devices. These devices are iterations or studies that precede, build up to, or facilitate the making or conception of something else—another iteration, or another conclusive product. The origin of the word *generate* lies in the Latin *generÇre*, meaning "to produce." However, the root is *gener–*, meaning "to give birth or beget." Two important connotations can be drawn from this history: that its relation to production correlates with craft, and that its reference to birth—or the creation of generations—correlates with iteration. Each successive generation is built upon those previous to it. It can also be inferred that each generation forms a foundation for those that come after.

What are the goals of a generative device in the design process? What makes a generative device different from one that is not? The generative device can be composed in many ways, using many crafting techniques

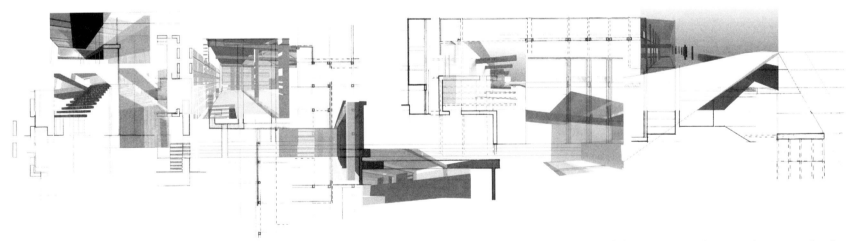

Figure 1.15. *This document is a hybrid drawing of an itinerary through the spaces of a project. It integrates fragments of plan, section, and perspective as a study of the spatial and experiential consequences of tectonic assembly. It is used as a generative document—one from which new ideas emerge for design. It provides a point of departure for future design iterations.* STUDENT: MARYJO MINERICH—CRITIC: JAMES ECKLER—INSTITUTION: UNIVERSITY OF CINCINNATI

and media. It is created with the intent to develop some spatial idea, to test an idea, or to investigate techniques for representing or refining the idea. It is a tool for architectural conception that contributes to the linking of making and thinking throughout the design process. For instance, if a diagram produces an idea for the way a space is to be used, and then several models are created to test variations of that space to accommodate that use, the diagram was used as a generative device. Just as process refers to both physical craft and conception, generation can refer to both physical conditions and ideas.

Generating the physical condition, the form or space of architecture, can be based in production or testing. Production most often refers to aspects of craft intended to represent ideas. They may or may not become generative devices; they are often the final iteration or the outcome of previous stages of a process. Testing refers to the sequential creation of iterative studies. Each study has the potential then to be the generative device for those that come after it. Techniques for representation are important throughout this stage of process as well, but they are deployed with the intent to create or resolve an idea rather than being used strictly for communication.

Generating ideas for design is closely linked to physical craft. A design concept might drive the functional, spatial, or formal characteristics of architecture. And the physical production of space—the act of making—might yield ideas for the way it is to function or be used. Concept as a generative device may be rooted in metaphor, precedent, or a desire for a particular

experiential event to be manifest in the architecture. Craft as a generative device can then resolve or refine those initial ideas.

» *See also* Iteration; Process.

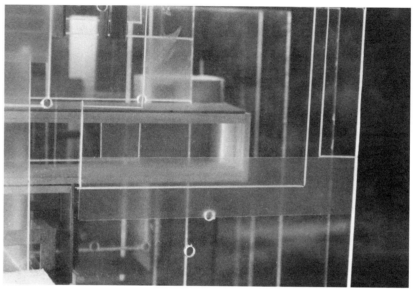

Figure 1.16. In this example, the student uses an analytical diagram as a generator. The original analysis is of compositional devices in a painting. That information is used as a guide for construction, assembly, and ultimately, for spatial composition. STUDENT: DAVE PERRY—CRITIC: JAMES ECKLER—INSTITUTION: MARYWOOD UNIVERSITY

GRAFT

To attach one part onto another

A means of combining two or more unlike elements

Generative Possibilities in Conjoining

The project involved the design of an addition to an existing building. The building was old, and it was created using materials and techniques that are no longer available. The new addition would have to relate to the original building in some other way.

The architect decided to graft the new addition to the building: it would be conceived as distinct structure from that of the original, yet it would be connected as if fused to the older structure. Any attempt to re-create the characteristics of the first building, he believed, would result in a poor imitation at best. So the strategy called for each building to advertise its role and its place in the evolution of the structure.

He chose materials that were noticeably different from those of the original. He composed the facades in a way that would immediately distinguish the newer portion from the older one. Similarly, spaces were composed using a very different set of guidelines so the new structure could accommodate different programs. At the point of connection between the old and new, pathways and corridors met one another to provide spatial continuity. The two were attached but maintained their individual identity.

Grafting is a technique of formal composition in which two unlike elements are physically attached. The process involves a physical transformation of both objects at the point of the graft. Connections of adjacency or simple assembly do not typically constitute a graft because the process of connection does not entail the physical transformation of the objects. Furthermore, in the typical scenario for grafting, an existing element receives a new element as an addition or augmentation. Grafting a newly designed component onto an existing one takes advantage of the previously established formal distinction between the two entities. Otherwise, two newly designed elements that are integrated with one another may provide the appearance of a grafted joint. However, because they were conceived as conjoined objects, they lack the distinction that makes grafting possible.

This augmentation can produce three types of relationships between the elements that are connected: synthetic, symbiotic, or parasitic. A synthetic relationship between components implies that the connection fully

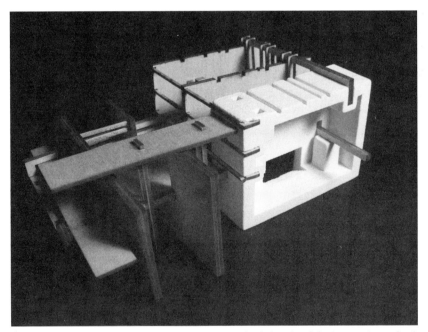

Figure 1.17. The wooden planar structure on the left side of the image is grafted to white mass on the right. Members are elements inserted into grooves in the mass, making a seam joining the two constructs.

STUDENT: TIM SMITH—CRITIC: JAMES ECKLER—INSTITUTION: UNIVERSITY OF CINCINNATI integrates their forms and functions into a singular construct. A symbiotic relationship between the components of a grafted joint implies that the two elements maintain some formal distinction but operate as complements to one another, both compositionally and programmatically. A parasitic graft implies that both components remain as distinct elements despite the physical connection between them, and that one is formally or programmatically dependent upon the other.

How might this act of joinery impact spatial conception? A graft is a technique for making; however, it might also be a reflection of the intent to relate elements. Grafting one piece onto another could be an appropriate method for combining the spaces that hold two distinct programs. It may also be one method of extending an existing spatial construction while maintaining the ability to recognize the original versus the addition. Formally grafting one element to another in order to achieve a particular compositional relationship might be driven by the need to define that same type of relationship between spaces, programs, or disparate organizational structures, or between experiences within a spatial sequence.

Figure 1.18. In this example, framing elements extend from the main body of the construct to penetrate the surfaces below and to the side of it, grafting it to them. STUDENT: KENDALL KLAUS—CRITIC: JOHN HUMPHRIES—INSTITUTION: MIAMI UNIVERSITY

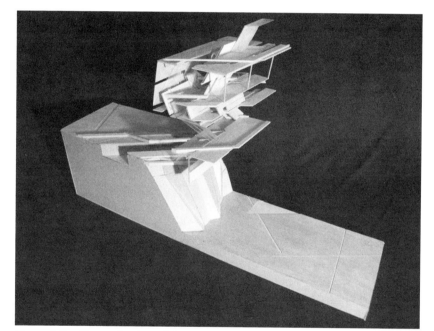

Figure 1.19. The projection of the spatial construct from the surface below it is accomplished using a graft. The lower portion of the model is attached to the ground plane using a series of stacked and embedded planes, grafting it to that surface. STUDENT: WENDELL MONTGOMERY—CRITIC: JASON TOWERS—INSTITUTION: VALENCIA COMMUNITY COLLEGE

INJECT

To place or force into

Generative Possibilities in Positioning Within

There was an old factory on Main Street. It had been abandoned for years. The people of this town had become apathetic toward it. When they walked from one store to the next, they ignored the looming brick building with broken arched windows. This perception changed when a local man purchased the old factory with the intention of turning it into residential units.

In an effort to keep the shell of the building undisturbed, except where it needed repair, the new units would be built within the existing outer walls. The design concept was to build a new building within the old shell. The interior of the factory was demolished, and new walls erected in their place. The joint between the older shell and the newer interior was made obvious.

The units varied in size; some had one of the big windows, and others had two. In some places the residences were moved toward the interior to provide circulation up against the old wall of windows. It was in those places that it was most apparent that the newer apartments were injected into the previous structure. They were designed without any intent to respond or be structured by the existing shell.

Figure 1.20. The small horizontal volume on the right side of the image is inserted into the main volume as if by injection. STUDENT: MICHELLE MAHONEY—CRITIC: JAMES ECKLER—INSTITUTION: UNIVERSITY OF CINCINNATI

Injection is a principle of formal composition in which an existing element is altered in order to receive another positioned within it. The implication of a forced placement of one element into another is a result of altering the existing element while maintaining the integrity of the new object. Additionally, after the process is complete, both components preserve their distinctiveness; one will always be read as being within the other.

In this instance injection implies that a form is being regarded as a kind of small-scale context within which another is inserted. How might this action influence the generation of architecture? This compositional principle is an act of making in which one element is placed within space that is created by another. This physical relationship between the form that receives and the one placed within it can also reflect a conceptual

relationship between programs or experiences. One spatial quality might be set within a larger volume, thereby defining a different zone that impacts sequence, progression, experience, and program. A smaller addition to an existing programmatic scheme might be manifest through the injection of small structures into a larger volume. As with other techniques for making, injection has the potential to frame a way of thinking about the spaces and forms that result from it, influencing the conception of architecture.

Figure 1.21.   The space in the background of the image is contained within an assembly distinct from those around it. It is brought into the larger volume as if injected into the space guided by the rails beneath it.   STUDENT: NICK REUTHER—CRITIC: JAMES ECKLER—INSTITUTION: MARYWOOD UNIVERSITY

Figure 1.22.   The smaller assembly of frames and planes are injected into the cavity within the larger white mass. STUDENT: NIKA BONAPOUR—CRITIC: JOHN MAZE—INSTITUTION: UNIVERSITY OF FLORIDA

INTERVENE

To interrupt or place between

To involve an element or event in a larger circumstance in a way that affects both

Generative Possibilities in Interruption

The town has a particular character. Street vendors line the sidewalk. Each table of trinkets is similar to the others next to it. Most buildings come right up to the sidewalk as if in unison. This creates a narrow walk between the vendors and the storefronts. Each morning the same group of people park in the vacant lot and have breakfast in the local diner before work. This would change however. The vacant lot was the proposed site of a new building. Construction would begin in a few months.

The designer knew about each of these systems to which his new building would have to respond. He was one of the morning patrons at the diner. Each system would be interrupted or altered by the addition of the new building. He could either use the project to try to change the way things worked or to reinforce the customs of the place. He chose the latter. The front facade was eventually placed right next to the sidewalk. The new clientele that it brought encouraged more vendors to hawk their wares on that side of the street.

Not all remained as it was, though. Every intervention leaves its mark in some way, and this new building was no different. Now people parked on the street. Traffic was a little more congested, and it took a little longer to get to work each morning.

Intervening is an act of placement, wherein an element is positioned between or within existing conditions. Intervening within an existing condition is a process for defining relationships between that condition and the addition. Unlike injection, intervention implies a reciprocal relationship. Both the element and the set of conditions it is set within will be altered by the presence of the other. A context is transformed to receive the element, and the element is made to conform to its surroundings.

Intervening implies the existence of context. That context is composed of whatever existing conditions are being impacted by the added presence. It may be as conventional as a new building intervening within an established city block. Or it can be an abstract process in which intervention is the study of conceptual relationships without the realities of built form.

In what ways might this process impact the development of spatial ideas? Placing an architectural intervention within a context, either physical or conceptual, forces the consideration of external relationships. The spatial relationships between the intervention and existing structures will be defined by placement, orientation, scale, and proximity, each of which is a consideration in the act of intervening. The organizational structure of a context will be impacted by the insertion a new element, one that has the potential to reinforce that organizational pattern or to interrupt it.

Intervention is also an act that implies transformation. The addition of a new element to an existing condition inevitably alters the characteristics of that condition. That transformation may be subtle or profound, depending on the design intent behind the development of the intervening structure. A context defines the limits to which an intervention must conform. It affects the production of the intervening element. Likewise, the act of placing the element is an augmentation of the context it is placed within. It affects the preexisting systems and functions of context. Intervention reflects a sequence of design decisions as much as it does composition.

There are three contextual scales to consider in a process of intervention: the scale of the site, the local scale, and the scale of the region or territory. Site refers to the immediate surroundings of the intervening element. The local context refers to the more broad surroundings of the site. And the region consists of any surrounding elements that have even minimal contribution to a context. Considerations at the scale of the site might include spatial connections between interior and exterior, or the direct physical association with surrounding elements. Considerations of a local context might include organizational structure, the compositional characteristics of the surrounding area, or programmatic relationships between context and intervention. Regional scale implications might include formal vernacular, or environmental issues. Any act of intervention guides a process of response. The

intervening element will respond to the conditions of its surroundings in one way or another. The act of intervention implies control over that response as a product of design intent.

» *See also* Context.

Figure 1.23. Intervention is the introducing something new or foreign to a context. It affects its new surroundings, transforming them. Likewise, the qualities and characteristics affect the configuration of the intervention. This example shows an acrylic construct marked and carved to receive a new construction. Its design is driven by characteristics of its context. STUDENT: MIKE STAUFFER—CRITIC: JAMES ECKLER—INSTITUTION: MARYWOOD UNIVERSITY

Figure 1.24. In a more conventional context—a field—the architecture is placed strategically to correspond to a larger organizational logic. The field is carved to receive the architecture. It is divided into territories around the intervention. The design is shaped by the characteristics of the field. STUDENT: NICK YOUNG—CRITIC: JASON TOWERS—INSTITUTION: VALENCIA COMMUNITY COLLEGE

INVESTIGATE

To examine systematically

To engage in a process with the intent to acquire knowledge

Generative Possibilities in Seeking Solutions

It was important to her that the building she was designing respond well to its surroundings so that it would be well received by the people of the small town in which it was to be built. She realized that if the design were rejected or *misunderstood, it would fail. People would avoid it when possible and seek the first opportunity to replace it. She wanted this to be a lasting contribution to the growth of the town—a step in its evolution. This meant that design decisions*

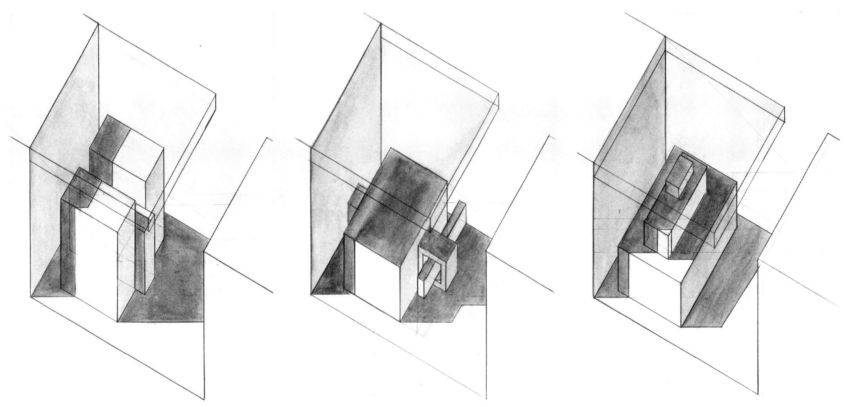

Figure 1.25.   Much of process is dedicated to investigation. It is an effort to test ideas relative to various design criteria. It is a way of generating new and innovative solutions to design problems. In this example, compositional variations are studied according to the behavior of light as it interacts with form. Shadows are shaped by the configuration of elements. Multiple scenarios are investigated.   STUDENT: KATHERINE CORMEAU—CRITIC: JOHN HUMPHRIES—INSTITUTION: MIAMI UNIVERSITY

could not be made without an understanding of local customs, traditions, and other social forces that direct the composition of built form.

The preliminary portions of the design process were rooted in documentation and analysis. She first mapped the locations of buildings, program types, public spaces, and access routes to her site. She documented the composition of the facade, the distribution of public and private spaces, and the means of access from the street to buildings in the immediate vicinity of her project. She spent many hours sketching, mapping, and photographing. Each of the products she produced at this stage constituted an investigation wherein she generated the information necessary to make decisions regarding her own design. The subsequent stages of the process were also investigatory, as she applied various ideas and tested them against the criteria inherent to the project.

Investigation is a fundamental driver of the architectural design process. It is a way that the designer seeks to understand a design-related issue, or set of issues, in an existing condition or within a developing project. The design process is a form of inquiry in which craft facilitates conception; the act of making is correlated with the way the spaces that are being designed are thought about. Investigation's role in this process involves testing design issues through iteration; investigation is the vehicle for discovery in process. The purpose is to test the outcome of decisions manifested in the architecture. An investigation can yield several possible answers to the questions that motivated it. Those answers are dependent upon the factors that determine the success of the design and can therefore be measurably evaluated. If the designer accepts the first solution without any investigation, a more suitable possibility might be overlooked.

Investigation might also take place through study or research. Studying various aspects of design through conventional research provides a solid foundation for the decisions that the designer makes. However, that study is most beneficial when it is translated into the process of iteration. The potential for investigation to influence the outcome of a design is limited when discovered solutions are replicated without accounting for the specific attributes of the current project.

How does investigation impact the evolution of a design? The primary motivation behind any investigation is to discover possibilities for design that were not considered before. Those possibilities can drive decision making, redirect the course or priorities of a design process, or resolve design problems in a project. These various discovered possibilities represent different stages of a design, different iterations in a process. Investigation facilitates the evolution of design intent by directing process and decision making.

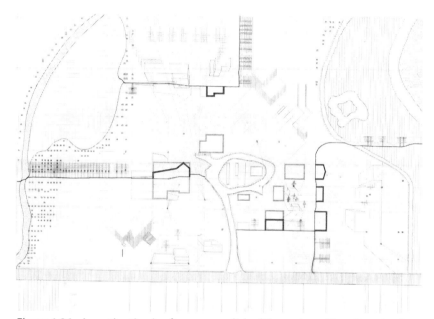

Figure 1.26. *Investigation is often accomplished through making. Drawing is a craft, and the techniques employed in this example integrate multiple drawing types in order to document various features of a site simultaneously. In integrating these drawing types, and techniques for producing them, the student is able to investigate different spatial and formal relationships between building and context.* STUDENT: KYLE CAMPBELL—CRITIC: JAMES ECKLER—INSTITUTION: UNIVERSITY OF CINCINNATI

ITERATE

To perform repeatedly

Generative Possibilities in Repetition

As a part of the design process, a student decides to make a model that illustrates the spatial composition of her project. In addition to communicating a compositional idea, the student uses this model as a way of better understanding the

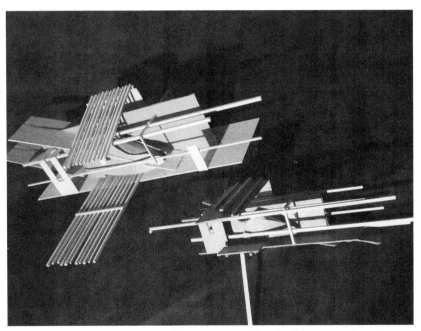

Figure 1.27.   Through iteration, designers are able to build upon and resolve ideas. This image shows two versions of the same project. One came earlier than the other; it was a vehicle for study and making discoveries that could be implemented in the next version.   STUDENT: MICHELLE BEAUVAIS—CRITIC: JIM SULLIVAN— INSTITUTION: LOUISIANA STATE UNIVERSITY

various applications of the idea to the construction and assembly of its parts. As a result, her idea develops further.

She begins by making generic volumes and positioning them relative to one another. This exercise allows her to see opportunities that she can exploit to more clearly present her idea for the project. She makes another model in which spatial configuration and tectonic assembly become more resolved. She is making decisions as she builds. This provides more opportunities she can take advantage of. She makes another model.

Iteration of the model further refines her idea. Each version builds on the lessons learned from the previous one. Each subsequent model more clearly represents the ideas of the project as well as the way that the architecture satisfies the aspirations inherent within her concepts for it.

Iteration is the basis of the design process. Making something repeatedly, incorporating ideas generated from previous versions, produces an environment for investigation and discovery. Each stage has the potential to advance the design relative to spatial and formal composition, representational technique, and conceptual intent. The progressive stages of an iterative process are the vehicle for design evolution and advancement.

How does doing the same thing repeatedly help resolve a design? What can be learned from that type of process? Each stage varies somewhat based upon information learned form the previous version. In turn, the current stage will provide new information to be used as a generator for subsequent versions. Consequently, each stage should not be thought of as a redesign, but rather variations of a single design.

The production of multiple variations allows the designer to evaluate them and determine which version functions the best, based upon specific design criteria. More often than not, each variation will have certain successes and failures. The manufacture of multiple versions facilitates the advancement of the design as the versions are combined to capitalize on different successful instances and minimize the instances of failure. Iteration becomes a way of recognizing and combining the best of each into a single, better design solution.

» *See also* Process; Discovery; Investigation.

Figure 1.28. In the iterative sequence, each version becomes progressively more resolved and refined. Each stage provides a foundation for the next. Each stage is also a result of those that came previously. STUDENT: JEFF BADGER—CRITIC: JAMES ECKLER—INSTITUTION: UNIVERSITY OF CINCINNATI

LAYER

A level or material in a stacked assembly

To make by stacking, laminating, or covering

Generative Possibilities in Making or Reading Strata

It is rare that any building element is crafted from a single piece of material. Walls, floors, and ceilings are a composite of parts joined together for structure, performance, and aesthetics.

In representing these elements the student crafts components of a model under the same limitations that govern construction. Instead of using a single plank of wood to connote an overhead or a wall, he layers different materials of structural armatures. He uses layers to achieve rigidity, create thickness, and facilitate joinery with other elements. In some places he cuts through layers to reveal the manner and logic of the element's construction.

Layering is a function of several facets of design process, thinking, and description. It can be a technique for making. It can be a strategy for composition and arrangement. It can be a component of formal assembly, or a descriptor of a formal typology.

As a technique for making it involves a repetitive stacking of components toward the assembly of an element. How can this technique inform a space? How might it generate new ideas toward the creation of architecture? Material in a layered assembly can determine many characteristics of the space it contains. Similarly, the manner in which that material is layered can impact spatial conditions dramatically. Consider the difference between material that is layered in thick slabs versus thin ones, or regular versus irregular thickness of material. The differences can impact the way the scale of a space is perceived or measured. It can determine compositional orientation—whether a space is perceived as horizontal or vertical. A layered assembly that provides gaps between strata might create the opportunity to filter light or relate distinct spaces through a limited view. Conversely, an assembly that is densely stacked might contribute to an impression of mass or spatial division.

Figure 1.29. Layering is an act of placing successive parts on top of one another. This example shows layering used as a strategy for arranging form. The plane is composed of layered panels that protrude to reveal the layers. STUDENT: NATHAN SIMPSON—CRITIC: JAMES ECKLER— INSTITUTION: UNIVERSITY OF CINCINNATI

The act of assembling material through layering can generate spatial ideas as well. The possibility for other components to be incorporated into the strata might provide ideas related to joinery and systems of assembly in the containment of space. At a larger scale, space itself may be the subject of layering. Can spaces be stacked? In this instance, layering can be a compositional device for relating multiple spaces within a larger construct. Spaces positioned adjacent to one another, giving the impression of parallelism or a similar orientation, might be understood as being layered.

This idea for the composition of spaces can be a tool to direct the way spaces are occupied or the way one transitions through them. The compositional relationship established through layering might reflect programmatic relationships. In order for this layered composition to successfully contribute to an experiential or programmatic intent, the layering of space must be easily perceived. This necessity will direct the way in which formal composition is employed to contain space, materials, proportions, and the positioning of openings.

The formal attributes of a layered assembly are clearly discernable material strata. This may contribute to assembly of parts, or to defining an object type.

Figure 1.30. This example shows layering used as a strategy for arranging spaces. Spaces are constructed between physical layers. Spaces are arranged as a progression, moving from one layer to the next. STUDENT: DAVE PERRY—CRITIC: JAMES ECKLER—INSTITUTION: MARYWOOD UNIVERSITY

Figure 1.31. In this project, layering is used as a strategy for assembling components and for organizing spaces. Containment is achieved by a series of skin structures layered over one another. Spatial organization is based upon layers of parallel horizontal spaces arranged between walls or column rows. STUDENT: HECTOR GARCIA—CRITIC: ALLEN WATTERS—INSTITUTION: VALENCIA COMMUNITY COLLEGE

MAKE

To craft or create

Generative Possibilities…

The piece of wood is found at a construction site where a building is being demolished. You check its surface for any nails or other objects that might be embedded inside. You clean it and sand it down a little to remove the debris from the outside. It is old and dense. You feel the resistance it provides as you push it over the saw blade. The friction makes it char a little inside the cut; you catch a slight smell of burnt wood. You are fashioning a set of interlocking wood components for a model. Gradually, finished pieces emerge from the timber. You assemble them as if they were a puzzle. There is a hole for a small peg that keeps them in position. The pieces are of various sizes and proportions. They all precisely fit together to create a composition of space and tectonic form.

The plaster is soft and dry. It has little weight. You begin sifting it over the surface of the water. You continue to sift it until there is an appropriate proportion.

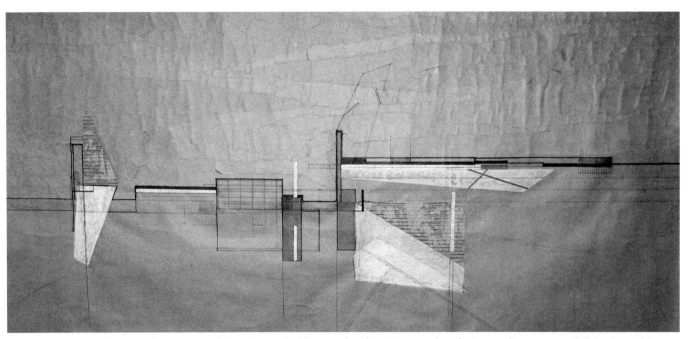

Figure 1.32.   To make something is to craft it, to invent it. The act of making is a way that designers discover possibilities in architecture. Making is not limited to construction. Drawing is a craft, and drawings are made. They are used to document, study, and create architectural environments. This example shows many methods of construction employed to make this drawing. Ink is applied to the surface. Other materials are layered onto it. The surface is cut and peeled away to provide texture.   STUDENT: RYAN SIMMONS—CRITIC: ALLEN WATTERS—INSTITUTION: VALENCIA COMMUNITY COLLEGE

The mold it is to be poured into creates a slab with undulating sides. One edge comes up into a wall-like structure. There is also a groove within which something else might be able to be inserted. When the plaster is removed from the mold it is cold to the touch. Its surface reflects the patterns of the material that was used to construct the mold. While looking at it, you realize there are other decisions you'd like to make regarding this piece. You begin chipping and carving material away in order to provide a place where the wooden interlocking construct can be joined to the plaster mass.

Craft is fundamental to architecture. The act of making enables ideas to become manifest in space and form. Through making, new possibilities become realized. Manipulating material and joining objects generates ideas for design. It is a part of a process of discovery and a method for design inquiry. It is a heuristic endeavor in which new ideas inspire changes to be made in subsequent iterations. New ideas are generated, and strategies for design and representing are developed, because making is haptic. Information is gleaned from working with a material. Every material has different tolerances that limit construction. Different materials present different limitations and possibilities; each will lend itself to being worked in specific ways. Each will also have certain functions it cannot perform and formal configurations for which it cannot be used. These characteristics are learned through the sense of touch, the act of manipulating a thing with the hands. The density of a material is felt when a blade is dragged through it. Elasticity is felt when pressure is applied. New ideas come from the crafting possibilities presented by materials and techniques for making.

Making can be either tectonic or stereotomic in nature. The tectonic involves the craft of joints. Multiple parts are assembled into progressively more complex components and formal structures for containing space. Stereomoic involves techniques for shaping or removing material. Space is created from the subtraction of material from a solid mass.

Drawing is an act of making that is representational of either tectonic or stereotomic craft. Drawing illustrates the products of craft. It communicates spatial and formal design intent. Even though drawing is a strictly representational medium, the thought processes used in drawing reflect those used in tectonic assembly or sterotomic sculpting. It is a facet of making that is associated with both.

Join

To connect or bring elements together

The joint is a fundamental aspect of architecture, and the act of joining elements characterizes many facets of the design process. Joining elements is an act of connection or assembly. However, as a foundation to the way designers approach architecture, it has taken on a larger role in the disciplinary lexicon. In the architectural process, the joint can sometimes refer not only to physical connection but also to spatial connections, variations in technique, stages in a process, or even to ideological overlaps.

For the purposes of this text (whose mission is to present foundation design principles), the joint will be discussed in terms of space and form. In these terms a joint refers to the physical connection between elements. That connection can be constructed as objects are assembled, or it can be spatial, referring to the transition from one space to another. How can a joint generate space? Can the

Figure 1.33.   The joint is not a simple connection between parts. A strategy for joint-making provides opportunities for designing assemblies, composing multiple materials, and defining relationships.   Student: Jennifer Hurst—Critic: James Eckler—Institution: Marywood University

joint, or the act of joining, influence the design process? The well-crafted joint is responsible for the realization of architecture in several ways.

Joinery in its most basic form serves the pragmatic function of structure and stability. The well-crafted joint will behave in a way that lends itself to the physical structure of space. However, the possibilities of joinery in architecture are not limited to this role. The act of joining can be predicated on a tectonic logic. This logic is a based on design intent; it explores the connection between the physicality of the joint and the spatial condition of habitation. Tectonic logic seeks to determine how a space is to be used, experienced, and understood by an occupant as a means of determining a strategy for assembly. It addresses compositional aspects of joint-making, that, when applied to the design process, has the potential to guide decisions.

The notion of tectonic logic can also be expanded to include issues of spatial opportunity within the construction of the joint itself, which can be a vehicle for the manipulation of space or the way it is occupied. For instance, it might be used to create a gap so light can be cast across a wall, or as a way of demarcating space. Spatial opportunities in joining are taken advantage of

Figure 1.35. ***The joint is an element of architectural design. In this example, several types of joints are used in making assemblies, but also to define the characteristics of the space.*** STUDENT: WENDELL MONTGOMERY—CRITIC: JASON TOWERS—INSTITUTION: VALENCIA COMMUNITY COLLEGE

Figure 1.34. ***The joint plays a significant role in the configuration and operation of space. It is a design tool in the invention of architecture. In this example, the joint is used to control light entering the volume.*** STUDENT: DAVID BURWINKEL—CRITIC: JAMES ECKLER—INSTITUTION: UNIVERSITY OF CINCINNATI

anywhere that the expression of the joint manipulates the physical or experiential characteristics of architecture.

In architectural process the act of joining reflects the intent behind the invention of space. As a formal or spatial construct, the joint performs a function of design.

Fold

To bend along a crease

Folding is a method of tectonic assembly. It involves the bending of a planar material along a crease. This act can be either actual or perceived. The actual fold refers to a form that has been folded along a crease. A perceived form is one in which multiple components are joined together as if they were a single form folded.

Figure 1.36. *Folding is used as a method for deforming a surface in a controlled and precise way. Through folding, planar elements can be made to wrap or contain. In this example, it is a strategy for making used to articulate surface.* STUDENT: NATHAN SIMPSON—CRITIC: JAMES ECKLER—INSTITUTION: UNIVERSITY OF CINCINNATI

Figure 1.37. *In this example, folding is used as the primary strategy in composing and delineating space and form. It is a model through which initial ideas for the dispersal of programs and means of containment across a site are studied.* STUDENT: MARYJO MINERICH—CRITIC: JAMES ECKLER—INSTITUTION: UNIVERSITY OF CINCINNATI

Figure 1.38. *In this image, folding is a strategy of forming spaces rather than elements; space is contained within interlocking brackets. The bracket is a folded plane, but where it connects with its interlocking counterpart, space is forced to turn the corner.* STUDENT: RYAN BOGEDIN—CRITIC: JAMES ECKLER—INSTITUTION: MARYWOOD UNIVERSITY

This technique for making has implications on spatial configuration. The act of folding material reflects a design position on space-making. The volume contained by the folded object may be understood as a single space that has been bent and organized along two intersecting axes. The fold itself might also be intended to contain space. As a plane is folded, space begins to be contained.

With two folds, a space is defined on three sides. Spatial proportion and configuration are determined by the angle of the folds.

Weave

To interlock or interlace

Weaving is a method of tectonic assembly. It involves the overlap, interlock, or interlace of multiple pieces in the construction of a single object. The result of a woven assembly is something akin to fabric. Surface is made articulate through the undulation or protrusion of specific pieces within the assembly. The density of the weave determines its permeability and has implications for its potential to facilitate various operations such as filtering or screening.

Stack

To build up or laminate multiple layers

Stacking is a method of tectonic assembly. It involves multiple parts that are piled or laminated to one another in layers. Stacking is a method for giving thickness to a material. That thickness can begin to take on characteristics of stereotomic massing. In this instance, material is not removed through carving but by editing the profiles of the many section-cut layers within the stack.

On the sides of the stack, the strata of parts will reveal the method the component's creation. The stratification of material can be used as a device

to establish scale; it might become a module by which other elements of the construct can be proportionally evaluated. Gaps or variations can be made into the layers of the stacked form as a way of using this technique for making or as a tool to produce a spatial relationship from one side to the other.

Figure 1.40. In this example, stacking is used to create a component of an assembly. A notch in the stacked component receives a cast object. STUDENT: BRITTANY DENNING—CRITIC: JAMES ECKLER—INSTITUTION: UNIVERSITY OF CINCINNATI

Figure 1.39. Stacking is a way of constructing from modules or units. This stacked project uses layered planes to understand surface characteristics. STUDENT: ELIZABETH SYDNOR—CRITIC: MILAGROS ZINGONI—INSTITUTION: ARIZONA STATE UNIVERSITY

Figure 1.41. Elements are variably stacked to investigate the material and spatial possibilities of voids. STUDENT: JOHN CASEY—CRITIC: MATTHEW MINDRUP—INSTITUTION: MARYWOOD UNIVERSITY

Cut

To divide, sever, or detach, as with a blade

Cutting is a stereotomic method for forming an object. It involves dividing an object or severing parts from it. A cut is a first step in a process of making. It begins the manipulation of an object. The cut carries with it decisions regarding formal configuration or a strategy for tectonic assembly.

The formal attributes of a cut are varied. The cut that completely severs addresses issues of proportion and size. However, there are other options for cutting besides dividing a single object into multiples. A score is a cut that marks a surface. It is a method for articulating a mass. A notch doesn't cut completely though. It provides opportunity for another element to be received. Creating a notch as a potential joint introduces tectonic assembly as an issue addressed by cutting.

Cutting informs tectonics. It is a way that the single mass can be modified to play a particular role in a larger assembly. It is also a way of creating moments where a joint might be fashioned between the form and another object.

Figure 1.43.   Cutting can also be a method for creating joints. In this image a joint is made as one element is passed through a slot cut from another. Student: Dave Perry—Critic: James Eckler—Institution: Marywood University

Figure 1.42.   In this example, the surface is cut to create a depressed trough. It is used to connect elements across the surface and imply direction. Student: Laila Ammar—Critic: James Eckler—Institution: University of Cincinnati

Figure 1.44.   In addition to the physical act of cutting, a void that resembles a cut can be crafted into an element. In this model the student creates a slot in the armature. Its proportion in length, width, and depth gives it the characteristic of a cut. It is also used to form a joint. Student: John Levi Weigand—Critic: John Maze—Institution: University of Florida

Carve

To form or shape a solid

To remove material from a solid

Figure 1.45. Carving is used to form the curved profile of the central component. It was a single piece from which material was removed in order to provide specific formal characteristics. STUDENT: RYAN BOGEDIN—CRITIC: JAMES ECKLER—INSTITUTION: MARYWOOD UNIVERSITY

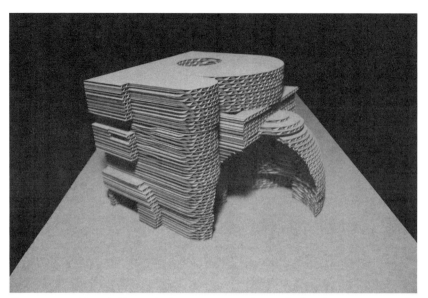

Figure 1.46. Material is stacked to create mass from which volumes are carved away. Spaces are contained within the mass rather than in a tectonic assembly. STUDENT: KIRK BAIRIAN—CRITIC: LAUREN MATCHISON—INSTITUTION: UNIVERSITY OF SOUTHERN CALIFORNIA

Carving or sculpting is a stereotomic method for forming an object. Carving a solid is the removal of material from it; this might be done to craft hollows within the solid. This method of carving can be representational of a spatial configuration or a strategy for making space that is defined by mass. It is representational or strategic in that any space constructed at a scale that would permit habitation would necessarily be an assembly of smaller parts.

Carving away material can also be a way of conditioning the solid to receive another object. It is one step in making a joint with another component in a larger assembly. Carving can also be a way of reconfiguring the form of the solid. Carving or sculpting can manipulate the physical attributes of an object in space. This is a transformational process through which the object is modified in order to give it a different purpose.

Cast

To create a solid by pouring material that is in a liquid state into a mold to harden

Casting is a stereotomic method for forming an object. It involves pouring material in a liquid state into a mold that determines its form. The material hardens within the mold before it is removed, leaving the newly created solid. This form of craft is not entirely stereotomic, however, because it requires the construction of a mold, which will be assembled of parts. Those assembled parts determine the surface quality and formal configuration of the resultant solid. However, the resulting mass resembles stereotomic craft. It functions in many of the same ways as a carved object; it takes on similar roles in design and construction.

Figure 1.48.   A particulate material can also be cast into certain forms. In this study, forming sand in a mold tests some of its material qualities. Other configurations result in failure because there is no bonding agent holding the particles together. STUDENT: JOHN CASEY—CRITIC: MATTHEW MINDRUP—INSTITUTION: MARYWOOD UNIVERSITY

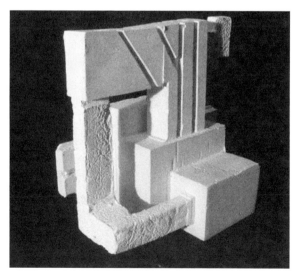

Figure 1.47.   In this example, form was created from cast material. The substance began as a liquid and hardened within a mold. The characteristics of form are the results of the crafted mold structure. STUDENT: THOMAS PETERSON—CRITIC: JASON TOWERS—INSTITUTION: VALENCIA COMMUNITY COLLEGE

Figure 1.49.   Individually cast objects are used as components in a larger construction. Each has its own formal characteristics that it lends to the assembly of a large wall surface. STUDENT: UNKNOWN, TEAM PROJECT—CRITIC: TIM HAYES—INSTITUTION: LOUISIANA TECH UNIVERSITY

Building a mold is a generative process. It is one in which ideas can be tested and iterated through multiple versions of a mold assembly. The craftsperson must understand the limitations of the material used in creating the mold as well as the limitations of the material being poured into it. Mold-making demands attention to craft, as joints must be completely sealed. However, when crafted with precision and built to remain intact when the form is removed, the mold can be altered and reused multiple times. When the form emerges, it can be evaluated, and changes can be made to its mold. It can then be cast again. It can be either a productive or generative tool.

MARK

A visible alteration of a part of an object or surface

A cut, score, line, spot, deposit, or any other circumstance that alters a part of an object or surface

To alter a part of an object or surface; a preliminary act of making

Generative Possibilities of a Blemish

He didn't know where to begin. There it was: a blank white sheet right in front of him. He had a few ideas, but they were unclear at best.

Once he begins, the sheet will never be that same blank white surface that it is now. There is no going back. Should he begin at the center or the edge? To the left side or the right? There is nothing to respond to, nothing to build upon. Finally, he gives up the contemplation and the cyclical questions that lead nowhere. He picks up a pencil and straight edge. He makes a heavy mark just off of center.

Suddenly the white expanse isn't so intimidating. There is something there now, something he can edit according to the unresolved ideas he has. The mark can be given thickness, or accompanied by other marks. This is a starting point. Ideas become clearer as he progresses. Eventually the mark is assigned a task within the scheme he is developing. The white expanse fills with more marks of varying dimension and thickness. The ideas from before are represented clearly as decisions are made.

To make a mark is the fundamental act in the process of design. It is the initial gesture of every craft. It is the primary vehicle for making, representing, and most importantly, architectural inquiry. It is through the mark that we, as designers, are able generate ideas, explore the possibilities of our decisions, and seek an understanding of the environments we inhabit.

There are two types of marks: those that we make, and those that we leave behind. Almost all aspects of the design process involve making a mark. It is the basis of analysis, investigation, and representation. The mark can be graphic or physical—a drawn line that denotes an element of a composition or a component of an assembly that indicates a characteristic of an object. The mark can be a way of inventing something new, or editing the existing. A mark that is left behind is a physical memory of a preexisting state. It is a residue.

It may be the stain of line that has been erased, or the imprint left by a construction that has been razed. It can either disrupt intent for future design or become an incorporated element, one that the next idea can respond to.

The two types of marks are different: one is the basis of process, and the other is the result of process. There aren't any specific ways that a mark impacts design process or thinking. There aren't any rules of thumb that govern its use. It is the one ubiquitous gesture in the production of space and form.

Figure 1.50. The simple act of making a mark can provide direction for intuitive exploration. Here ideas are quickly iterated. As they approach resolution and complexity, intuition gives way to decision making. STUDENT: ELIZABETH SYDNOR—CRITIC: MILAGROS ZINGONI—INSTITUTION: ARIZONA STATE UNIVERSITY

Figure 1.51. A mark is also a record. It is a memento of ideas and observations past. In this small drawing the marks are documentation. They narrate the experiences in travel. They record those experiences as intertwined vignettes as well as corresponding text. STUDENT: KYLE COBURN—CRITIC: JOHN HUMPHRIES—INSTITUTION: MIAMI UNIVERSITY

OBSCURE

To make something inconspicuous

To cover up from sight

Something that is not plainly seen

Generative Possibilities in Hiding

The objective of the project was to position a space for meeting at the center of an office. It was to be something that was accessible and visible to employees and clients alike. It also needed to shield some meetings from view.

The team tasked with setting up the office began by positioning the work desks around the central meeting space. They were arranged so that the primary paths of circulation aligned with the points of entry into the room. This allowed it to become integral to the way people navigated the office. Glass walls provided visual access to any event that occurred within the confines of the central space. The panes were framed in an irregular grid, and most of them were translucent. There were several that remained clear, but they were small and provided only a glimpse of activities within. Light could come from within or without. Silhouettes could be made on the surface to provide some level of visual access. However, lights made to shine into the space erased the silhouettes and obscured the activity within.

Something that is obscured is disguised, hidden, or otherwise inconspicuous. The act of obscuring some object, element, or spatial condition can influence or direct design thinking in several ways. Obscurity can be a tool for distributing program. It can be a process that executes a design decision or intent. Or it can be a process that generates spatial characteristics or conditions.

The desire to obscure a space or object is a programmatic consideration, an act of differentiating between what is displayed and what is not. What is being obscured? Where is it placed in relation to other programmed elements of the design? Obscurity in design could address social issues of privacy and access, or it could address pragmatic issues

of function. This application of obscurity to the design process has the potential to generate spatial separation between programs, as well as a system of arrangement.

Figure 1.52. Obscurity is a state of being hidden. This study demonstrates the potential of material properties to become a tool of selective and controlled obscurity. The writing behind is obscured or revealed based upon the flow of sand. Interruptions are placed in the sand's path, which controls those portions that are hidden or revealed. Student: John Casey—Critic: Matthew Mindrup—Institution: Marywood University

Obscurity can be a means of facilitating some larger design intent. Certain elements may be obscured to emphasize the presence or function of others in order to establish hierarchy. Obscuring a structural system gives precedence to the surface that it supports. A space that is held away from or behind another can divert focus toward the primary volume that conceals it. What determines a system of hierarchy that can be established by obscuring certain spaces or elements? How might that system affect the arrangement or composition of spaces or the forms that contain them? This application of obscurity in the design process has the potential to generate order, organization, and sequence.

What space, or spatial condition, is to be obscured? How might that obscurity lend itself to the conception of space, sequence, or perception? The obscured space may be a product of narrative or experiential intent. Considering obscurity as a tool for prescribing the way an occupant perceives or interacts with space or form has the potential to direct decisions regarding spatial experience. Obscurity can facilitate discovery—something hidden suddenly revealed. Obscurity can also be a design tool used to give an occupant only a subliminal awareness of some condition. Obscurity can be one facet of a larger spatial narrative that defines the way space is conceived.

» *See also* Reveal.

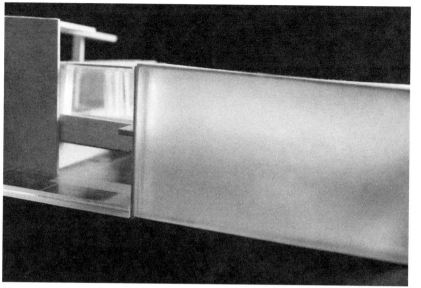

Figure 1.53.   Obscurity can be a result of position and obstruction. The subject positioned behind a barrier will be obscured by it. The opportunity for revelation comes through the ability to move around the barrier. In this example, obscurity is achieved both by position and material quality. The construct is plainly visible on one side, but the other disappears behind a translucent plane. It is known that the construct extends behind because of the silhouette that shows through the plane. Details, however, are not apparent until the other side is revealed.
STUDENT: CARI WILLIAMS—CRITIC: JAMES ECKLER—INSTITUTION: MARYWOOD UNIVERSITY

PRECEDENT

An example used for justification for future instances

A subject of a study of an existing example; a guide for future development

Generative Possibilities in the Study of Previous Instances

He was getting frustrated with the project. He was trying to integrate a large atrium space into the building. The project leader advised him to do a little research and find a few examples to help him. Not knowing what else to do, he went to the library. There he found images and explanations of projects with atrium spaces. They were interesting, and he resolved that his current project should include something similar.

But that was not enough. These images couldn't be copied just because he liked them, nor would just having them as inspiration contribute to a solution to his current dilemmas. These projects were governed by different intents and

limitations. If he were to use them, they had to be the subject of more rigorous study.

He drew plans and sections of the buildings. He studied their composition, proportion, and the relationship between the atriums and the surrounding spaces. He used these drawings to evaluate the successes and failures in the various designs. This set of studies yielded very useful information that he then adapted and applied to his current project. He wasn't copying the examples he'd found, but discovering other possibilities and opportunities that he had not previously considered. It gave new direction and focus to the design process.

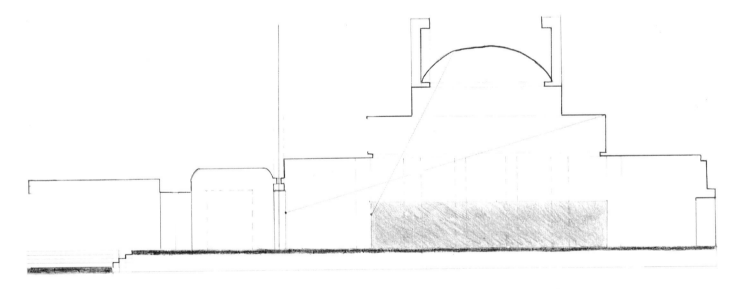

Figure 1.54. Precedents are examples studied and analyzed to understand possibilities for new design. This image shows a precedent building examined for the principles of composition employed in relating space. STUDENT: JENNIFER HURST—CRITIC: JAMES ECKLER—INSTITUTION: MARYWOOD UNIVERSITY

Precedents serve as exemplars in a design process. They can be existing buildings, methodologies, or ideas that guide some aspect of a current design. A precedent study is typically a procedure for investigating an example of a design issue that is evident in a previously developed project. This is done in order to understand different ways that principle might be applied to a current project. However, precedents may also be used as a communicative device for the illustration or justification of a design decision.

How can a precedent study contribute to a design process? How does the study of an existing building help the creation of a completely different one? Precedents can contribute in a variety of ways. At the very least they constitute a form of research in which different design possibilities can be found and examined. Precedent analysis can provide opportunities for extensive influence over the invention and development of a design project.

It is common for a precedent to be used simply for imitation. This is often the result of precedent studies that are primarily based in conventional

research. A designer wants to create complex component of a building, so he or she finds another that uses a similar idea in order to imitate it. This can be a valuable communicative device: it gives critics an immediate understanding of the design intent because they can see an existing result. However, this type of precedent use has less potential to influence architectural conception. It relies completely on observation rather than generative study.

Precedents can become generative through analysis. This process occurs when design decisions are identified in an existing structure and graphically evaluated based upon certain design criteria. Successes and failures of a building, technique, or system can be taken into account when new spatial information is generated for a current project. Design principles can then be variably applied to the evolving project based upon its specific characteristics. Precedent analysis can thus guide the conceptual or strategic development of a design.

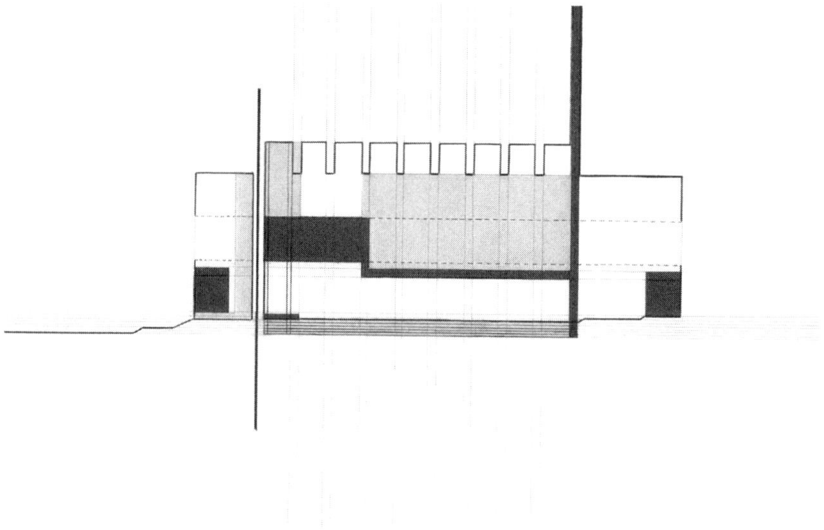

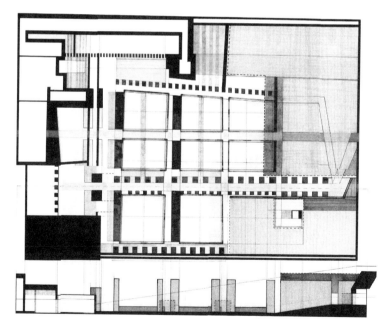

Figure 1.55. *In this example, the student synthesizes precedent information from previous analyses to understand the relationship between tectonic assembly, spatial profile, and the operations of space.* STUDENT: GEORGE FABER—CRITIC: JAMES ECKLER—INSTITUTION: UNIVERSITY OF CINCINNATI

Figure 1.56. *This precedent study shows the organizational network of spatial and formal systems. It studies correlations between the position of form and the facilitation of movement and program.* STUDENT: DEREK JEROME—CRITIC: JAMES ECKLER—INSTITUTION: UNIVERSITY OF CINCINNATI

PROCESS

A sequence of actions in which each action is based upon discoveries from the one before it

The application of techniques for representing concepts that guide decision making and production in design

Generative Possibilities in Applied Technique

The student produced many sketches, diagrams, drawings, and models. She began with just a few ideas for ways in which her project could be composed. She researched her ideas through precedent study. She tested them through sketching and drawing. She studied and reevaluated them through diagramming. Each time she made something, her ideas would become more resolved, and she'd develop new ones that would help her move forward with her project. From the initial stages of conception to the final stages of resolution, the design process was a means by which she could research and inquire about the possibilities presented in architecture. Her final product could be traced through these steps, and the evolution of thought would be reflected in the evolution of the space and form of her project.

The word *process* has evolved in meaning, from referring to the content or meaning of a dialogue to referring to a journey, or to moving forward. It currently refers to a set of steps or actions taken in a specific order to yield a result. Each of these meanings can be seen in process as it pertains to design. Process is the means by which architecture is conceived, the way that it is embedded with content. Process is an exploration of the possibilities of design—a journey. Process also consists of techniques and methods by which ideas and possibilities are realized.

Design process is a form of architectural inquiry performed through various acts of making. How does one inquire about architecture through process? How does this impact a design? Inquiry, research, and decision

 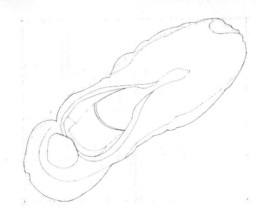 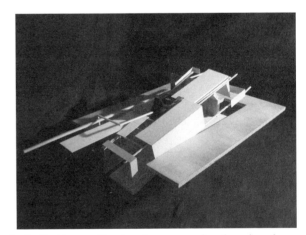

Figure 1.57.   The design process is a heuristic investigation of possibilities in spatial and formal composition. In the first image the shoe is measured and analyzed. The second image documents the shoe as an articulated surface. The third is a container that holds the shoe, which has become integral to the design. Each stage built upon those that came before. Each stage was a generator of iterations that followed. That gradual accumulation of information is the foundation of the design process. Student: May William and Charles Jones—Critic: Jim Sullivan—Institution: Louisiana State University

are all pursuits of intellect. This thinking about a design is guided by various pursuits of craft. Techniques for making are a way of testing ideas and discovering possibilities that were previously unknown. Making and thinking are intrinsically linked in a process of design because technique is used as a frame for architectural conception. Various media can be employed to explore different aspects of a design problem. Ideas can be constructed, tested, and reconfigured based upon the performance of the crafted item. Most importantly, craft is generative. New ideas for design are a result of making something and observing an unanticipated outcome. Design is rarely perfect in its first permutation. Through necessary iteration, craft is a vehicle for the resolution of ideas.

Process is a broad term, a composite of many design principles. Each of these principles refers to some manner of design thinking or making. Taken in its entirety, the design process is the exploration of potential and possibility for architectural space. Process in design is not a linear sequence of events with singular outcomes. Unlike a method, it has no definitive goal. Instead it seeks to discover possible solutions to a design problem through iterative making. It demands that decisions be revisited over and over again as new discoveries are made. Exploration in process is achieved when intuitive decisions are measured against or determine design intent. An iterative process will refine those intuitive gestures into architecture with purpose.

Certain skills will be favored as the designer evolves. Individual priorities in design will emerge. This evolution results in the development of an individual process. The individual's process might make use of a particular methodology, or design language. The emergence of an individual's process reflects a specialized understanding of technique and ways that techniques are applied to foster invention.

PROGRAM

Events that take place within a space; the function of space

To create, code, or define events that are to take place within a space; to script a function of occupation

Generative Possibilities in Function

He interviewed the family. He asked them about their jobs and work habits, and the ways they interacted with one another. He was trying to find out about their lifestyle and what was important to them. He discovered that they were social people; they entertained frequently. Often entertaining was a way of sharing the experiences of their travels. When alone, they would sit for some time around the table talking and sharing food.

Their answers told him about the ways they used space. The information shared by the family provided a script for him to follow as he designed their new house. He began with the social spaces and the way they interlocked with the dining area. The more public spaces were large enough to hold quite a crowd, but they were divided into smaller areas appropriate for the family when they were by themselves. The dining table was in one of these areas. It was contained in a way that gave it access to the larger public spaces but would also provide enclosure and an intimate setting for the family to converse on their own. Some of these spaces were divided by display cases that showcased the various treasures they had gathered while traveling. To guests it was a centerpiece of conversation. The house was programmed specifically for the family's needs.

To program space is to assign function to it. Programming has the potential to be a generative component of the design process, a way of outlining requirements for the characteristics of space and form. When a space is charged with housing an event, that space can be precisely configured toward meeting the requirements associated with the event. Proportion, spatial and formal relationships, and experience may all be factors that are influenced by program.

Program can be manifest in many degrees of resolution, from the generic to the specific. Over the course of the design process, that level of resolution may evolve according to the decisions made regarding spatial and formal composition. In what ways might a generic program facilitate decision making as a part of process? In what ways might a specific program do the same? The considerations of a generic program can be generators of composition. The priority in creating spaces for a generic program lies in the composition of the space itself rather than in meeting a set of criteria based upon programmatic needs. It is gestural in nature and invites interpretation and exploration. However, a specific program establishes a set of standards by which success can be measured. For instance, a space for reading is a generic program. It is a point of departure for experimentation with dimension, proportion, access to light, placement within a spatial sequence, and formal composition. On the other hand, a reading room designed to store a certain number of books and provide room for a specific number of people to study establishes the standards by which success can be measured. In this case, there is a definite set of requirements to be met by the spaces that house this program and may introduce a formulaic logic to the design process.

Evolving design implies that programmatic considerations may also evolve. The ability for program to provide both a point of departure and a measure of success can be valuable in providing direction to the design process. Program may begin as a space for reading; as the design evolves from that point, various spatial and formal characteristics may be defined. Those characteristics might then inform the gradual resolution of the program. Using this logic, design thinking continually shifts between defining function and composing the spatial construct. The conclusion would be a point at which the demands of a particular function of a space are met through a thoughtful development of composition and experience. Applied in this way, program becomes both a tool for architectural inquiry and a specific set of design criteria.

RESPOND

To act or make decisions in reaction to a previously existing condition or circumstance

Generative Possibilities in Reaction

The site was near downtown. Most of the buildings in this area were row houses. If they didn't share common walls with their neighbors, only a narrow alley separated them. The entry to most of them was directly off the sidewalk, elevated a little by a front stoop.

The site had very narrow side yards separating it from neighboring structures. The architect thoroughly documented the neighboring buildings on that block. His observations yielded several key pieces of information that he used to generate a strategy for responding to the new building's immediate surroundings. First, both neighboring structures had small windows facing the narrow side yard. Second, there were gardens and terraces, often used communally, in the center of the block. Finally, the terrain sloped, positioning the project site somewhat below the houses on the opposite side of the block.

He responded to the windows on either side by recessing the walls immediately opposite them. This allowed more light into the side yard. There he placed his own windows to take advantage of the light, but positioned them in a way that wouldn't permit a view into the neighboring dwelling. He responded to the central communal space by creating access to the gardens in back, both from the house and from neighboring yards. This allowed gathering to continue, but he also designed markers to define ownership. And he decided to have the height of the house fall below the roof decks of the houses farther up the slope so that their vista overlooking the town wasn't impeded.

Architectural response is a process through which multiple elements are made to relate to one another. That relationship can be spatial or formal, compositional or programmatic. The process involves the identification of spatial, formal, compositional, or programmatic characteristics in an existing condition. Those characteristics can then be used as a guide for new design.

What is the objective of a process of response in the generation of architecture? Directing the design process toward a response to another condition can have one of two objectives. It can be a method for integrating a new design into an existing condition, or it can be a process-related device for developing cohesion between components in a design.

Figure 1.58. Architecture has allegiances to the characteristics of its surroundings as well as those of the elements it is to hold. In this image a path is clearly visible, marked in the surface of the ground. The intervention is configured in response to the topography and the location of that path. STUDENT: BRITTANY DENNING—CRITIC: JAMES ECKLER—INSTITUTION: UNIVERSITY OF CINCINNATI

Responding to an existing condition is a process that promotes the integration of a design into a context. The design may augment, reconfigure, or occupy a site's existing spatial structure. The process of response may be a way of adapting design intent to the formal limitations of a context. Spatially or formally responding to an existing organizational structure can compositionally integrate the new design into an existing context. The new design may be charged with providing a new set of spatial conditions to contain an existing program. Each of these scenarios implies a process in which a characteristic is identified and a corresponding component of the design is generated to accommodate it.

However, a response doesn't necessarily need to be between an existing condition and a new one. It may be a way of simultaneously developing components that are related to each other through space, form, composition, or program. It can be a method for ensuring the integration of various components in a single design.

The process of response is a way of defining architectural intent for interaction. Interaction between spaces or the events within them can be a product of response. Response can direct the registration or relationship between formal elements. It can be a strategy that governs the physical connection of designed components. As a part of a larger process, response is likely iterative: it can facilitate editing and can play a role in the transformation of parts and ideas.

» *See also* Dialogue.

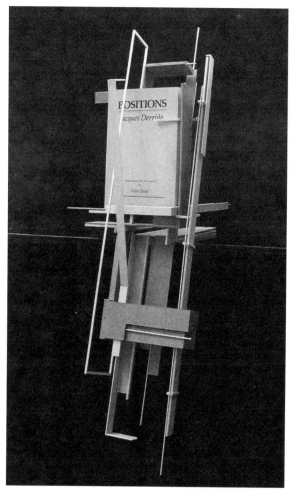

Figure 1.59. The book has certain dimensions, weight, and requirements for display. The architectural armature that holds it in place is made in response to the book's specific characteristics. STUDENT: RICHARD JONES—CRITIC: JIM SULLIVAN—INSTITUTION: LOUISIANA STATE UNIVERSITY

RETAIN

To keep or hold

To preserve; to keep unchanged

Generative Possibilities in Preservation and Memory

The building was slated to be demolished. It had outlived its usefulness and would be replaced by one better suited for the desired function. The older building had occupied that site for some time. It had become a fixture in the community; it was therefore important to community residents that it be preserved in some way.

A fragment of the older structure's facade was retained, kept as a memory of what it used to be. The new facade was designed as an extension of the remnant. New construction was built off the old, using many of the compositional characteristics of the fragment in the new construction. The new facade was divided into intervals, with a scale based upon that of the fragment. Where the fragment was thick or thin, so were the new walls constructed around it. The fragment contained a window; it acted as a guide for the construction of new openings. They aligned with the older one and correlated with each segment of the new facade.

Even though details were changed, materials were different, and elements rearranged, there were enough compositional cues taken from that fragment to recall the previous building. As for the piece retained from the older structure, it was set back from the surface to indicate its difference from the rest.

Retaining something is an intentional act of preservation. An element can be preserved despite the removal of others around it. Retention can also be a more generic idea of resistance to removal. In order for retention to be identified it must exist in juxtaposition to change or removal. It is measured in relation to the degree of change that it resists. How can the retention of some design component impact design process or intent? A retained element might mark the evolution of a design idea within a larger process,

become a catalyst for conceiving of architecture, or refer to an existing state of architecture.

Ideas change throughout the design process; that is, indeed, the point of the process. However, as ideas change they also inform those that come after them. As a project grows in sophistication, some ideas or elements are discarded, some changed, and some retained. As the designer iterates aspects of the project, elements or ideas that prove to be more successful than others will be kept and the others discarded. The decision to retain some component of the design or idea and not another is one way that the a project's evolution can be determined and controlled.

Alternatively, a retained element may become the foundation from which a design idea is built. Much of design is devoted to relationships between forms, spaces, or functions. Retaining some aspect of a previous design or preserving a fragment of an architectural context in its present state can give the designer a valuable set of limitations. These limitations may guide the composition of the project; they may also provide a point of departure for the generation of new ideas.

As a descriptor for a current condition of architecture, retention may refer more generally to preservation. Portions of a reconstruction might be preserved from alteration. Or elements of architecture might resist the some changing force, such as time or weather. In this regard, retention can reflect an architectural condition at any scale. A small detail of an object might be retained in the midst of larger alteration. Similarly, one particular hillock retained of a filed might be retained while others are altered to reduce their slope.

Figure 1.61. *This image is of a model generated from an analytical diagram. In it the diagram is retained and integrated as an element of the construction. It acts a guide for the aligning, relating, and organizing elements of the design.* STUDENT: DAVE PERRY—CRITIC: JAMES ECKLER—INSTITUTION: MARYWOOD UNIVERSITY

Figure 1.60. *This model was generated from an analytical diagram. The diagram established a compositional language that translated into strategies for making space. Instances of that original diagram were retained as surface articulations seen on the plane in the image foreground.* STUDENT: TAYLOR ORSINI— CRITIC: JOHN MAZE—INSTITUTION: UNIVERSITY OF FLORIDA

Figure 1.62. *The model is built around and through the folded leaves of a phonebook. The printing on the pages is retained without manipulation to act as an organizational pattern, a texture, and a surface characteristic.* STUDENT: MATTHEW RABALAIS—CRITIC: JIM SULLIVAN—INSTITUTION: LOUISIANA STATE UNIVERSITY

REVEAL

To make known or visible

A conscious effort to show or display

A physical cut or slot through which something has been made visible or its presence implied

Generative Possibilities in Awareness

He was making another model for his latest project; this one focused on the design of the building shell. It was going to be an elaborate series of layers that thickened the wall. They would also ensure that the building's primary structure would remain along its outer edge to free up space in the interior.

He began by constructing the structural components. They occurred at even intervals, and each had a different profile as they were used to support the undulating surfaces of the wall. After he had built the structural components, he began making the panels that would serve as an outer skin of the assembly. When he was finished, he held the construction in his hand. The wall was well crafted, and various surfaces jutted in and out on both sides. They were all uniformly white. But he was disappointed. There had been something captivating about the structural armature before he had covered it. Its complexity showed the way the jutting surfaces were defined. Its interval provided a measure to the entire assembly. All of that was now covered.

He began making a new model. In this one he created cuts positioned strategically in the skin panels to reveal, in different places, particular characteristics of the underlying structure.

Something that is revealed is uncovered, displayed, or otherwise conspicuous. Intentional revealing reflects a conscious decision on the part of the designer to control access to, or perception of, space or form. Additionally, in common usage, an architectural element that facilitates visual access to something that would otherwise be obscured is referred to as a reveal. A reveal is usually some detail or joint that expresses structure that would otherwise exist below a surface. The act of revealing some object, element, or spatial condition can influence or direct design thinking in several ways. The act of revealing can be a tool for distributing program. It can be a process that executes a design decision or intent. Or it can be a process that generates spatial characteristics or conditions.

Figure 1.63. This is a study of the way material and assembly can reveal information. The thread is a material that provides opportunities through density to create components that permit or deny visual access. The act of spooling the thread is a vehicle for controlling the density of wraps and awareness of the image beyond. STUDENT: BART BAJDA—CRITIC: MATTHEW MINDRUP—INSTITUTION: MARYWOOD UNIVERSITY

The desire to reveal a space or object is a programmatic consideration. Revealing a space or object is an act of differentiating between awareness and obscurity. Revealing can be a function of space that makes an occupant aware of a condition yet to be encountered, as opposed to the discovery of an obscured condition.

What is being revealed? Where is it placed in relation to other programmed elements of the design? To reveal in design could address social issues of privacy and access, or it could address pragmatic issues of function. In this respect, the intent to reveal might be a strategy for organizing space so that a mechanical system is put on display or a celebrated object is highlighted.

As a design principle, revealing can establish an organizational relationship between spaces. There is a connection between the space that houses an observer and the one being observed. This application of revelation to the design process has the potential to generate spatial continuity between programmatic elements as well as a system of programmatic arrangement.

An act of revealing is also a tool for establishing hierarchy in space or form. Certain elements may be revealed in order to emphasize their presence or function. Revealing a structural system informs space by displaying the mechanics of its composition. That same reveal can establish the assembly as primary within the composition of space. A space that is opened to another can communicate a spatial relationship. The revealed space may also be a product of narrative or experiential intent. Revealing can facilitate the spatial extension of sequential continuity, disclosing a space beyond.

Something that is obscured may not be completely hidden. A combination of revealing and obscuring may be employed to communicate a limited awareness. The presence of an obscured space might be hinted at through a reveal. What space or spatial condition is to be revealed? How might that act of revealing lend itself to the conception of space, sequence, or perception? Considering the act of revealing as a tool for prescribing the way an occupant perceives or interacts with space or form has the potential to direct decisions regarding spatial experience. Revealing the spatial conditions or details of an assembly can be one facet of a larger spatial narrative that describes experience or directs process.

» *See also* Obscure.

Figure 1.64. *In this example, gaps have been left between elements of a stacked assembly. The gaps function as small reveals through which one can look.* STUDENT: JEFF BADGER—CRITIC: JAMES ECKLER—INSTITUTION: UNIVERSITY OF CINCINNATI

Figure 1.65. *A reveal does not always display something on the other side of it. The shift in height shown in this image is a part of a joint between components of a design. It reveals the nature of each and the way they are joined.* STUDENT: JENNIFER HURST—CRITIC: JAMES ECKLER—INSTITUTION: MARYWOOD UNIVERSITY

SUBMERGE

To place under

To bury or inundate

Generative Possibilities in Covering

The place was prone to harsh winds. They'd whistle around any obstacle placed above the surface of the flat terrain. Sometimes they'd carry stinging sand. The pavilion, as designed, couldn't fulfill one of architecture's fundamental responsibilities: to provide shelter. The open sides would permit the wind and sand flow through it freely. It would provide no respite.

To create an enclosure that would repel the winds and sand would require materials unavailable for this project. Those that were available would quickly succumb to the eroding forces of windblown sand. The design team decided upon a solution that began with a cut in the ground. Within that cut, the pavilion could be constructed. The wind would pass right across the top of the crevasse. In submerging the pavilion in the ground, a small tranquil space was created as an escape from the wind.

Architecturally, submergence is a way of defining a formal relationship between a surface and an intervening element. This relationship is inherently contextual. It can be an act of additively covering the element, creating an extension of the surface. Or it can be an act of subtracting from the surface in order to position the element within or beneath. There are three ways that an element can be submerged relative to a surface: it can be fully within or beneath, it can become a component of the surface, or it can be embedded.

Full submergence implies that the element exists entirely on the other side of the surface (the inside, or underside). Making the element a component of the surface implies that it occupies a space within or beneath, but that its uppermost face occupies the same plane as the surface to which it relates. Embedding an element implies that portions of it are not submerged or are exposed. How can this process be used to inform design intent? Submerging an element defines a relationship between the element and the surface it is being submerged within. This relationship can occur at two

scales: the scale of the space being submerged in a larger contextual condition, or the scale of that part of the assembly that might be submerged within or beneath a tectonic plane.

Submergence at the scale of habitable space most often refers to the relationship between intervention and ground. The intervention can be entirely subterranean—a position beneath the surface of the ground. As

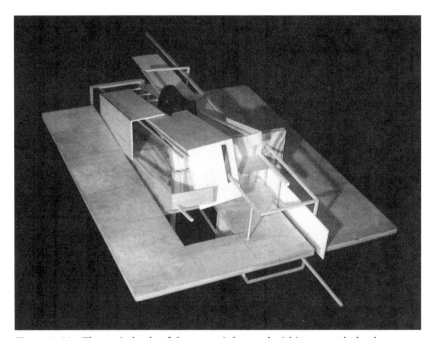

Figure 1.66.   The main body of the space is housed within an angled volume. The lower end of the volume is partially submerged beneath the surface of the base plane.   Student: Charles Jones—Critic: Jim Sullivan—Institution: Louisiana State University

described above, a submerged element can be beneath, at, or embedded within the surface of the ground. Each of these positions describes a different formal relationship to the ground and to the context as a whole. They stand in opposition to a relationship with the ground where the intervention is placed upon the surface or held above it.

In any of these positions there are spatial, experiential, and programmatic implications to be considered. Issues of spatial sequence are raised in the design of the transition between above and below. Issues of experience are raised as the filtration of light is designed for the submerged spaces. Both of these issues impact the events that might occur in the submerged space. Because of the issues that are raised as a result of submerging space within the ground, this process of making can also be a

method for controlling those aspects of a design. Submerging something provides an opportunity for spatial transition, for the filtration of light in a specific manner, and for the prescription of events that can occur in the space.

At a smaller scale submerging something within an assembly can be a method for crafting a joint. It can speak to the assembly itself. Or it can describe the way in which an object occupies a niche created through assembly. A compositional structuring device or system might be submerged within a thick planar assembly. Or, an artifact might be reside within a niche, submerging it within another object. As an act of making, submerging can reflect design intent or guide its conception.

» *See also* Suspend.

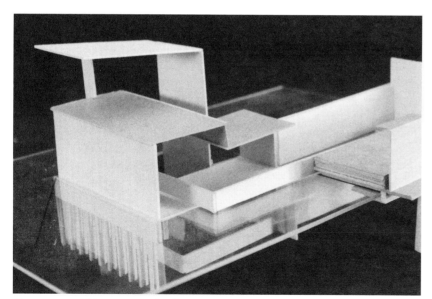

Figure 1.67.   This project is divided into two portions. One is submerged below the base plane, the other positioned above it. Some points within the project spaces exist in both the upper and lower portions, creating a series of spatial relationships across the base plane. STUDENT: JENNIFER HURST—CRITIC: JAMES ECKLER—INSTITUTION: MARYWOOD UNIVERSITY

Figure 1.68.   This section model reveals the profile of spaces as they descend into the ground. Some are partially submerged, while others are completely beneath the surface. Spaces relate to one another across the surface of the ground, and circulating through spaces provides an occupant with different vantages for viewing the surroundings. STUDENT: SETH TROYER—CRITIC: JAMES ECKLER—INSTITUTION: UNIVERSITY OF CINCINNATI

SUBTRACTIVE

A process of making that is characterized by removal

Generative Possibilities in Removal

A block of clay lay on her desk. She had shaped it many times. But it was still a solid object. It had no voids within which she could imagine habitation. She used a wire to slice into the mass of clay. Slowly and precisely, she removed material. Using this subtractive method, she was able to invent a complex set of interlocking spaces within the shaped clay mass. From this point forward, her process was an additive one. She attached other elements to articulate the volumes she had created in the mass.

Subtraction is a simple process that allows a designer to quickly iterate a design through intuitive decision making: ideas can be generated as an object is carved or as fragments are removed from an assembly.

This strategy for iteration fosters discovery. Because it has the potential to become more about the forms that define a space than the space itself, it can be a distraction to the primary design objective. In what ways might this, as a technique, propel a design to another level of resolution or begin the next iterative step? Perhaps, as a preliminary design technique, it could be employed to discern variations in spatial composition as in the narrative. Or it might be used to develop a tectonic language for the communication of spatial information that could be employed in a design's future iterations.

Beyond this strategy for making through subtraction, it can also describe a strategy for making at a smaller scale. A single large piece can be carved

Figure 1.69. In contrast to the illustration presented in the "Additive" section, this example depicts a notch or depression created in an element through the removal of material.

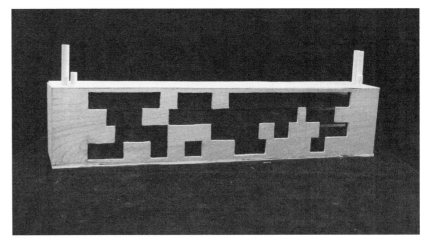

Figure 1.70. In this example, subtraction is used in order to articulate and detail this facade. The removal of parts of the plane creates a frame for viewing the movement of sliding panels. STUDENT: BART BAJDA—CRITIC: MATTHEW MINDRUP—INSTITUTION: MARYWOOD UNIVERSITY

to create individual components. This contrasts with the additive techniques of layering, or the building up of material to create architectural elements. The additive and the subtractive speak to the difference between the tectonic and stereotomic methods for crafting.

    » *See also* Additive.

Figure 1.71. **In this example, subtraction is the method used to craft a joint between components. One is cut away, and the resulting voids are then filled by the other components.** STUDENT: ZACH FATZINGER—CRITIC: REAGAN KING—INSTITUTION: MARYWOOD UNIVERSITY

Figure 1.72. **This model uses subtraction as a compositional strategy. The armature is achieved through assembling planes to create an intricate formal volume. However, these crafting techniques are employed in a way that imitates subtractive making. The armature is filled with small compartments of space, some of which are filled by other parts of the model.** STUDENT: TAYLOR ORSINI—CRITIC: JOHN MAZE—INSTITUTION: UNIVERSITY OF FLORIDA

SUSPEND

To hang something

To stop or pause an action or sequence

To cause something to float, or imply that something floats, without apparent structure

Generative Possibilities in Elevating

The library is row upon row of book stacks. In the far corner is the librarians' desk. There you can ask questions or check out a book to take with you. The door is immediately next to it, along with a display of this week's featured books.

You move into the stacks, looking for a particular book. The space between shelves is narrow, and they rise well over your head. You are immediately cut off from sight and isolated within the labyrinth of books. Finding the one you've come for, you go to seek out a place to study it.

A stair leads you to a mezzanine. Here a field of tables replaces the rows of dimly lit stacks. Each table has too many chairs around it, but the space is tall and well lit, a stark contrast to the stacks beneath you. The mezzanine itself is supported above the stacks by columns positioned directly within the shelves of books. The shelves disguise those columns so that they are never seen. Instead, it is as if the mezzanine were a floating island, suspended above the shelves.

Suspension can be one of two processes. It can imply a slowed or paused movement. It can also describe a technique for formal composition that creates a relationship between a surface and an element in which the element is held above the surface.

As it pertains to movement, suspension is not a matter of slowing or pausing as much as it is a process of creating space for pause. Moments of pause may inform zones of circulation. Movement may be suspended to accommodate program within a spatial sequence. Slowing circulation may be a function of transitioning from one space to another—turning a corner, proceeding down a stair, or stepping through a gap in a wall.

Suspension can also be an act of making in which an element is held aloft. This process can be a response to context or an act of both spatial and formal composition. How is this process able to generate space or design

intent? Using suspension as a strategy for engaging a context presents a formal composition of removal from, or minimal association with, the existing surface. To some extent, this strategy might lessen the obligation to respond to existing formal or organizational characteristics of a site. Instead, the design relies upon an assembled, mediating structure that holds the element above the surface or ground plane. It is that intermediate structure that might respond to contextual characteristics as opposed to the element

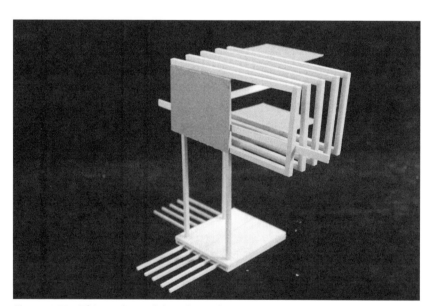

Figure 1.73. This study model explores the possibilities of suspension, with the main body overhanging the supports that hold it aloft. Space is made within the body of the model as well as below it. STUDENT: ASHLEY CAVELLIER—CRITIC: KATE O'CONNOR—INSTITUTION: MARYWOOD UNIVERSITY

that it is holding. This may reflect, or generate, a design intent that imposes a new ordering system onto the existing one. It may also be a response made necessary by some incompatibility between the context and the needs of the design. For instance, the ground surface may not be proportioned in a way that accommodates a particular program, so the act of suspension might provide an opportunity to design within a set of dimensions not possible at the surface. Or a spatial need for the continuity of a plane may not be feasible on an undulating surface.

Suspending elements can also be a means of composing space. Regardless of whether one element is suspended within a space or above a contextual field, there are implications on habitation; the most immediate is that it creates the opportunity to inhabit the space below the suspended element. This impacts spatial composition and sequence through the compression and expansion of space. As one moves beneath the suspended object, space is compressed; proportions are reduced relative to the occupant. As one moves out from under that suspended object, space is expanded; proportions are increased relative to the occupant. That also creates differences in spatial type and has consequences for sequencing space as one moves from expanded space to compressed space and back again. What programs might be housed within the compressed space versus the expanded? Can the influence over spatial sequence be used to facilitate a larger transition or provide a place of encounter?

There is also the question of the nature of the suspended element. It may be an object suspended to provide a way of controlling these issues. It may also be a space itself, which incorporates another programmatic type and possibility for habitation. It forces a consideration for how an occupant moves from below the suspended space into it. All of these issues reflect decisions of both spatial and formal composition and operation. As an act of making, suspending can reflect design intent or guide its conception.

» *See also* Submerge.

Figure 1.74. *The orthogonal volume at the center of the image is slightly suspended above the model's base. The sliver between the base and the volume creates a distinction between it and the other elements around it.* STUDENT: GRACE DAVIS—CRITIC: STEPHEN GARRISON—INSTITUTION: MARYWOOD UNIVERSITY

Figure 1.75. *In this example, space is differentiated using suspension. The volume at the center of the image has a counterpart suspended above it. This creates a space between upper and lower volumes that is dramatically reduced in size from the spaces around them.* STUDENT: RYAN BOGEDIN—CRITIC: JAMES ECKLER—INSTITUTION: MARYWOOD UNIVERSITY

SYNTHESIS

The process of combining parts into a unified whole

Generative Possibilities in Combination

An architect has just received an addition project about which he is very excited. A couple has purchased an older historic house and has asked him to design a new addition that will better suit them while preserving the character of the original structure. Before design can begin however, an extensive study of the existing conditions has to take place.

The architect begins by analyzing the site, breaking it up into several categories of study: dimension and topography, existing site features, as well as adjacent buildings and public access. The addition will also have to respond to the existing spatial composition of the house, so he analyzes using circulation, program, and degrees of privacy. Since the new addition has to efficiently respond to the environment, he analyzed it in terms of daylight, solar orientation, and climate. All of these studies enable him to conceive a design strategy through synthesis. The product of that synthesis is a single diagram that incorporates the information gained from each individual study into a spatial composition. He then uses that diagram to develop the first set of process drawings and a model.

Synthesis is a type of abstraction in which a designer is able to unify distinct pieces of information into a single, complex whole. Through a process of synthesis, isolated pieces of information are studied relative to their potential to affect one another. How is the process of synthesis generative? How does it generate information? How does it generate design?

Synthesis begins with identifying related parts that have been studied or documented independently of one another. Synthesizing them into a single element permits the different ways they impact one another to be investigated. After synthesis occurs as a part of a study, the designer is then able to create another iteration of the project accounting for new information generated in the overlap and connection of different systems.

Through synthesis, a designer can apply knowledge gained through research or analysis to a design process. It is that application that drives testing and iteration. Success of a formal or spatial composition is measured by testing the various arrangements of components brought together toward the fulfillment of a design objective.

» *See also* Analysis

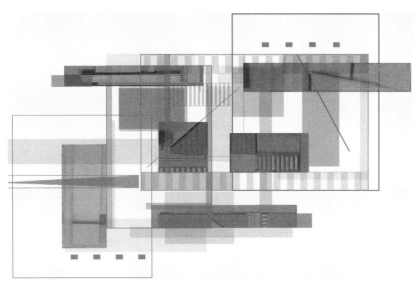

Figure 1.76.   Synthesis is a combining of information or media into a single, integrated construct or document. This drawing synthesizes model photos with a digitally crafted diagram. STUDENT: RACHEL MOMENEE—CRITIC: JOHN HUMPHRIES—INSTITUTION: MIAMI UNIVERSITY

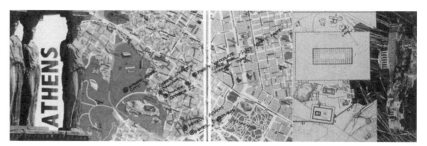

Figure 1.77.   This example synthesizes a map, plans, and images as a means of documenting travel and encounter. STUDENT: KYLE COBURN—CRITIC: JOHN HUMPHRIES—INSTITUTION: MIAMI UNIVERSITY

TRANSFORM

To drastically change formal characteristics

To make physically or functionally different

Generative Possibilities in Alteration

The saw grinds through the metal panel in a cloud of sparks. In time a piece is removed completely, leaving a rectangular hole. This process is repeated several times. Each hole that is cut is of a different dimension and orientation, but the process of cutting it remains the same.

The metal itself is corrugated to make it rigid. This permits it to bend in only one direction, along a seam that runs parallel to the folds. In some instances the pieces are not removed entirely, but are instead bent out, acting as a louver to limit the entry of light to a particular direction.

The pieces that were removed are eventually reattached in a new orientation. They are used as overhangs to shield the openings caused by their removal. The openings are framed in wood to soften the sharp edge of the shorn metal.

What had been a steel shipping container has become a pavilion. More just like it are made and distributed throughout the park. Benches and tables are placed within them. People sometimes use them as a place to stop for lunch. Other times they are needed as shelter. People will retreat within to escape the sun, or run toward one to escape an unexpected rain shower.

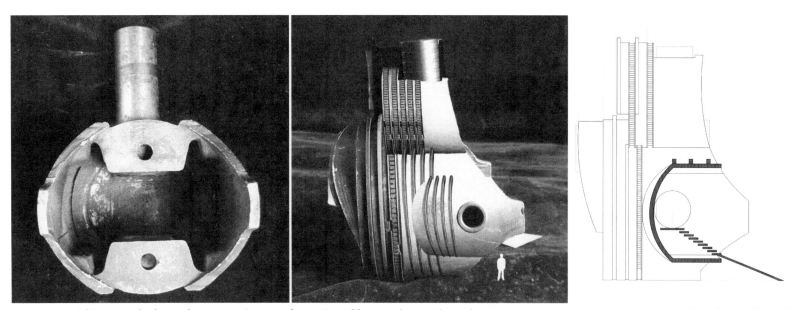

Figure 1.78. *This example shows the progressive transformation of form and space through an iterative process. The exercise began with a found object. The student then acted upon that object to transform it into a spatial construction.* STUDENT: JOE GIBNEY—CRITIC: JAMES ECKLER—INSTITUTION: MARYWOOD UNIVERSITY

Transformation is a process by which an element is altered in either form or function. The altered element retains some basic characteristics of the original form, differentiating this process from one in which the subject is replaced by another. If the transformation extended to complete reinvention, the process would be replacement rather than transformation, as there would no longer be any remnant of the original form.

A physical transformation is one in which formal characteristics are manipulated. Compositional properties might be transformed to affect spatial or formal relationships between elements. Properties of an assembly might be transformed in order to influence spatial characteristics or the capacity of the joint to inform space.

A functional transformation is one in which an element is altered in order to influence the way it operates in space. Functional transformation can be a product of process or a formal operation. In terms of process, the program of a space, or the way an inhabitant occupies it, may be transformed through subtle manipulations of its physical attributes. In this instance alteration of function speaks to reassigning the purpose of the architecture and frames considerations for the way space and form may be manipulated in order to serve that new purpose. However, functional transformation may also be a mechanical condition of form. Moving parts, or some other reliance

on a physical reconfiguration, may be a strategy for making, composing, or programming space. A plane that slides through a space may divide or unify depending on its position. Operable louvers may block or filter light in response to different events in a space. These formal manipulations reflect the intent to design an architecture that is able to actively accommodate many uses, or respond to different conditions of use, such as proportion, sequence, experience, or environment.

How does the transformation of design elements influence invention? How can transformation, as a physical act of manipulation, influence the way space is conceived? Transformation is a critical component of the design process and is typically a result of iteration. Transformation of design elements through various stages of process is the primary vehicle of design development; decisions are tested and the architecture is transformed to better meet design criteria. This evolution through process resolves not only physical aspects of a design, but can also resolve aspects of design intent. Transformation as a function of iteration is a vehicle for discovery. As unexpected conditions of a design are found, new ideas are able to augment or replace those that had driven the process to that point. As design operations change, the intent for the design may also evolve.

TYPE

To associate, group, or categorize based upon a common set of characteristics

An embodiment or quintessential example

A generic model used to illustrate certain characteristics

Generative Possibilities in Grouping

The project was very complex and consisted of a variety of spaces and functions. There were so many different programmatic responsibilities for the building that organizing the layout was proving to be very difficult.

The designer used typology as a strategy for overcoming these difficulties. She divided the various programs into more generic types. She organized the scheme by grouping spatial types, using typology to reduce a long list of spatial characteristics and programs to a simpler set of generic spatial attributes and programs. These spatial and functional groups became the primary elements composed in the overall scheme.

To assign a type to a component of design is to define it as similar or dissimilar to other components based upon certain characteristics. This process enables certain associative relationships to be made between elements even prior to any act of composition or assembly. The designer is able to realize that certain components will have one relationship or another based upon their type. In what ways can typology impact design process or thinking? How can the act of giving something a type generate new design ideas?

One way that typologies can aid in the design process is through representational language. Maintaining consistent language throughout a construction aids in the way that spaces are read; additionally, consistency better enables the designer to evaluate different aspects of a design and make changes. A component's type can determine the way it is made, which is a direct extension of design intent. For example, typology might dictate that similar things be made in similar ways. This consistency of language provides a common standard by which different spatial conditions can be evaluated, and it aids in the development of relationships between parts of a design. Understanding the way different components within a design relate to one another is a catalyst for experimentation, as those types can be arranged and rearranged. That process of arrangement and rearrangement will result in new ideas about the way spaces are composed.

Grouping components by type can also be a precursor to a more sophisticating organizational strategy. Various types can be arranged prior to the realization of specific details within spaces. The resulting scheme can provide insight into ways that different spaces might interact compositionally or functionally. That insight becomes a vehicle for iteration, as different scenarios can be tested even at the very initial stages of process. Eventually, patterns will emerge that can govern compositional decisions: an organizational strategy rooted in typology.

STUDENT: RENEE MARTIN—CRITIC: JOHN HUMPHRIES—INSTITUTION: MIAMI UNIVERSITY

2. TERMS OF ORGANIZATION AND ORDERING

ANCHOR

A point used for support or stability

A primary point in an organizational hierarchy

Generative Possibilities of a Focal Point

The fair comes to town, and you know that it will be good this year because the organizers have been advertising a new ride for months. Upon arriving you stand in line to purchase tickets, and you can see the promised attraction standing above the other rides; it is on the other side of the midway. Once the tickets are purchased, you weave your way through the other rides, vendors, and games in order to navigate to the new addition.

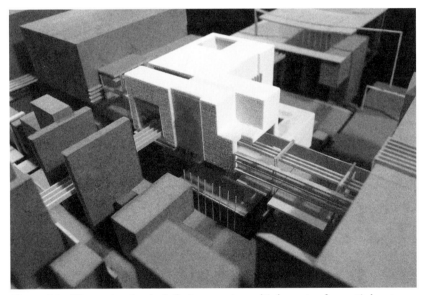

Figure 2.1. The anchor is a hub that connects multiple parts of a spatial system. The white volume in this example receives extensions from spatial components around it, redirects them, and uses them to define its own spatial character. If it were removed, this model would be a collection of disassociated parts. As it is, the white volume is the primary component that anchors the project; all other parts are dependent upon it to define their role within the composition. STUDENT: DAVID BURWINKEL—CRITIC: JAMES ECKLER—INSTITUTION: UNIVERSITY OF CINCINNATI

No matter where you are, you can always see some part of it up over the tops of the other rides, hear the commotion associated with it operation, or find a convenient sign that directs you toward your goal. It seems no matter where you walk, you will inevitably find your way to that new ride. Along the way many other attractions and distractions will cause you to deviate from your intended path; other rides catch your eye, or a desire to win a prize prompts you to play a carnival game. But all of these events are subordinate to the main attraction, the anchor of the entire midway.

Any organizational structure is dependent upon the establishment of a system of hierarchy; some pieces are more important than others. This hierarchy will determine the arrangement of design components and the relationships that exist among them. Assuming that a component serving the role of anchor is the primary piece of a project, what possibilities exist for the organization of other elements around it? An anchor can be employed in several ways as a project is organized. It can be a point within the organization that is prominent (as illustrated in the narrative text), or it can define a pattern for the organization itself (such as a nucleus in a radial organization pattern, or a terminus in a linear one).

The fair midway mentioned in the narrative, the common shopping mall, or any other collection of architectural elements can, and often does, make use of anchors to define a system of organization. Even a town square has the ability to be seen as an anchor to the surrounding commercial or residential portions of the town. These different uses can have an extensive influence on the architecture of the fragment being used as the anchor. The designer's challenge is to use an anchor piece to develop relationships between other components. The generative possibilities rooted in the term *anchor* are linked to the question, How does this one element negotiate the relationship between other associated components?

Figure 2.2. In this project, there is a central space around which all others are organized. Paths lead to it, and form defines it within a set of brackets and screens. This nucleus or core is highlighted as the primary component of the project. As such, it acts as an organizational anchor and possibly a structuring device. STUDENT: LeStavian Beverly—Critic: Tim Hayes—Institution: Louisiana Tech University

ANOMALY

An abnormality or inconsistency

Something that deviates from the rule, or something that is different from, interrupts, or disrupts a pattern

Generative Possibilities in Abnormality

A woman arrives at a building. The facade is divided into five equal bays. Each of the three bays to the left have a single large window, making them identical to one another. The bay to the far right is blank, and the second bay from the right holds the main entry.

She walks in. A rigid orthogonal grid that corresponds to the five bays of the facade organizes the interior spaces of the building. Walls and columns are arranged on the grid lines of the five-bayed building, making the grid apparent. Each column falls at an intersection of perpendicular grid lines that are inscribed into the floor. Walls are positioned so that they either end or turn a corner on those same intersections. Windows are cut into the exterior walls at regular intervals

determined by the grid structure. Everything, except one component, is dependent on this grid.

Ahead, and off to the left of the where she entered, the woman sees a box made of a different material from the rest. It is off-axis from the grid by about 60 degrees and is taller than the rest of the structure by about 10 feet. Steps are needed to access this volume, which is raised just above the floor plane of the rest of the building. This spatial anomaly is the primary space of the entire structure, and it is her destination.

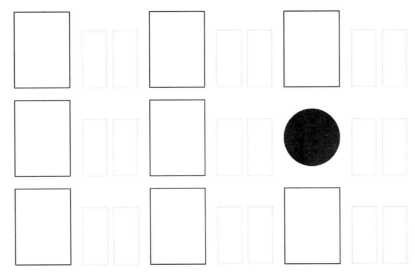

Figure 2.3. An anomaly is an isolated change in an established pattern. It can serve to establish hierarchy by highlighting an important element, or it can be a disruption that severs relationships between components or alters the way a system functions.

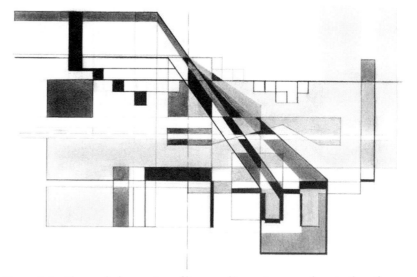

Figure 2.4. The angled grouping of lines and tones is anomalous to the otherwise orthogonal field. This serves to provide contrast between the angled set of elements and those that they cross. It highlights the angled elements as primary within the hierarchy of the drawing. STUDENT: ANGEL ORTIZ—CRITIC: JASON TOWERS— INSTITUTION: VALENCIA COMMUNITY COLLEGE

If an anomaly is something that violates a rule or standard of a design, how can it be used in a way that does not undermine the design? An anomaly is the purposeful deviation from a rule, convention, or norm governing a design. Few design decisions can better establish the clear prominence of one element than making that element different from everything in its surroundings. Primacy is given to the anomalous element by virtue of its difference from the norm. In most cases, however, the anomaly will be regarded as a primary element, whether it is intended to be or not. As such, it also has the ability to undermine the clarity of a design.

For instance, if an otherwise inconsequential component of a design is set apart as an anomalous entity, it will serve little use other than to confuse. When the use of anomalies is applied to a design as a strategy for establishing a hierarchy of elements, the designer must first set up the standard from which the anomaly is to deviate. What is the norm established in a design? What elements are important enough to warrant an exception to that norm? How might that exception be created without moving completely away from the design strategies already in place?

Another consideration is one of quantity. How many anomalies can be present in a design before the original standard is lost or becomes one of inconsistency? An anomaly's success is rooted in the fact that it is uncommon and easily identified as different.

Figure 2.5. A change in material, construction technique, or geometry can create an anomaly within a project. It calls special attention to that element. In this instance, the contrast established through the change in both material and geometry in the lower-right, stacked triangle serves to delineate areas within the project. STUDENT: GRACE DAVIS—CRITIC: STEPHEN GARRISON—INSTITUTION: MARYWOOD UNIVERSITY

Figure 2.6. The object suspended within the wire structure is an anomaly established by change in form and opacity. The curvilinear form of the object immediately calls attention to it. Its opacity and perceived weight, compared to the relative transparency of the wire structure, establishes it as the primary component of the project. STUDENT: JOHN DAUER—CRITIC: TIM HAYES—INSTITUTION: LOUISIANA TECH UNIVERSITY

ARRANGE

To order elements

To place elements in relation to one another

Generative Possibilities in Organizational Logic

Whenever the market comes to town, vendors set up their small pavilions in the town square. It is a large, paved public space with buildings along each side. The position of each vendor is predetermined and highly organized. The pavilions are arranged in a way that defines circulation for the shoppers and orientation for the vendors. Each booth has an obvious front that faces a path and an obvious back that abuts a neighboring booth. The vendors choose the most advantageous sites for the wares they are selling before the market arrives. This arrangement results in a carefully choreographed pattern of movement and series of encounters.

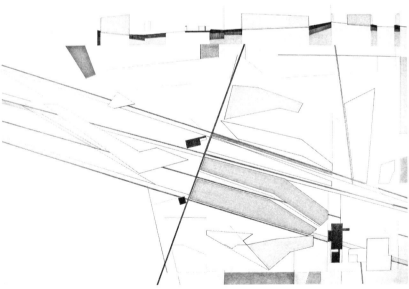

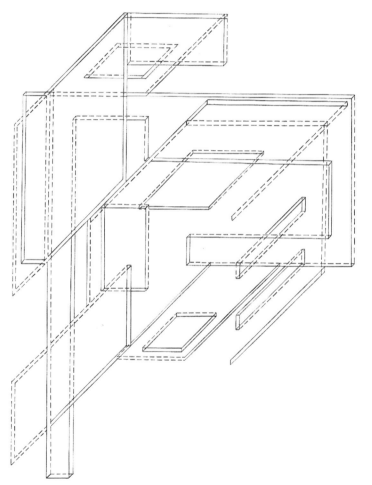

Figure 2.7. Arrangement speaks to an act of placing, positioning, or organizing pieces of a design. This drawing uses patterns of arrangement to investigate possibilities for the distribution of program across a site. Within it, zones of the site are understood and given emphasis according to program, circulation, and the placement of interventions. STUDENT: NATE HAMMITT—CRITIC: JAMES ECKLER—INSTITUTION: UNIVERSITY OF CINCINNATI

Figure 2.8. Arrangement can refer to form. In this example, the arrangement of parts within an assembly are used to make space. STUDENT: JIHYE CHOI—CRITIC: MILAGROS ZINGONI—INSTITUTION: ARIZONA STATE UNIVERSITY

Every design process involves an act of arrangement. That arrangement can be the position of spaces in relation to one another or the positioning of objects in space. The act of arrangement speaks to a strategy of organization. How does an organizational strategy influence the arrangement of objects and spaces? The organizational strategy of any design will define intent for the relationships among components. Arrangement is the act of making that tests the possibilities of that intent. Relationships are established between forms or spaces through grouping or association, orientation, proximity, or proportion. Through arranging spaces, a designer is able to determine not only the relationship between those spaces but also the sequence in which they are encountered.

Arrangement can occur as a pattern. A pattern of arrangement is an organizational strategy. It can use one of the five organizational types, or it can be a pattern that hybridizes several of them.

Physical structures or elements of a design can also be used to define arrangement. They are components of a design that define relationships—spatial, formal, or functional—among multiple elements of a project. The datum acts as a device for linking and sequencing other parts. The barrier acts as a way of dividing or separating parts from one another. Any element of a design that acts to relate multiple components is an organizational element—a structure that determines arrangement.

Figure 2.9. Arrangement can also refer to the organization of spaces. In this example, it is the arrangement of spaces around an open area. STUDENT: GEORGE FABER—CRITIC: JAMES ECKLER—INSTITUTION: UNIVERSITY OF CINCINNATI

ASSOCIATE

To join or group

Association: A relationship established through joining or grouping

Generative Possibilities in Designed Relationships

Your flight lands and you find yourself, with your bag, standing in front of the information desk. You realized on your flight that you had forgotten to make hotel reservations, so you're looking for a last-minute option. The only rooms still available are in the hotels associated with the airport. The hotels aren't physically a part of the airport but are nearby, with shuttles running all day to create connections between them. Eventually you're able to secure a reservation, and you board the appropriate shuttle. Upon arriving, you notice that the hotel has a large volume extending from the lobby out to the street. In that extension there is a small café, a restaurant, and a gift shop for tourists. None of these businesses are operated by the hotel, but associated with it by virtue of being connected at the lobby.

Why would a design require elements to be associated? An association of elements is a relationship that enables the designer to group or categorize pieces. This method of organization is one way that a consistent formal or spatial language can be used. Similarities and dissimilarities between pieces are acknowledged in the way those pieces are associated—or not associated. Additionally, association—physical or implied—is an organizational tool that identifies the most important characteristics of a form or space. It communicates that importance by using those characteristics as the baseline for determining similarity or dissimilarity.

How can an associative relationship be designed? Design possibilities exist both tangibly and intangibly. The association of two similar things can be physical or implied. Association can be determined based upon programmatic characteristics, similarities in function that cause different spaces to be categorized together: an implied association. Spaces and forms can also be associated compositionally, through similarities in spatial or formal configuration: a physical association.

What aspects of form or space cause components to be grouped or otherwise related? Are the similarities of form or space better expressed through an implied association, such as aesthetic similarity, or a physical association, such as a spatial joint creating an intersection between elements?

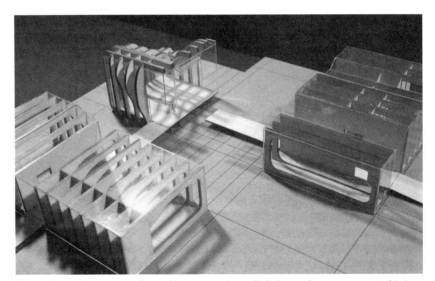

Figure 2.10. A common formal language (parallel ribs and a transparent skin) associates the different volumes that comprise this project. Organizationally, they are associated through the marked grid that governs their placement relative to one another. This association provides consistency that makes it easier to understand. STUDENT: COREY KOCZARSKI—CRITIC: VALERY AUGUSTIN—INSTITUTION: UNIVERSITY OF SOUTHERN CALIFORNIA

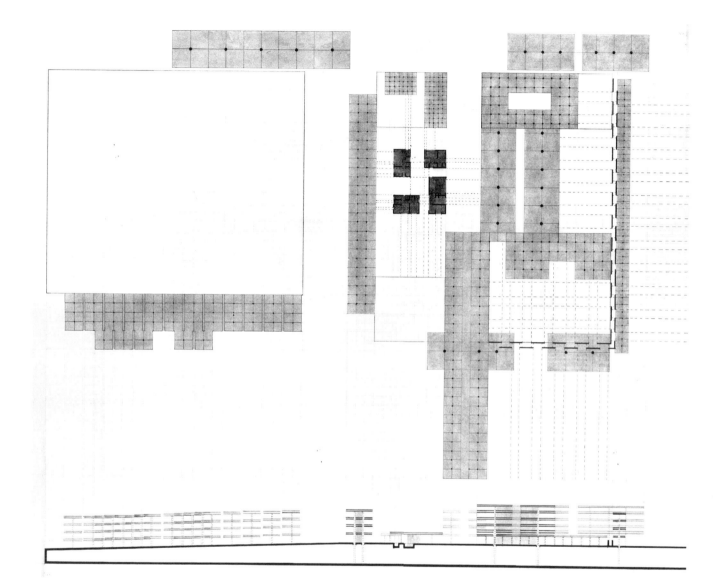

Figure 2.11. Association describes the characteristics by which elements are grouped, categorized, or related to one another. In this example, association between elements occurs in several ways. It is an analytical site plan and section. The position of each drawing on the page allows the characteristics to be read in both section and plan simultaneously. Through composition, the section is associated with the plan. And within the analysis itself there is a series of elements distributed across the site. Similar elements are represented using a similar graphic language, thereby associating them. Elements are also shown to be associated within an organizational grid structure by the use of a lightly dashed line that links aligned objects. STUDENT: BRITTANY DENNING—CRITIC: JAMES ECKLER—INSTITUTION: UNIVERSITY OF CINCINNATI

AXIS

A center line, used to relate different parts

An alignment of objects or spaces

Generative Possibilities of Alignment

The street doesn't follow the typical grid pattern of the city. Instead, it is angled diagonally. As a result, many of the adjoining city blocks are wedge shaped. It is a thoroughfare for both cars and pedestrians, ensuring that it is always crowded. Wherever it intersects with any other large street, there is a traffic circle. Each circle holds a monument to a historic event or achievement of citizens of the city. In this manner the street stretches from one side of the city to the other. At one end there is a museum; at the other is a group of governmental buildings.

While standing at the top of one of the monuments that acts as an observatory, several things can be observed. One is the straightness of this street in contrast to the others: although most roughly follow a grid pattern, they are often curved to accommodate terrain or some other existing feature. And from one particular vantage point, each monument perfectly aligns; it is this alignment that defines the axis.

The museum is connected with the government buildings through the precise arrangement of the monuments. And the main entry to the museum lies directly on the axial line. Likewise, the governmental buildings surround a courtyard, the center of which is also on the line.

An axis is a simple tool of alignment and relation. It can exist at a very small scale or, as in the narrative, a very large one. An axis is simply a single line, either physical or conceptual, that can connect, organize, or orient the various pieces and parts of a larger condition. How can an axis generate design? How can an axis be used effectively used in a design process? The simplicity of the concept makes an axis applicable to design in a wide variety of circumstances. An axis can be employed to frame a view of something specific, an experiential intent for the creation of, or orientation of, space. It might also be used as a line connecting multiple pieces together; it could be a path, a structure, or just a visual alignment. In this instance the axis becomes a tool that facilitates

the process of design and conception as an organizational strategy. It could also be an organizational structure unto itself, as we see in the narrative, where it directs the composition of elements in a design.

Although there are many possible applications of an axis to both the process and craft of a design, its use implies a single decision on the part of the designer. When an axis is employed in design, an inherent linear quality will result. With that understanding, several questions drive the use of an axis. What can an axis become other than just an imaginary line? An axis created by a line of sight could be used as a generator for a project; it could also be a path that connects one element to another. There are many possibilities, and

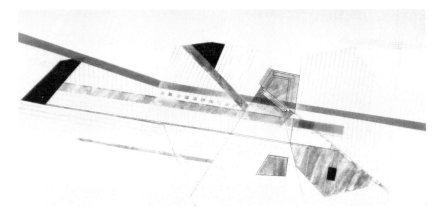

Figure 2.12. **An axis is a straight line that links two primary foci. In this example, a site is structured using an axis that links a programmed area of the field at one end (the black tone on the left side) with the entry to an intervention (the black rectangle along with lines linking it back to the axis) at the other. This provided an organizational element along which other designed components of the project could be distributed.** Student: Laila Ammar—Critic: James Eckler— Institution: University of Cincinnati

it is one of the design challenges presented by the use of an axis to understand the physical and spatial implications of this system of organization.

How does one distribute elements along the line? Is the axis being used to create an alignment of similar pieces, or is it to be used as a compositional tool to arrange elements around a center? Does the axis physically cut through pieces, pass by them, or present a common thread that they can be placed upon or near? Is the axis intended to create symmetry among elements or an asymmetrical balance of elements? Each of these questions speaks to the use of the axis to generate space and form and can be used to consider the use of the axis as a tool for design, as well as to identify different ways in which the axis has been used in existing design.

Figure 2.13. The axis in this image is created by contrasting tones across a regulating line (functioning as an axis from the upper left to the lower right). Elements are distributed to either side of this axis, providing compositional balance. Student: Unknown—Critic: Jason Towers—Institution: Valencia Community College

Figure 2.14. In addition to large-scale site applications, an axis can also be used to govern the relationship and distribution of spaces within the smaller-scale spatial construct. Here an aperture marks one focal point; a point of entry marks the other. This type of visual connection can establish a pattern or sequence of movement through spaces. It can also define direction within an organizational pattern. Student: Nick Reuther—Critic: James Eckler—Institution: Marywood University

BOUNDARY

A border that marks a limit

A border that defines one area as distinct from another

Generative Possibilities in Defining a Limit

The grassy field extended to a row of trees far in the distance. The field was actually several pastures owned by different farmers. A fence stretched across it to separate the pastures and keep the herds apart. There were gates placed intermittently along the length of the fence. They provided opportunities for the farmers to cross into one of the other pastures to lend assistance or to chase down the occasional stray animal. Not only did the fences divide the field into constituent pastures, they marked the limits of different territories as well. The fences were boundaries between areas as well as elements that bound the individual pastures.

In Middle English, *boune* referred to a stone marker used to define territories or borders. Presently, *boundary* has several subtle variations in connotation can prove valuable to design. A boundary can be, as its etymology implies, a demarcation between one region and another. On a smaller scale, a boundary can refer to a dividing line, or some device used to divide. However, it can also reference something that is bound, in which case (and in spatial or organizational terms), the boundary is the element that binds—a kind of perimeter. The difference between a perimeter and a boundary is that *boundary* implies that there is some continuation beyond it, that the boundary is being used to set areas apart. In contrast, *perimeter* refers only to the limit of one area without any reference to anything beyond. *Edge* is different, too; it implies a limit to an area without referring to anything beyond that limit, whereas a boundary is clearly a divider. Because of these many subtle variations, boundary can have complex implications as it applies to design process.

What opportunities does boundary present to design process? How can it be applied in a way that generates space instead of being a result of other design ideas? A boundary consists of any component that contributes the definition of one area relative to another. It can be used to mark

one space from another within a building just as it can delineate regions in a landscape. It can be a physical construct that separates, or an implied

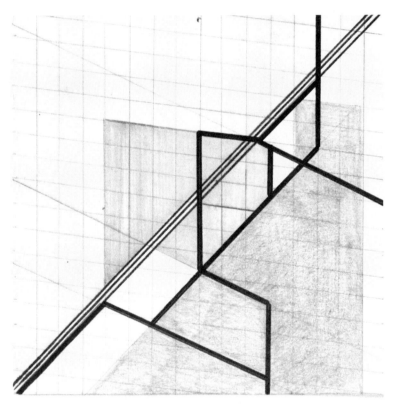

Figure 2.15.   In this diagram, the student explores possible configurations of zones for holding various site programs. The overlapping of systems creates boundaries that divide the various zones from one another and provide opportunities for intervening architecturally. Student: Derek Jerome—Critic: James Eckler—Institution: University of Cincinnati

border. There are two commonalities throughout all of these variations. As an element that defines or divides, it creates a designed relationship between two areas. And as something that implies multiple regions, there is also an implication of access—some way across. Even as it makes two or more spaces distinct through division, it links those spaces by defining transition.

The boundary can be generative as an organizational tool, as well as through its ability to define spatial relationships and experiential transitions. Relationships between spaces or areas can be established through intent and reflected in the physical properties of the boundary. A boundary might be thick in order to exaggerate the distinction between spaces. It might be porous, granting more opportunity for movement across, in order to reinforce the linked relationship between spaces. Or it might be subtly implied to provide an understanding of territory without compromising spatial continuity.

In terms of organization, the boundary can be used to define larger contextual issues of composition and placement. The boundary can act as a guide for programmatic considerations throughout the design process. The function of a boundary, either spatial or organizational, can be established by design intent and act as a standard of evaluation for the invention of space and form through an iterative process.

» *See also* Edge.

Figure 2.16. *In this relief model, the depressed areas define a boundary that contains designed constructions. The boundaries define the places to build, but those boundaries are not absolute. There is one point on the right side where the boundary is crossed and a linkage between constructions is formed.* Student: Brittany DeDunes— Critic: Tim Hayes—Institution: Louisiana Tech University

CIRCUIT

A circular line that moves around or encloses a center space

A cyclical path, or the region defined by such a path

An indirect route, typically characterized as being long, that is peripheral to its destination

Generative Possibilities in Designing the Way Around

The house sat at the center of a large estate. It had stood in this place for a very long time, and now attracted visitors to the historic gardens that surrounded it. In the house itself there were people willing to share information about the estate or to act as guides.

On the approach to the house there was a juncture in the gravel path. One could continue straight to the house or take a more circuitous path through some of the gardens. She chose to turn away from the main walkway and use the garden trail. While on it she encountered many different arrangements of plants, sitting areas, and sculptural fountains. Periodically there was a placard that marked a rare plant specimen.

Before long she arrived at the front of the house, having taken the indirect circuit to get there. The other members of her party were inside speaking with a guide. They had elected to take the direct route.

A circuit is a peripheral or indirect pattern of movement. It refers specifically to a pattern of movement that goes around something. If a circuit specifically references movement, how is it an organizational tool? If it is limited to an outer periphery, how can it be used to generate space? The circuit is a notion that engages aspects of organization and program at the same time. It is an organizational strategy in that it defines the periphery of an element, thereby marking a region. It is programmatic (potentially a strategy for making space) in that it is a constructed means of circulation.

As an organizational structure it is understood to contain a region. In doing so the circuit is something that informs a boundary—that is, it defines a boundary that is also required to act as a circulation corridor. In addition to the operation of movement, the circuit might also designate an area of influence for a design. The circuit is not just movement: it is an indirect movement toward something. There is a dependence on that destination. With the destination as a focal point and the circuit as a periphery, everything in between becomes an area impacted by the central design. As a boundary, the regions to the other side of the circuit are not directly influenced by the focal destination. These operations are tools for designing organizational relationships within a contextual field.

Figure 2.17. **The spatial construct is nested within a depression on the site. The path of approach takes a circuitous route around the circumference of that depression rather than a direct line to the point of entry.** STUDENT: LAILA AMMAR— CRITIC: JAMES ECKLER—INSTITUTION: UNIVERSITY OF CINCINNATI

The programmatic considerations of path and itinerary immediately precede the making of space. If the circuit is an indirect path toward a destination, then there must be experiential and spatial consequences to this extended approach. The circuit can create a ceremony of approach wherein an occupant is, in some way, prepared to encounter the destination. There may be a series of events along the path; perhaps the path itself provides a gradual spatial transition from one environment to that of the destination. Whatever programmatic scenario characterizes the circuit, it is the result of the purposeful creation of space.

Figure 2.18.   This study model is characterized by a pair of intersecting pieces and the distribution of spaces and assemblies around that point of intersection. A bracket wraps the composition around the right side. The way this bracketing component moves around the central intersection is characteristic of a circuit if it is considered as a potential path or other spatial construct, rather than as a formal assembly. STUDENT: SAMANTHA ENNIS—CRITIC: STEPHEN GARRISON—INSTITUTION: MARYWOOD UNIVERSITY

DATUM

A line or plane that is generally centered and used as an organizational device; a spine

The primary element of an organizational structure

A linear design component off of which other components branch

Generative Possibilities of a Constructed Reference

A wall runs the full length of the structure. It is thick; in some places it is wide enough to permit someone to occupy it. In those places it acts as a passage connecting various parts of the design.

Different spaces extend off of the wall on either side. The wall is scored and marked to reflect the module that governs the size of those spaces. It varies in dimension, shifts in height as well as thickness, according to that module.

In order to move from one space to the next, one must travel through the wall, along it, or in some cases, within it. It provides the primary organizational structure for the design. It is present in every space. It governs most of the relationships between different spaces, and between the events they house. It is a datum, a structure that functions as a spine linking and arranging all other elements of the project.

Datum, in common usage, refers to a single fact or piece of information; it is the singular of *data*. Its role in design terminology is only loosely related. It originated as a surveying term for a reference line or point. It has since come to be used more generically, as an organizational element characterized as a linear component around which other elements in a composition are arranged. Its function is analogous to that of a spine in relation to ribs: a linear construction (spine) that acts as a reference or structure for extending pieces (ribs).

Architecturally, the datum consists of any linear piece, space, or assembly that organizes other spaces or forms in a composition. In what ways can a datum be used a generative device? Can it play a role in architectural process or thinking? A datum can be spatial, formal, or compositional. The spatial

datum is one composed of primary spaces arranged in a row or a single linear space from which others extend or connect. The formal datum is one in which an object or assembly becomes a linear, centralized structure that

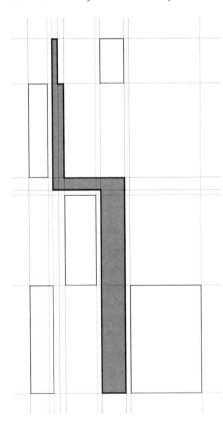

Figure 2.19.
In the illustration, several elements are arranged about a central bar. That bar functions as an organizational datum. Some elements are placed in alignment with the different edges of the bar. One is bracketed by the interior angle as it turns a corner. The datum incorporates each element into a common organizational system.

holds spaces or forms in place around it. A compositional datum is a gesture that functions as a reference line in a larger composition.

In each of these there is an implied hierarchy, where the datum piece is primary and other extending pieces are secondary or tertiary. This idea is both organizational and typological in nature. Process can be used to assign importance to design components, and the function of datum can become a role for the primary parts. This is, then, a strategy employed at the very beginning of a design process from which more resolved spatial relationships would emerge.

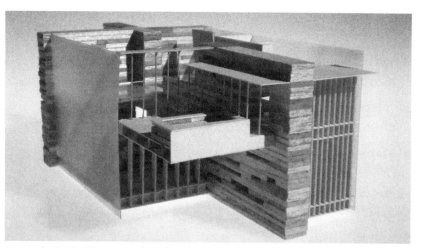

Figure 2.21. In this example, a datum wall divides spaces according to program. The wall is perforated to allow light to pass through. It is also cut to create a threshold between public and private spaces arranged to either side. STUDENT: JEFF BADGER—CRITIC: JAMES ECKLER—INSTITUTION: UNIVERSITY OF CINCINNATI

Figure 2.20. The central wall functions as a datum, with spaces distributed to either side. It is selectively punctured to provide opportunities for circulation from one side to the other, providing a linkage between spaces in the project. STUDENT: WENDELL MONTGOMERY—CRITIC: JASON TOWERS—INSTITUTION: VALENCIA COMMUNITY COLLEGE

Figure 2.22. In this example, the datum is an extension from the spatial construct across the field within which it is placed. The extending piece follows a single line that correlates to the edges of different zones that compose the contextual field. This aligns aspects of the spatial composition with conditions of its surroundings. STUDENT: MARY-KATE HART—CRITIC: JAMES ECKLER—INSTITUTION: MARYWOOD UNIVERSITY

DELINEATE

To define, outline, or represent graphically

Generative Possibilities in Marking

There is one main space in the building, twice as long as it is wide. The space is so tall that on one side two other floors look out onto it. It is a space for large events. Groups of vendors periodically come to sell their wares from booths. There are also occasional displays. At one end there is a café where people stop for lunch or coffee.

When empty, the room is completely uninterrupted. The only indicators of the temporary installations are the red lines on the floor that delineate the stalls for booths. Permanent program is delineated by a change in the finish material of the floor. The polished stone becomes wood to mark out the territory of the cafe.

Delineation is the marking out or graphic definition of a space or region. Marking a surface with the intention of defining a relationship between spaces or regions is an organizational act. Marking in order to outline or define is also organizational, in that it sets one area apart from another. Delineation can also be a generative process or a communicative act. How can delineation be used as an organizational device? What is its role in process? How does it aid communication of the architectural idea?

The act of making a mark to define regions follows an organizational design idea. It is in the character of the mark that delineation can establish complex relationships between spaces or areas. Although delineating is graphic in nature, it can be a component of a larger strategy for articulation. Within that strategy it may contribute to nongraphic construction. A surface may fold to differentiate the upper portion from the lower; the act of folding is a constructed articulation. The seam that forms the joint between areas may have begun as a graphic delineation. That seam may even register with other aspects in other areas of the design, causing it to transition from constructed fold back into a graphic language.

Hierarchy and other compositional principles also contribute to the character of a delineating line. It may vary in thickness or tone. It may be broken.

Figure 2.23. The volume is broken down into segments. Between each segment is a gap that delineates the sections of the project. The gaps both hold a structural piece and permit light to enter the space. Student: Matthew Sundstrom— Critic: Jason Towers—Institution: Valencia Community College

It may be doubled at certain points. These characteristics work to inform the relationship between regions that the delineating line marks.

As a process, the act of delineation relies on convention, either created or commonly accepted, to investigate possible spatial and organizational relationships. It is a way of quickly outlining, defining, and differentiating aspects of a design in an iterative way. It may also be used as a precursor to more complex construction later in the process. The reliance of delineation on graphic conventions also makes it communicative. It is a way of representing an organizational scheme through a commonly accepted graphic language that can be easily read and understood by those outside of the process of the scheme's creation.

» *See also* Mark.

Figure 2.24.   The separation between different spatial types is delineated by a wall in conjunction with a gap between areas of the lower plane. STUDENT: KEVIN UTZ—CRITIC: JAMES ECKLER—INSTITUTION: MARYWOOD UNIVERSITY

DIRECTION

Orientation relative to north, south, east, and west

Orientation of movement; orientation of a vector or trajectory

Generative Possibilities in Orientation

The building was long and narrow. Spaces were arranged in a linear fashion along a central axis. Circulation was primarily located at the center of the building between spaces.

Because of the building's proportions, most of the various spaces that composed the building were also long and narrow. Each was arranged in the same direction. Movement through the building was defined by its rigid directionality. Spaces were encountered in a particular sequence. Advancement from one space to the next occurred in the direction of the central axis. Moving in one direction

meant that one was venturing farther into the building, whereas moving in the opposite direction implied that one was leaving.

Direction refers to orientation or movement relative to north, south, east, and west. It impacts the organization of a design by providing a method for measuring relative position between multiple elements or a single element within its context. Direction correlates with orientation; however, orientation refers to the resulting physical relationship between elements, whereas direction refers to the measure of rotation. This difference is so subtle that the

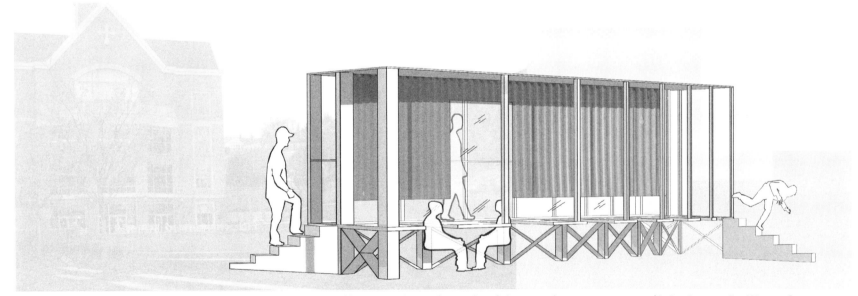

Figure 2.25. Direction of movement through space is established by proportion and an order of elements that are encountered in it. STUDENT: JOE WAHY—CRITIC: MATTHEW MINDRUP—INSTITUTION: MARYWOOD UNIVERSITY

two words are often used interchangeably. But there is another characteristic of direction that sets it apart from orientation: it is also a way of describing or measuring movement along a vector. In what ways can this term influence the organization of a design? Are they different from the applications of orientation?

Using direction in organizing elements of a design has much of the same potential to generate ideas as orientation. However, the direction of movement has the potential to generate design ideas that are independent of orientation. Movement can be that of an occupant or that of a design component. Using organizational and compositional principles to direct the movement of the individual is one way of linking ideas of structure with those of spatial encounter or path. Using organizational principle to control the movement of objects can be a way of constructing relationships among multiple components of a composition.

» *See also* Orientation; Movement.

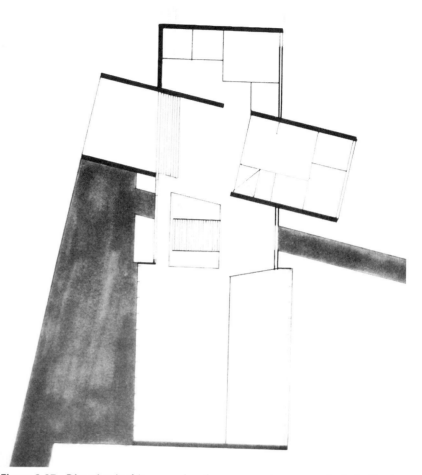

Figure 2.26. In this example, direction is understood as an orientation toward a point. The linear bands, cuts, and ribbons collaborate in defining horizontal directionality toward (or perhaps away from) the black-and-white construct to the left of the image. Student: Hanying Lu—Critic: Tim Hayes—Institution: Louisiana Tech University

Figure 2.27. Direction in this example references an element not included in the image. It is reinforced, however, in the orientation of the angled bar relative to the orthogonal one. In addition, its alignment with the path that extends off the page insinuates that the angled bar is directed toward a distant point or element at the terminus of the path. Student: Allen Fee—Critic: James Eckler—Institution: University of Cincinnati

EDGE

An outermost limit; an ending

Generative Possibilities of a Terminus

To the small child, it seemed that there was nothing beyond the confines of the garden. It was ringed by a stone wall that soared well over his head. He could not see anything on the other side, nor did he ever hear anything.

In reality there were neighboring gardens on the other side. And the wall was not so tall to an adult. But to that child it marked an absolute edge defined by the limits of his experiences. The wall did mark an edge to the garden, but only because there were no gates or access of any kind to the other side. It marked the limit of ownership as well as the composition of the garden.

An edge is an outermost limit, or anything that defines an extent. In the way that an edge defines an area, it is similar to a boundary, with one primary difference: an edge doesn't imply any relationship to the other side. If an edge refers only to what it contains, in what ways can it generate space? Edge can be discussed in three categories: the organization of space, the organization of field, and as a physical characteristic of objects (which, although self-explanatory, has implications in both assembly and composition).

As it pertains to the organization of space, the manipulation of edges and boundaries determine a spatial profile in both plan and section. Where a boundary establishes the way one moves from one space to another, an edge is one of the factors that defines the way in which one occupies space. How does one occupy an edge? The edge may be constructed as layers of space creating circulation around the perimeter. Perhaps the edge is constructed to capture the attention: even a person in the center of the space is oriented outward. The edge may be sculpted to create different ways and opportunities for interaction. The spatial edge is a container. Its composition defines the way that space may be used or occupied. Designing the edge is an exercise in determining spatial character.

The regional edge is a marking of scope. Whereas the contextual boundary distinguishes one territory from another, the edge marks a limit of influence. That may be a project scope—the area to be designed. It may mark the limit of a territory without regard for what exists beyond it. The design implications of this type of edge lie in defining it. How is the edge announced, the end point made apparent? Perhaps a wall is erected to halt movement and bar visual access. Perhaps the edge is implied more subtly as merely the point at which the design stopped. In either case the edge becomes a valuable limitation to design, one that determines the extents of a project and provides focus.

» *See also* Boundary.

Figure 2.28. In this example, edge is manifest as the articulate wall on the far side of the image. It denotes the extents of the project and provides enclosure for the spaces within those extents. There is no reference to anything on the other side. It marks the end of the designed space. STUDENT: THOMAS HANCOCK—CRITIC: MILAGROS ZINGONI—INSTITUTION: ARIZONA STATE UNIVERSITY

Figure 2.29. In addition to the large-scale organizational qualities of an edge as it pertains to site, it can also reference the end of a space. In this example, individual spaces have defined edges that mark the point at which they terminate. These edges take the form of assembled wall-like structures. They divide the horizontal plane into sections and illustrate the edge of space. Additonally the edges of the horizontal plane mark the limits of the project. STUDENT: VICTORIA TRAINO—CRITIC: KATE O'CONNOR—INSTITUTION: MARYWOOD UNIVERSITY

FABRIC

Something that possesses a texture or pattern that is similar to cloth

An underlying structure or organization

Generative Possibilities in an Organization of Interrelated Parts

The buildings were arranged in an orthogonal pattern. Perpendicular structures intersected one another, forming open courtyards. Grass covered the courtyards except where a narrow path was paved in concrete. It ran down the center of the open space, connecting the buildings' entries on opposite sides of the courtyard. In the middle of each path, it widened to form a larger area. Sculpture was displayed in these central paved areas.

The entire campus was a fabric of intersecting and overlapping paths and spaces. Some were exterior, such as the paved walks and outdoor sculpture rooms at the center of the open spaces. Others were interior halls connecting classrooms and auditoriums. The fabric ordered and organized the disparate buildings and exterior spaces into a single, unified campus.

Fabric refers to a complex, layered underlying structure. It is an organizational pattern not unlike the threads in a cloth. The complexity of interrelated parts recalls a weave, in which multiple organizational structures exist simultaneously through overlap and intersection. If a fabric refers to a elaborate set of intertwined organizational patterns, is its use as a design tool different from the basic grid, radial, center, cluster, and linear patterns?

The fabric implies a structure that couples two or more of those basic patterns. Since they rarely exist in a pure state, the fabric is a way of understanding how multiple types are combined—their compositional relationship to one another. The fabric becomes an analytical tool and is primarily used as a means of reading and responding to a context.

It is almost impossible to visualize a built environment composed purely of one of the five primary organizational structures. Consider nearly any neighborhood as a composition of various organizational structures. The street grid might be one, as it controls access and negotiates various scales and modes of movement. The distribution of buildings may be in

Figure 2.30. Sometimes referred to as an urban fabric, the system of street blocks determines an underlying structure that directs the position, scale, density, and program of buildings inserted within it. Variations in city zones can be determined by considering the patches of differently configured buildings and the functions they serve. Student: Jihye Choi—Critic: Milagros Zingoni—Institution: Arizona State University

direct relationship to that street grid, or have a designed deviation from it. Within that grid and field of objects there may also be a public center or commercial district. There may be demographically or culturally defined zones. Each of these may take on a different organizational pattern, and yet one doesn't have less influence on the operation of the place than any other.

The fabric can be used as a way of discerning relationships between contextual information sets through structural overlap, coincident points, and deviations. That information can then be used as a way of determining the role a new architectural design might have within a complex built environment. The fabric can indicate strategies for architectural response to the multiple organizations.

» *See also* Palimpsest.

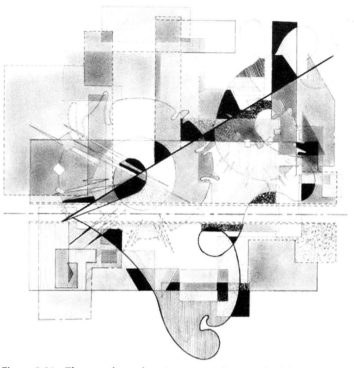

Figure 2.31.   The toned, overlapping rectangles reveal a fabric that structures this analytical diagram. The diagonal and curvilinear shapes move across and disrupt the underlying fabric, but it does govern the shading that surrounds those shapes. It reintegrates the nonorthogonal shapes into the orthogonal fabric. STUDENT: DANIEL GUTIERREZ—CRITIC: JASON TOWERS—INSTITUTION: VALENCIA COMMUNITY COLLEGE

FIELD

An open landscape; an expanse

A plane or surface that receives a smaller component

Generative Possibilities in Placement and Openness

The design team developed an idea for the project they were assigned. Instead of creating a single building to house so many unrelated programs, they decided to try making a set of buildings arranged across the site. Each structure would be dedicated to, and specifically designed for, its assigned program. It would relate to the others through a series of paved and covered paths stretching across the site. The set of smaller structures would be arranged around a central open space.

This organizational logic caused the team to reevaluate the way they understood the site. Instead of an area meant to receive a single building, they began to consider it as a field of arranged objects. Instead of being one component in the larger plan of the city, it was now a field subdivided into multiple sites for the smaller structures.

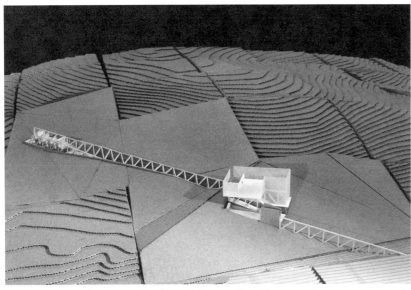

Figure 2.32. In this example, the architecture is an intervention to a contextual field. The filed is minimally modified to receive the architecture that is set within and upon it. STUDENT: HOUSTON BURNETTE—CRITIC: PETER WONG—INSTITUTION: UNIVERSITY OF NORTH CAROLINA, CHARLOTTE

Figure 2.33. In this example, the field presents opportunities that shape the architectural intervention. Simultaneously, the field is modified to receive and interact with that intervention. The result is integration between architecture and field. STUDENT: NICK YOUNG—CRITIC: JASON TOWERS—INSTITUTION: VALENCIA COMMUNITY COLLEGE

A field, in the most literal sense, is any open area. However, with an assumption that the field actually contains many different components, it can be understood as a contextual composition—a field of objects. This understanding is more generic and can refer to any sort of expanse. So then, how does using this term in a more generic sense aid design thinking? The intent is to strip away connotation in order to create opportunities for the discovery of design possibilities that were previously not considered.

The field, as a generic expanse, is one in which a new design can be placed. It can remain a flat conceptual plane, in which case it becomes a vehicle for generating contextual strategies for a design. Or it can be understood to be composed of a wide array of elements that mirror an actual context, in which case it becomes an analog for that environment and a testing ground for the application of contextual strategy.

Retaining a generic understanding of field can help guide design thinking by increasing the number of potential applications to process. It can be used as a tool for reading and understanding an existing environment, or it can be a manufactured environment. It can be composed of a predefined organizational structure, or it can be a blank slate meant to be marked, articulated, and reconstructed to meet the needs of architecture. As a contextual idea, it will reflect more specific information as the design process advances and the ideas driving it become more resolved.

» *See also* Context.

GRAIN

A texture produced by the accumulation of fibers

A pattern or direction of texture derived by the arrangement of pieces or particles

An arrangement or organization that implies a predominant direction; the directionality of an arrangement

Generative Possibilities in Directional Patterning

All of the primary streets downtown run north and south. They are two-way streets, each several lanes wide. Most people park along these streets. The sidewalks are wide to accommodate more pedestrians. Because these streets handle so much traffic, the shops in the area always have as much frontage as possible along them. The long sides of the blocks run parallel to these primary streets. The result is that the city has a definitive graining structure that corresponds to the direction of the north/south streets. The block structure, building orientation, and patterns of habitation are determined by it.

Graining refers to a common pattern of orientation among elements in an organizational structure. Just as the grain in a piece of wood is made evident

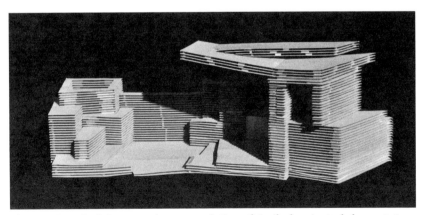

Figure 2.34. Graining uses the accumulation of similarly oriented elements to imply direction. In this example, the method of construction is stacking, and the elements that are stacked provide a distinct horizontal grain structure. STUDENT: THOMAS HANCOCK—CRITIC: MILAGROS ZINGONI—INSTITUTION: ARIZONA STATE UNIVERSITY

by bundled long fibers, graining as it pertains to an organizational structure implies a kind of large-scale directionality in a set of pieces. What consequences does graining have on design or design process?

Graining implies a system of hierarchy. Although most organizational patterns will be multidirectional in some way, a single direction may be more prominent than the others. Graining, as a system of hierarchy, can be used to establish design parameters, both at the scale of the larger composition and at the scale of the single object.

Placing the elements of a design in accordance with a grain structure establishes relationships between those elements. It also creates opportunities for design in the development of the interstitial spaces between elements. For instance, if a grain structure is applied to the arrangement of pieces, the way one navigates that structure can be determined through design. Defining the spatial and experiential difference between traveling along the grain and traveling across the grain is one consideration. In those differences hierarchy is reinforced, and an order of encounter, path, or sequence can be established. This use of graining can become a kind of way-finding tool.

The small-scale implications of orientation can also have an impact on large-scale implications of direction. Through the design process, graining can be used as a strategy for placing and orienting the spatial or formal components of a composition. Those components are then considered individually, and the impacts of that directional strategy will be better understood as the design becomes more resolved. This process can develop a nonlinear pattern of thought and development. It promotes decision making at both the large and small scales, which have a reciprocal influence on each other. Decisions made will be continuously challenged and revisited, developing an integrated relationship between component and composition.

Figure 2.35. *This drawing is a diagram in which the student created a grain structure in order to communicate direction and sequence.* Student: Brayton Orchard—Critic: John Humphries—Institution: Miami University

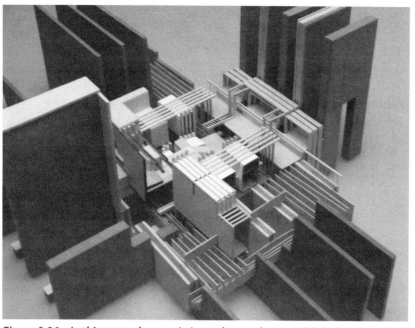

Figure 2.36. *In this example, a grain is used not only to establish directionality but also as an organizational structure. The context piece has a definite grain, and there are moments within the intervention that coincide with that contextual grain, or run counter to it. The contextual grain functions as a guide toward the placement and orientation of project components.* Student: Staci Carrier—Critic: James Eckler—Institution: University of Cincinnati

HIERARCHY

A ranking of elements

Any system by which the importance of elements is represented graphically

Generative Possibilities of Assigning Relative Importance

Modern libraries have changed dramatically from those of previous generations. The primary function of the library is to store information and make it available for consumption. But information is no longer exclusively in the format of books.

This consideration helped the design team generate their proposal for the library project program. In it, book stacks and reading areas were still primary functions of the library, but they were to be surrounded by a series of secondary functions. Each was defined by a different way in which information could be stored and consumed. There was an Internet lab, a room for video screening, and an audio room. Other support spaces, such as restrooms and maintenance closets, were interspersed throughout this arrangement. The way the design was organized was a direct reflection of the hierarchy of library program elements.

Originally, *ierarchi* was a religious term that referred to a ranking of angels. Later it came to refer to a ranked organization of things. This notion of ranking based upon importance or type is one that is present throughout every stage of architectural design process and communication. It is a notion that defines design development, architectural intent, and project parameters. Why does an idea as simple as a ranking system saturate architectural design so completely? How can it be used in a way that generates ideas for space rather than just documenting them?

Hierarchy is a system of relative importance. It is simply an act of defining and communicating elements of a project that are of primary, secondary, or tertiary importance. That importance is determined based on many criteria—for instance, the subject of study or experimentation, design goals, or emphasis in communication. A primary element is one that is most important or relevant: a significant space or the dark line of a section cut. A secondary element is one that is important and serves the larger goals of the primary element: a support space or the mid-dark line of an uncut wall in a

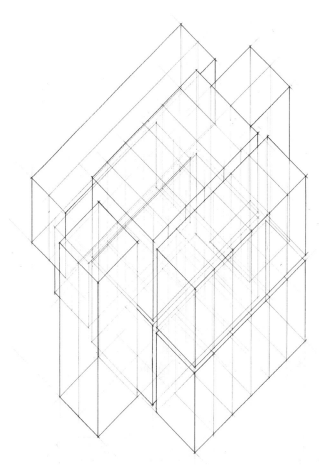

Figure 2.37. Hierarchy is used in two ways in this drawing. First, as a graphic convention, line weight distinguishes primary lines from secondary lines. The primary lines show the outer edges of the object or space, and the secondary lines show where those larger volumes are divided. Second, hierarchy is established through the relative size of volumes. This might indicate the relative importance of different volumes to the overall design intent. STUDENT: MICHELLE ARNONDIN—CRITIC: JIM SULLIVAN—INSTITUTION: LOUISIANA STATE UNIVERSITY

section drawing. A tertiary element is one that serves minor importance to the goal of the design or the communication of a document: a storage space or a construction line in a section cut.

Hierarchy is established and represented in a variety of ways. Consider a programmatic hierarchy. There are many types of spaces that a building must have; however, it probably has a primary purpose that motivates its design. A theater will have many different spaces serving a variety of functions, but the one that is most important is probably the auditorium. It will be larger than the others to accommodate more people. It might be more heavily detailed, or finished with better materials. It should be the easiest to find, with the other spaces serving as support for that one primary use. Without a hierarchical strategy, this same building would have the auditorium (primary), the box office (secondary), and the maintenance closets (tertiary) equally sized, detailed, finished, and accessible. Confusion on the part of the occupants would be one of many problems.

Hierarchy is also a consideration of representation: it is used to express the relationship between different conditions or sets of spatial information. It is built into the conventions that dictate the ways architecture is documented and understood. Line weights are an obvious hierarchical convention. But hierarchy in representation can be established in many other ways as well: the density of lines, the darkening of a tone, or the strategic use of color in a drawing. Those are only a few examples; there are many more conventions that can be created to indicate importance. The exaggeration of elements

can also establish a hierarchical system as a tool for studying or generating new ideas—for testing possibilities.

Hierarchy is an inescapable aspect of design. However, when it is considered as a strategy for developing design it has the potential to uncover different possibilities for spatial character, organizational structure, or communicative technique.

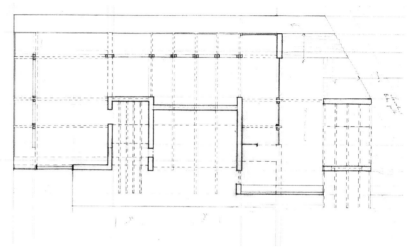

Figure 2.38. Hierarchy in graphic convention is applied to both line weight and line type. These standards help in the communication of architectural information. Student: MaryJo Minerich—Critic: Karl Wallick—Institution: University of Cincinnati

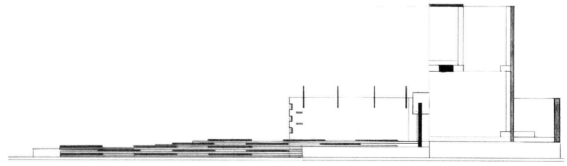

Figure 2.39. In addition to using hierarchy as a standard convention for graphically communicating architectural information, this student uses it as a means of defining prominent components of the design. Those elements that contribute the most to the overall architectural intent are highlighted to show they are more important. Consider the dark extension from the left side of the drawing to its center. This is the primary connection to the project's surroundings, and is therefore marked as a prominent aspect of the design. Student: Bernie Gurka—Critic: James Eckler—Institution: Marywood University

JUXTAPOSE

To place two or more elements near one another for the purpose of comparison

To arrange elements in a way that relates them through comparison

Generative Possibilities in Comparison

City hall had been in the same building since the city was founded. As the city grew, so, too, did the requirements of the building, and it became too small to house all of its new roles. The citizens of this community were faced with a dilemma. They could demolish the building and build a new one to suit their current needs. They could move city hall to a new location. Or they could expand their current structure. Few people liked the options available to them. Demolishing the building would remove an icon of the city. Moving the functions of city hall would render the current building useless and perhaps abandoned. The reluctant majority settled for expanding the building, fearful of losing its importance to the community due to its transformation.

Making this sentiment a priority, the designers decided to create an addition that was unmistakably different from the original. It was made in a way that housed all of the necessary new programs required without compromising the qualities of the older building. It was largely transparent and functioned as a display for the original structure. It is an addition that has minimal contact with the original building in order to preserve it to as great an extent as possible. The end result was a single building composed of two juxtaposed wings.

The original French term *juxtaposer* was a hybrid between the Latin *juxtÇ*, meaning "beside," and the Old French *poser*, meaning "to place." In contemporary use, *juxtaposition* still depends on proximity and placement, but it is used to compare. This correlation between position and comparison has direct implications on the organizational structure of architectural design. How can a comparison influence the way a project is organized? More importantly, how can it be a design tool?

The juxtaposition of two or more design components links placement with communication. They are positioned in a way that makes similarities or differences between them more apparent. This creates two types of juxtapositions: the comparison and the contrast. Juxtaposition might be used to illustrate similarities between elements as a way of announcing a consistency of use. It might be a way of presenting different element typologies within a design. Two juxtaposed elements might also articulate an intersection between regions characterized by element type. In any event, juxtaposition is an organizational design tool for the strategizing, construction, and communication of relationships within a design. Because it is based upon a comparison of characteristics, the relationship it establishes can be spatial, formal, or programmatic.

Figure 2.40. *Juxtaposition is a placement of two or more things for the purpose of comparison. In this example, two surface treatments are positioned side by side so their differences can be easily understood. The juxtaposition reveals a similar representational language, as well as a change in size and proportion.*
STUDENT: SETH TROYER—CRITIC: JAMES ECKLER—INSTITUTION: UNIVERSITY OF CINCINNATI

Figure 2.41. *In this example, two towerlike constructs are juxtaposed across a shared plinth. Variations in size and complexity are made more apparent by their proximity to one another.* STUDENT: ELIZABETH SYDNOR—CRITIC: MILAGROS ZINGONI—INSTITUTION: ARIZONA STATE UNIVERSITY

Figure 2.42. *Juxtaposition can be an organizational tool for relating multiple components of a design. In this example, two distinct elements are connected at one point. They are different in many ways, but similarities in material, scale, and size are understood by comparison.* STUDENT: JIHYE CHOI—CRITIC: MILAGROS ZINGONI—INSTITUTION: ARIZONA STATE UNIVERSITY

MEASURE

A standard for evaluation that uses common units for the purpose of comparison

A device or system of units by which a single characteristic of an element is evaluated

Generative Possibilities in Standardization

He used his pace to determine the dimensions of the site for his project. This system of measure carried through other stages of the design process as well. As he sketched and modeled ideas for the project, he continued to use the pace as a unit of measure. Eventually, this became one of his design objectives: to use the proportions of the human body as a basis for the configuration of space.

To this end he began studying reach, height, grasp, and pace as dimensional measuring tools. By the project's conclusion every aspect of its design was dictated by human proportions. Spaces were configured according to the height of an arm stretched above the head. They were also considered according to the number of paces and the length of time it would take a person to walk through them. Shelves and cabinets were positioned according to the limitations of a reach. Handles and knobs were measured by the width of a palm or the distance between spread fingers. In using this system of measure, the interface between form and occupant was considered to a much greater degree than would otherwise be the case.

Originally *mesuren* meant "to control, govern, or regulate." *Measure* has since come to refer to a method of evaluating an element based upon a physical characteristic. Both of these uses are relevant as organizational and ordering devices in the architectural design process. Since measurement is a process, as is its predecessor, how is it an organizational device?

Organization is a compositional structure. It is reliant upon a set of parameters. Establishing a unit of measure is a possible parameter upon which an organizational structure can be based. This application refers back to the origins of the word; measure is used to regulate or govern arrangement and composition.

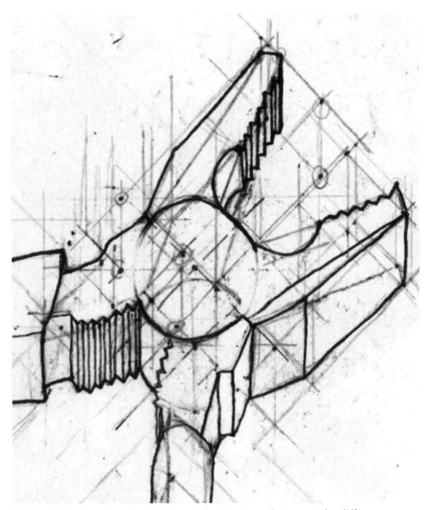

Figure 2.43. Construction lines reveal a structure that maps the different characteristics of form in this drawing of a set of pliers. It is used as a system of measure for the drawing as it is crafted. STUDENT: CAREY GIVENS—CRITIC: JIM SULLIVAN—INSTITUTION: LOUISIANA STATE UNIVERSITY

To operate in this way, the unit of measure must be explicit; it must be *measurable*. That unit is a standardized module used to evaluate a type of physical characteristic. That module can be dictated by convention, or it can be based upon a project specific meter.

In terms of generating space, the unit of measure is an important tool in determining and representing proportion. It does not have to be used strictly to evaluate decisions already made or an existing condition; it can also be used as a variable set of guidelines within the process of design. For instance, if a determination is made regarding the height of a space in relation to the size of an occupant, the occupant's height can be used as the unit of measure. In a sectional study, that unit of measure can be used to determine many characteristics of the spatial profile. Measure is not just a technique of evaluation; it can also be a criteria for design determined by strategy, concept, or intent.

» *See also* Meter; Module.

METER

A technique or device used to measure

A regulating principle or device that uses a system of units or modules

Generative Possibilities in Repetition

A colonnade dominated the entire front facade of the building. The columns extended the height of the first two levels of the building and were spaced at even intervals. They were identical to one another. To enter, one ascended a flight of steps to the edge of the colonnade and walked between the massive columns. The distance between the two center columns was exactly the width of the front doors.

The building was organized symmetrically about the front doors. It was divided into bays, each with a window that was positioned perfectly in each gap between the columns of the front facade. The repetition of columns provided a meter by which the entire building could be measured. The distance from one to the next corresponded exactly to the size of the bays of the building. The building continued to follow that module throughout its other sections. The columns of the front were a device for regulating and measuring every aspect of the structure. They provided a unit of measure and were a physical manifestation of that unit— a meter.

A meter is any system or device used for measuring. As a device, the meter is a physical manifestation of measurement manifested through the repetition of elements, or an articulation based upon a unit of measure. As a system the meter is a compositional logic used to regulate the proportion and placement of elements. Are there opportunities for a measuring device to influence design thinking or conception?

As a compositional logic a meter can act as a guide to process—a set of rules or limits to direct design thinking. Similar to its application to poetry, the meter can be a rhythm established as a framework for the arrangement or ordering of parts. When used in this manner, the meter becomes a kind of procedural formula, and the units of measure are actually components of design that act as variables in that formula. This use requires that design components be divided into types. Relationships between types are then determined by the formula.

The consequence of using this kind of compositional logic is homogeneity. Specificity in spatial function or characteristic is often sacrificed in an effort to make each component conform to the variable type to which it is assigned. In addition, relationships between parts are often not considered or tested through design process and are instead a result of the formula. In any event, there is ample opportunity for a metering system to act as a procedural framework, or even a protocol for actions in process.

The metering device has more varied—and sometimes subtle—applications to design. Its basic characteristic is rhythm and the repetition of elements. This may manifest as a constant module that is arranged to meet the goals of a design. Or it may be a distinct assembly of repeated parts that provides a way of measuring space and form as one occupies the architecture. These devices can be deployed in a design as a way of establishing a scale that can be perceived by an occupant, as a way of delineating spaces, or as a way of communicating an ordering system that relates parts of a composition. It may even be as subtle as a formal articulation that acts as a graduated measuring device.

These design elements and decisions for the way spaces and objects are assembled are methods for establishing scale in design. They have the potential to influence the way space is perceived by an occupant and communicate spatial relationships of proportion. It is because of these potential influences that the idea of a metering device can act as a catalyst for spatial investigations in design process.

» *See also* Measure; Module.

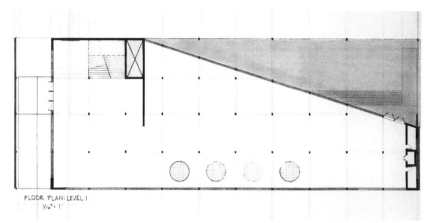

FLOOR PLAN: LEVEL I
1/16" = 1'

Figure 2.44. *The column grid in this drawing indicates both physical and organizational structure. The repetition of elements makes it a meter for the measurement of space. The columns divide the space into segments, which permits occupants to gauge distance and dimension within the environment they occupy.* STUDENT: SETH TROYER—CRITIC: JAMES ECKLER—INSTITUTION: UNIVERSITY OF CINCINNATI

Figure 2.45. *The structural supports along the side act as a meter for measuring distance along the path.* STUDENT: WENDELL MONTGOMERY—CRITIC: JASON TOWERS— INSTITUTION: VALENCIA COMMUNITY COLLEGE

MODULE

A repeated unit used for measurement

A compositional organization that is based upon repetition

Generative Possibilities in Unit Arrangement

The house was made as if it were a series of stacked volumes, each intended to hold a different part of the program. The volumes were not the same size, but they were based upon a common measure. The size of sleeping spaces equaled the common measure in both length and width. The main gathering space was two units wide by three units long. The kitchen was one unit by two units. The dining area was the same size as the sleeping spaces. Circulation threaded between these volumes, connecting them. It was one-quarter of a unit wide.

The entire building was a modular construction. The dimension used to regulate the size of volumes was the module that ensured that the various parts would interlock in a particular way. Because the entire building was based upon this module, parts could be interchanged and reconfigured. Throughout the process of design, the spaces had been arranged and rearranged many times before an arrangement that satisfied the requirements of the project was discovered.

The module is a standard of measurement. As it pertains most directly to architecture and design, it is an interchangeable part, or unit. The module is closely allied with both meter and measure in that it constitutes a system wherein an entity is broken down into units. Those units can be divided based upon dimension, proportion, or type. A module as a standard of measurement is a simple concept, but it seems to be strictly for documentation or evaluation. Are there ways in which the module can be a principle that generates design ideas?

A modular construction is one in which a part-to-whole relationship is principal to its design. Throughout the process of design, the role that each part has within the project must be decided. That role can then direct the way those modular pieces are assembled and the way they connect to any components that are common to multiple parts. The module becomes a way of expressing a particular idea about the proportional relationship

Figure 2.46. The space is created from a single sheet of material divided into equal squares. The edges of the squares are the only places where the student is permitted to cut or fold. From that module the student creates a series of interlocked spaces with distinct sizes and configurations. The module is still evident in the spaces that are created. Student: Cari Williams—Critic: James Eckler—Institution: Marywood University

between the small and the large. The module might be based on the proportions of the human body, the required space for a particular program, or the dimensions of an object held in the space. The basis of the module, combined with the arrangement of modular parts, can create an architecture that expresses its purpose, one that physically relates to the basis of the module.

A modular system is organizational in nature because of its use in creating relationships among the elements of a design. It is also an organizational system in that it provides a strategy or pattern of arrangement. Within a modular system there is a limited number of ways that one module can connect to another one. Those connections can therefore be scripted in a way that speaks to the specific functions of each unit, or the collaboration of units toward a single purpose.

» *See also* Meter; Measure.

Figure 2.47. This project is completely organized using a modular system. In the overhead plane, each panel is divided into four equal quadrants. Those quadrants are then evenly subdivided. Spatial composition adheres to the modular organizational structure. Student: McKinley Mertz—Critic: John Humphries—Institution: Miami University

MOMENT

A specific point in time or space

A single condition within a larger set of conditions

Generative Possibilities of a Singular Occurrence

In the plaza between two large buildings there is a sandwich shop. Every day there is a line at both lunch and dinner time that wraps around the tiny structure. The buildings on either side are tall office towers. There is a hotel immediately behind one of those towers. In one corner the plaza branches to lead visitors to several entertainment venues a short distance away. Pedestrians use the plaza as a short-cut to the buildings offering entertainment. Some stop here. Others pause and rest in the plaza on their way to some other part of the city. Most are from the hotel or the office buildings.

All of these surrounding structures are significantly larger than the sandwich shop, and yet it acts as an organizational and programmatic anchor for all of them. It is a single moment within a complex system.

Moment is commonly used to refer to a finite period of time. However, it can also refer to the passage of time, movement, or an event. This is a broad set of potential uses of the word. So how can these diverse meanings influence design or, more specifically, design organization? Each of these uses of the word has commonalities that inform a design principle. A moment in design is a relatively small, spatial event set within a larger pattern of arrangement (usually associated with aspects of movement, such as a path or an itinerary).

An event is correlated with the passage of time as a definitive beginning and end characterize it. It exists within a context of other events and experiences that tell a story. Consider a vignette, a single scene that builds upon

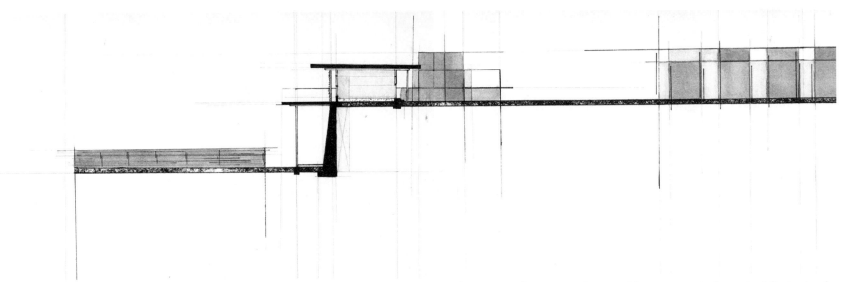

Figure 2.48. *The single space depicted in this section cut is one moment within a larger and more complex system of spaces. They are a part of a context that extends to either side of the small structure.* STUDENT: SETH TROYER—CRITIC: JAMES ECKLER—INSTITUTION: UNIVERSITY OF CINCINNATI

others to inform a longer scenario. Architecture is similar in nature. It is a composition of spaces. Each space has an assigned function and experiential condition. As a person moves from space to space, he or she plays through a kind of spatial narrative composed of various experiences ordered through sequence of encounter. Each of these spaces—each event—is a moment that provides an opportunity for design to take place, for the experience of space to be sculpted by the architect. The way in which those moments are composed implies an ordering system, or an organization based upon the spatial and programmatic relationship of one to another.

Figure 2.49. *The small curvilinear space is a single moment within a larger construct, part of which appears at the lower-right side of the image.* STUDENT: UNKNOWN; TEAM PROJECT—CRITIC: TIM HAYES—INSTITUTION: LOUISIANA TECH UNIVERSITY

NETWORK

An organizational strategy of interconnected elements

An organizational device that relates multiple elements to one another

A larger fabric based upon such a strategy or device

Generative Possibilities of Interconnectedness

The entire park was laid out as a network of paths and points. At each point there was a pavilion dedicated to presenting information on a particular point of interest. Because it was a network, any path we took could lead us to any one of the points in the park as long as we made the correct choice at each intersection we encountered. We looked at the map and pointed out which subjects we were interested in. We plotted our route from one node point to the next. Looking out away from the main gate we found the appropriate path and began to navigate through the system of walkways that structured the events in the park.

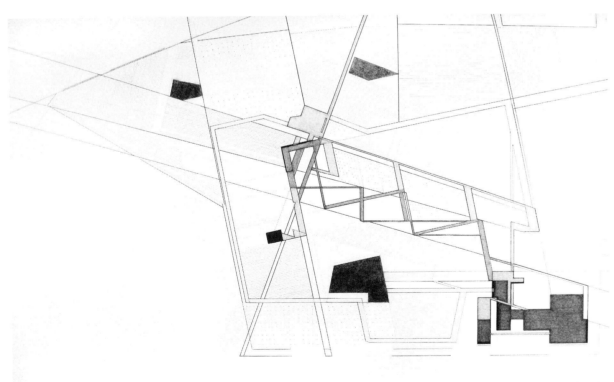

Figure 2.50. This plan is composed of a network of paths extending across the site. Each of those paths surrounds a fragment of the larger field, which is then devoted to a particular site program. STUDENT: NATE HAMMITT—CRITIC: JAMES ECKLER—INSTITUTION: UNIVERSITY OF CINCINNATI

A network is a set of interrelated elements dispersed across a field. Dispersal is important to the network. Its organizational structure implies a composition of open spaces and constructs: a mass-void arrangement in which the void area is relatively large. This type of structure may seem simple, or even self-explanatory. But how can it be used as a strategy for creating architecture? The elements in a network are related either through arrangement or associated characteristics.

For those related through arrangement, it is the structure of the network itself that defines the connection. They may lie on some axis or other organizing structure, or they may have some other physical registration or reference. Elements that are related through some associated characteristic, such as program, rely on the network for compositional cohesion. In either case, the dispersal of elements develops a correlation between the network and a field.

The network structure can be used in several ways to affect design. It can be used as a device to interpret an existing field of elements; in this case it can be an analytical tool to determine the way a new element may fit into the existing structure. The network can be used as a compositional strategy for relating elements in a design; this is a strategy linked to architectural intent. It can also be deployed as a way of using relationships between design elements to delineate a region, territory, or project scope.

Figure 2.51. In this model, there is a network of spaces that are interconnected through a series of paths and stairs. The network interconnection of parts prevents any single specified sequence or order to be established. Instead each moment is dependent on those that surround it. STUDENT: DAN MOJSA—CRITIC: REAGAN KING—INSTITUTION: MARYWOOD UNIVERSITY

NODE

A point of intersection between multiple lines or systems

Generative Possibilities in Intersection

We were making our way along one of the many paths in the park. They wound their way from one side to the other, linking the different points of interest that attracted people to the place. At each intersection between paths there was a pavilion. The paths expanded to create a paved rectangle that was larger than their typical width. A thick wall was built on one side of the paved area. On it there were information cards detailing some aspect of the park that was visible or accessible from that point. There were also columns opposite the display wall that supported a roof and bound the space of the pavilion.

The paths continued on. We knew that if we chose any of the options available to us, we would inevitably encounter another, similar pavilion. At every point of interest there was a pavilion that acted as a node within the network of paths and points. Each had information; each had two paths leading to different points within the park.

The word *node* comes from the Latin *nÿdus*, meaning "knot." As it applies to design, *node* refers, more generically, to an intersection or center point. There is also the potential for a node to be a part of a larger network, which differentiates it from a central organization. In an organizational pattern, a node acts as a hub linking multiple components together and consists of any element that contributes to the structure of that intersection.

In what ways can the use of a node be a design strategy? As with any other organizational pattern, the node presents a means for defining physical and spatial relationships between components of a design. It acts as a focal point, often within a larger network of other linked focal points. That focal point may be programmatic, such as a public gathering space that anchors other programmatic components distributed around it. It may be a spatial strategy meant to create complex transitions between multiple spaces simultaneously. Or it may be an organizational device that groups

or associates various elements of a design based upon a typological system.

There are several design considerations that arise when using a network of nodes as an organizational strategy. Defining elements associated with one node as opposed to another is an issue of language, representation, and type. Scripting the spatial, programmatic, and experiential transition from

Figure 2.52. A node is a point of intersection between multiple parts within a system. In this example, the node is made evident in several ways and within several systems. The physical intersection between elements forms the node. However, the spaces adjacent to those physical elements also intersect and overlap at that point. This creates a node within the organization of spaces. STUDENT: SAMANTHA ENNIS—CRITIC: STEPHEN GARRISON—INSTITUTION: MARYWOOD UNIVERSITY

one node to the next is necessary to the development and design of components within the composition.

Through the design process, the constructed elements that will be used to address these considerations within the architecture are created. This creates the possibility that the node as an organizational strategy might also become a point of departure for smaller-scale spatial ideas.

» *See also* Organization; Network.

Figure 2.53. Multiple spaces within this project intersect at the central stair. Upper, lower, and adjacent spaces are all connected through this one common point. STUDENT: MATTHEW SUNDSTROM—CRITIC: JASON TOWERS—INSTITUTION: VALENCIA COMMUNITY COLLEGE

ORDER

An arrangement of parts based on sequence or ranking

A logic by which parts can be arranged sequentially

Generative Possibilities in a Designed Sequence

There is one point of access to the stadium; booths for selling tickets are set up there. After their tickets are checked, people are admitted at a bank of turnstiles contained within a long covered pavilion. From there people ascend a long enclosed ramp to the tier where their seat is located. Exiting the ramp, they encounter vendors of all kinds who populate the outer ring of the stadium. People stop to purchase food or memorabilia before continuing around the building and finding the appropriate gate and eventually, their seats.

Entry to the stadium is structured by an ordering logic. Spaces are arranged to house programs that sequentially prepare the visitor for the event they are about to see.

Order refers to a logic of ranking. It is organizational in the application of that logic in determining the arrangement of elements. When order is imposed upon a set of components, a system of organization is created. In it, each component has a designated role in establishing organizational logic in the composition. Therefore, when components are in disarray according to that organizational structure, the entire system is in disorder; it is acting contrary to the established ranking logic.

In what ways can an ordering system be applied to an organizational structure? An ordering system might be a result of design intent, creating a caste system of elements that are to be included in the design. That ordering system might also be scripted by spatial or experiential relationships between elements in a design. In either scenario, order can be based on either hierarchy or sequence, and acts as a guide for testing variable patterns of arrangement.

An order based on hierarchy is a caste system. In the design process this works to divide design components based upon the degree of their contribution toward the primary design objectives. As a measure of design contribution it provides a logic for determining relationships between elements. This is important in determining ways that those elements might be positioned within an organizational pattern.

Sequence might be the most direct application of an ordering system to the organization of design components. Determining which spaces or objects are encountered before or after others speaks directly to their placement within an organizational scheme. This sequence might be determined based upon program, spatial operations, or compositional rhythm. Sequence can speak to occupation and movement from one space to another. Or it can speak to methodology and the order in which actions are performed.

» *See also* Hierarchy; Sequence.

Figure 2.54. *This hybrid section collage unfolds a design along a given path. It is an investigation of the sequence and order of programmatic components. The order in which one encounters a space is determined by the relationship that space has with others along the path. Order is an organizational logic that determines relationships between parts of a design. The sequence is dependent upon the path one takes from one space to another. Its variability is documented in the deviations from the primary section cut.* STUDENT: JESSICA HELMER—CRITIC: JAMES ECKLER—INSTITUTION: UNIVERSITY OF CINCINNATI

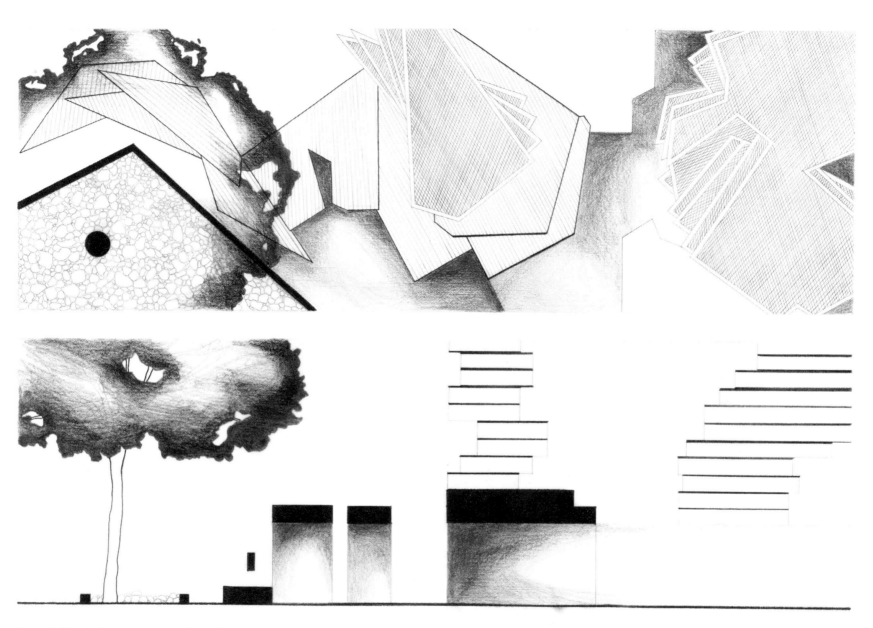

Figure 2.55. Order is present as a logic for arranging the three parts of the design. The lowest segment houses the tree. Adjacent to that, a higher area has been constructed. Upon that plinth, spatial constructions have been placed. Although this might not define a sequence by which an occupant would encounter these aspects of the design, it does illustrate an ordering logic. STUDENT: ELIZABETH SYDNOR—CRITIC: MILAGROS ZINGONI—INSTITUTION: ARIZONA STATE UNIVERSITY

ORGANIZATION

A structure or system that guides the arrangement of parts

A set of relationships between multiple varied components

Generative Possibilities in Structured Arrangement

While visiting the city, each student was to find and document examples of different organizational types. The first type he chose was the grid. He used the city plan as his example. He measured the length and width of several blocks and found that they were identical to one another. The city was planned as a regular grid.

In his travels he discovered and documented a building that was a long horizontal bar. In it, each space was arranged in sequence along a circulation corridor. He documented this building as an example of a linear pattern.

He came across another building that fit one of the patterns he was looking for. It had a large central atrium and from it, five wings were extended. Between each wing was a lawn. It was an apartment building of some kind. He documented this as a radial scheme.

He received a tip from a classmate about another building that could be used for his project. When he arrived he realized it wasn't one building, but a group of them: there were four identical office buildings dispersed across an entire block. He measured them, as well as their distance from one another, as an example of a clustered organizational pattern.

The hotel where they were staying was his example of a centralized organizational pattern. All of the guest rooms were arranged around a central core that housed a restaurant and the front desk.

In the fifteenth century, *organysen* meant, "to give structure to," or "to provide with organs." Similarly, *organizacioun* referred to "a bodily structure or composition." The origins of the word speak to biological structure or a relationships between organs. The current meaning is different only in that it does not exclusively refer to biological structures. Instead it has come to refer to a physical pattern of arrangement, or principles that direct an act of composition. It is a strategy for composition. That strategy may be a set of compositional principles or a formal ordering system.

Compositional principles are a set of rules that outline the intentions of a composition. They might set limits over scale: the design cannot exceed certain dimension, or cross a particular line, for example. Compositional principles might provide conditions for positioning design elements, if, for instance, two particular programs must be connected. They might establish a procedure for relating elements—new spaces must be aligned with existing spaces. There are many possible compositional principles governing the distribution of design elements; they are determined by the nature of every project. These principles can be used to determine the way space responds to context or the way elements are related within a project. A set of compositional principles represents a strategy of regulation in which an organizational pattern represents a formal ordering system to arrange design elements.

Francis D. K. Ching describes five patterns of organization: central, linear, radial, cluster, and grid. These patterns of arrangement can be used to describe spatial and formal relationships at any scale. They can be used to describe the connection or relationship between small spaces, or the positioning of different buildings at a civic scale. Within each of these systems of arrangement there are different types or variations, as well as hybrids. A grid may be regular or irregular. A linear arrangement may be along an axis or curved. A centralized pattern may also behave as a cluster. However, these systems of arrangement provide a key for both reading and generating space and form.

How are project elements distributed in relation to one another? How is a new element received within an existing organizational structure? These patterns of arrangement represent a method for relating elements through proximity, hierarchy, and registration. The distribution of elements according to a compositional logic of an organizational structure has the potential to guide decision making in design. Movement from one space to another, programmatic relationships, or contextual response might all be governed by one of these organizational systems. Similarly, discovering the organizational structure in an existing condition provides a key for understanding spatial relationships or determining the way new design might respond.

Central

An organizational pattern composed of a primary nucleus and a periphery

Something that is internal; a portion of a region that is not peripheral

Something that is important within a hierarchical system; a primary element

The central or centralized pattern is characterized by intersecting lines or linear elements. The central pattern's primary use is as an organizational structure for determining the placement of, and relationship between, design elements. A central organizational pattern is any ordering system consisting of a primary nucleus that acts as an anchor for a surrounding periphery.

A central organizational pattern can be used to affect design in two ways: design as a center, and design toward a center. Designing the center of an arrangement can give structure to an existing field of elements. Or it can be used in anticipation of elements within a field that will come later. The former implies that the center of the pattern is being deployed in order to define relationships among existing elements that were previously undefined. Or perhaps it is a tool to change the way in which elements relate to one another. The latter implies that the design prefigures future development and exists as a way of determining the pattern of that development.

What relationship will the designed center have to the elements peripheral to it? Is it being used as a transformative tool, one that restructures the existing? Or is it being used as a generative tool, one that facilitates expansion? Similarly, design may happen in response to an existing central ordering system. The intervening design then has several possible associations with the center. The pattern may be identified as a way of generating a

design that is to be incorporated into it. The pattern may also be identified as one that will be altered as a result of the new element. There is also the possibility that the inclusion of a new piece within the ordering system will exist as a counterpoint to that structure, an element that behaves as an anomaly. What role will the new design play relative to the existing organizational structure? How is that role defined through the composition of space?

Within this logic that a design can exist as a center or as dependent upon a center of an organizational structure, there is a question of scale. What defines the field? That field of elements can be considered a context that receives a new element. However, it can also be considered as a set of limits

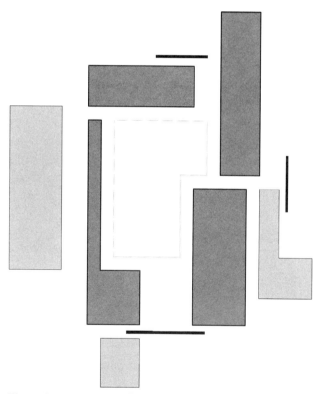

Figure 2.56. *In a centralized organizational pattern, parts of a design are distributed such that a nucleus is defined. When not being synthesized with other patterns, the characteristic that makes a centralized pattern distinct from the others is a focal point enclosed on all sides by the other components of a design.*

internal to the design of the element itself. A centralized organizational structure can be applied to the relation of spaces and forms, just as it can be applied to the relation of objects within a larger context. In this capacity, centralized organizational structures also speak to a system of hierarchy. The nucleus is of primary value, and the periphery is a composition of secondary and tertiary value. What spaces, forms, or events, are of most importance to the design overall? How do the other spatial components arrange themselves around that key moment?

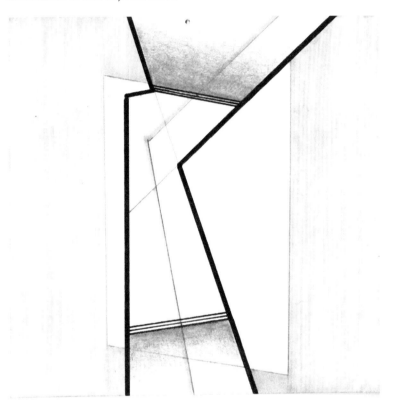

Figure 2.57. The white void in the middle of the page is defined on all sides by regions of shading. Lines passing through the center serve to further narrow and define the central space. The small area between the two thick lines to the sides, and the group of thin lines to the top and bottom, reinforce the centralized organization. Within that, a still small space can be seen at the point where the angled lines overlap. This intersection is the focal point of the centralized diagram.
STUDENT: DEREK JEROME—CRITIC: JAMES ECKLER—INSTITUTION: UNIVERSITY OF CINCINNATI

Cluster

A grouping of similar things

Elements bound into a group that is distinct from other groups or elements

The cluster pattern is a grouping of elements. The cluster pattern's primary use is as an organizational structure for determining the placement of, and relationship between, design elements. A cluster organizational pattern is

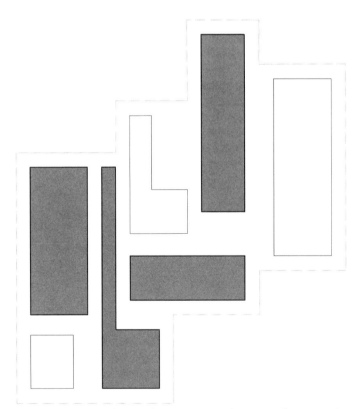

Figure 2.58. In a clustered organizational pattern, the parts of a design are distributed in groups. Each group is defined by its proximity of elements and its difference from others.

any ordering system consisting of a group that defines a territory or is otherwise held as distinct from other systems around or near it.

The cluster pattern shares some characteristics with both central and radial organization patterns, so it is useful to identify those characteristics that differentiate the cluster from the other two. The cluster is different from the central in that it is not dependent upon a clearly defined nucleus. It is different from the radial pattern in that it is not dependent upon a discernable pattern of direction or graining. But the cluster is different from these other two patterns mainly in that its periphery, rather than its core, defines it. The cluster, as a grouping of elements, is made distinct by the perimeter, or outer profile. The grouping may lack a clear internal structure and still be considered a cluster by virtue of proximity or type of elements. The two ways a cluster can be defined are through density of elements (proximity) or by element similarities (type).

As a generator, a cluster pattern can be used as a way of structuring components internal to the design, or be a way of reading a context that is to receive the design. When directing the positioning of design components relative to one another, a cluster pattern has potential as a way of codifying and delineating territories of space. Groups of formal or spatial elements will define regions within a design based on the type or composition of cluster profiles. When elements are being grouped, what characteristics classify them? How are groups deployed relative to one another in order to generate particular spatial relationships? As a contextual pattern, the cluster might identify spatial, formal, or typological conditions of a field that a design will have to respond to. Compositionally, the intervening design will play some role in the contextual pattern. Is it placed in one cluster or another? What determines its placement in one cluster rather than another? Is it used within a cluster or as a way of redefining the perimeter of the cluster? Is it used as a way of breaking the pattern or bridging between previously distinct groups? The role the design is to play in the existing contextual field should determine the placement of the design in the pattern and its relationship with the elements that compose the pattern.

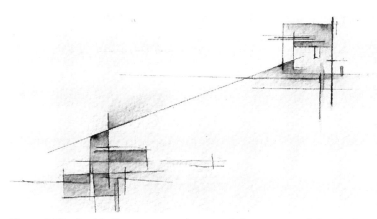

Figure 2.59. In this diagram, two clusters of elements are defined. There is no apparent organizational logic that governs the placement of elements within each cluster, but there is in the way the clusters are defined relative to each another. In this example, the clustered groupings remain separated. STUDENT: CLAIRE SHOWALTER—CRITIC: JOHN HUMPHRIES—INSTITUTION: MIAMI UNIVERSITY

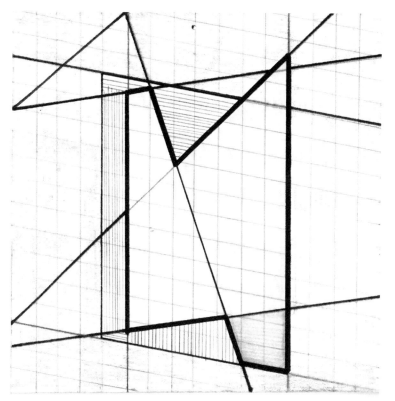

Figure 2.60. Overlapping lines and shaded areas are grouped together in this diagram. The extending lines serve to define the outer edge of the cluster. STUDENT: DEREK JEROME—CRITIC: JAMES ECKLER—INSTITUTION: UNIVERSITY OF CINCINNATI

Grid

A pattern of horizontal and vertical intersecting lines

An organizational structure derived from a pattern of intersecting elements

The grid is a pattern of intersecting lines or linear elements. The grid's primary use is as an organizational structure for determining the placement of, and relationship between, design elements.

There are two types of grid structure: regular and irregular. In a regular grid, the lines and the modules they define are uniform; regular grid lines are spaced at equal intervals, are parallel to one another, and the modules they create are identical. In contrast, the irregular grid's lines are spaced at different intervals, resulting in many varied dimensions of the modules between them. The irregular grid does not necessarily imply that the lines that compose it are parallel to one another.

The design implications are that the regular grid, a rare natural occurrence, is one that imposes order, whereas the irregular grid is a response to some existing order. In a field divided into identical zones, the existing context is replaced by this new ordering system. However, a grid structure that is multiply varied may be in response to an existing ordering system: the grid as a tool for integrating a new system into an existing one. The irregular grid might be a contrived composition without regard to some existing structure; however, its greatest potential within a design process is for generating a specialized and particular response between elements, both new and existing. What is being related within a grid structure? What principles are being used to define those relationships? The relation of elements within the system should determine grid type and deployment.

Grid structures have the potential to determine organizational hierarchy. Particular modules, intersections, or lines may be more important than others. As a grid negotiates spatial and formal response to an existing condition, hierarchy may be a result of existing primary and secondary conditions. As a grid negotiates the relationship among spaces and forms internal to it, hierarchy between elements may be generated by the grid structure itself.

Hierarchy can be represented through the positioning of elements within the grid structure and relative to one another, a line or module made more prominent than others, or variations in density within the grid.

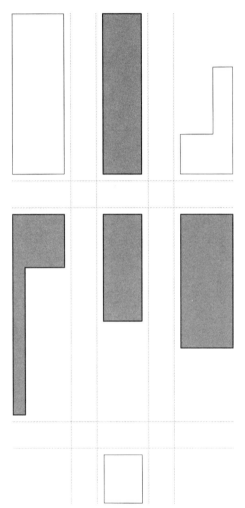

Figure 2.61.   A regular, orthogonal grid.

Grids can influence design process both in the development of singular spatial conditions and the organization of the larger field. The module of the grid can lend itself to establishing a unit of measure, scale, or assembly. That unit can be a way of dividing a space, a repeated programmatic module within a structure, or a composition of territories within a field. The grid lends itself to the process of composition and decision making at virtually any stage or scale of the design process.

Figure 2.63. In this example, a grid structure with different values in each section intersects with another organizational structure coming from the left side of the image. This diagram might be an analysis of an existing condition or the beginning of the development of an organizational strategy for a new design. STUDENT: CLAIRE SHOWALTER—CRITIC: JOHN HUMPHRIES—INSTITUTION: MIAMI UNIVERSITY

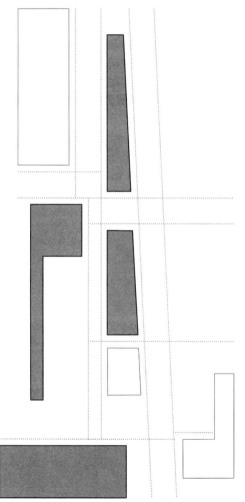

Figure 2.62. An irregular, nonorthogonal grid.

Figure 2.64. In this example, the grid is translated into three dimensions. It is a scaffold structure that holds elements in space. It is also manifest as a marking of surface wherein the treatment of surface is regulated by the grid structure. This model indicates a strategic development in a project; the student is examining the different ways the grid can be used to organize. STUDENT: ALEX HOGRETE—CRITIC: JOHN HUMPHRIES—INSTITUTION: MIAMI UNIVERSITY

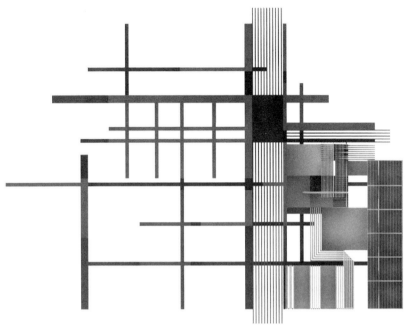

Figure 2.65. An analysis of an existing grid structure of a context provides insight into strategies for intervening within that context. A grid also regulates the new design, which is indicated by the densely packed grid lines on the right side of the image. The intervening grid is derived from its context and knits the design into its surroundings. STUDENT: STEPHEN DOBER—CRITIC: JAMES ECKLER— INSTITUTION: UNIVERSITY OF CINCINNATI

Linear

An organizational pattern structured about a line

A formal gesture defined by straight lines

A form, space, or sequence without diversions or branches

The linear pattern is a set of elements arranged around a line or forming a line. The linear pattern's primary use is as an organizational structure for determining the placement of, and relationship between, design elements.

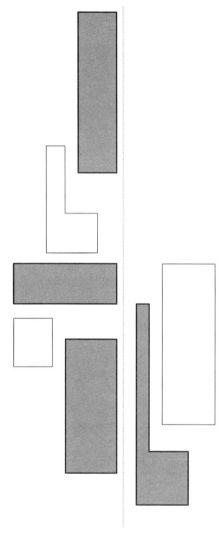

Figure 2.66. Elements arranged along a vertical line.

A linear organization structure follows a line or causes the elements that compose the system to create a line. That line may be an axis, a vector, or a curve. In an axial linear ordering system, elements are arranged about a straight line; direction is determined by the orientation of the axis. The vector linear organization is similar to an axial pattern except that it has an origin and a terminus, with a single direction from beginning to end. In a curvilinear organizational structure, orientation is constantly changing along an arc. Elements are still ordered along a continuous thread.

A linear pattern can be deployed as a way of organizing a design or as a way of reading and extracting contextual information from a field intended to receive the design. The linear ordering system represents a simple gesture for relating different components within a scheme. Whether it is an axial, vector, or curvilinear pattern, multiple components are arrayed along a thread. What are the components that are being arranged? In what order should they be placed? The various possibilities for orientation and direction will determine sequence within the ordering structure.

Is the linear pattern a tool for directing the repletion of elements or modules? The linear pattern can be divided as a way of measuring units of space. In terms of contextual reading, the linear organization might be an existing system to direct formal and spatial response. Depending on the type of linear structure identified in a context, the new design will play different roles within that pattern. Is the new design to be a point of

origin or termination of a vector system? Is it to be a unit along an axis? What orientation will it establish along a curve? Determine the relationships the designed spaces are to have with their surroundings in order to determine the role the design is to play in the contextual pattern of arrangement.

Figure 2.68. Spaces in this project are arranged in a linear fashion within an armature. The armature is derived from an observation of direction and graining in the context. The linear structure serves to reinforce the surrounding grain at the scale of the intervention. STUDENT: LAUREN WHITEHURST—CRITIC: JAMES ECKLER—INSTITUTION: UNIVERSITY OF CINCINNATI

Radial

An system of arrangement characterized by a relation to a common center

In a radial organizational pattern, elements move around or away from a focal point. There should also be multiple directions of movement or an arrangement of elements relative to the focal point. The radial pattern's primary use is as an organizational structure for determining the placement of, and relationship between, design elements.

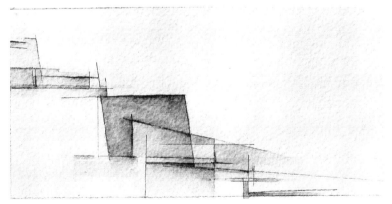

Figure 2.67. This diagram is a hybrid between the linear and grid patterns of organization. However, the grid sections are distributed in a linear fashion. This diagram might be an analysis of an existing condition or the beginning of the development of an organizational strategy for a new design. STUDENT: CLAIRE SHOWALTER—CRITIC: JOHN HUMPHRIES—INSTITUTION: MIAMI UNIVERSITY

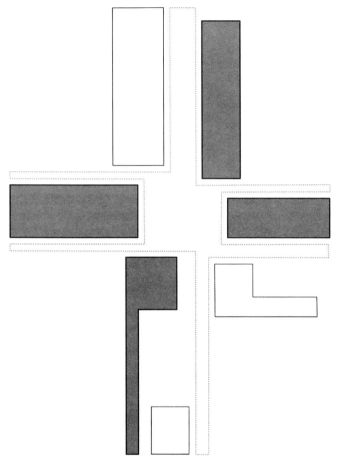

Figure 2.69.   Radial extensions from a centralized focal point.

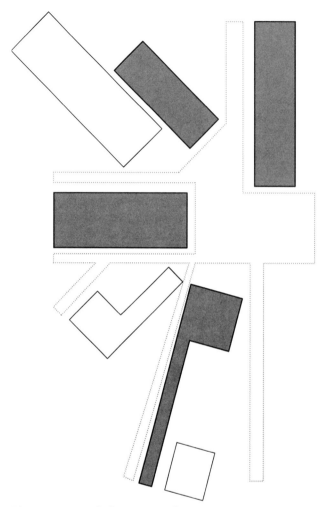

Figure 2.70.   Radial extensions from a noncentralized focal point.

The focal point in a radial system is not necessarily toward the interior of the pattern, which is the primary factor in determining its difference from a central ordering system. The primary characteristic of a radial pattern is that elements are arranged either around, or moving away from, the focal point in multiple directions. Concentric expansion, or a continuous spiral from the focal point, describes a system in which elements are arranged around it. In a system with different axes radiating from the focal point, elements are organized in multiple directions from the focal point. In either scenario, direction away from and toward the area of focus is the predominant factor in identifying the radial pattern.

The radial pattern can be integral to the process of design as either a generator of spatial relationships internal to a design or as a method for reading and responding to a context that is to receive an intervening design. When used internal to a design it can be a generator of relationships by directing the placement of components. Inherent to a radial pattern is a notion of hierarchy. As elements are dependent upon a focal point, whatever comprises the focal point is of more importance than the other components within the composition.

What design component is to define the focal point? How are other components positioned in relation to it? What other hierarchical categories might be present within the design and how might they govern placement of other components? A radial ordering system permits the designer to position units and components in a way that determines sequence, program, spatial relation, and formal composition. In terms of contextual reading, the radial organization might be an existing system to direct formal and spatial

response. Depending on the type of radial organizational structure identified in a context, the new design will play different roles within that pattern. Is the new design to be a focal point or a unit along an extension from that point? How is it to be related to either the focal point or its surrounding territories? Determine the relationships the designed spaces are to have with their surroundings in order to determine the role the design is to play in the contextual pattern of arrangement.

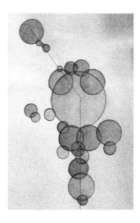

Figure 2.72. In this diagram, smaller circles, each with a different value denoted by tone, are arranged in a radial pattern about a larger circle that acts as the focal point. This diagram might be an analysis of an existing condition or the beginning of the development of an organizational strategy for a new design. STUDENT: CLAIRE SHOWALTER—CRITIC: JOHN HUMPHRIES—INSTITUTION: MIAMI UNIVERSITY

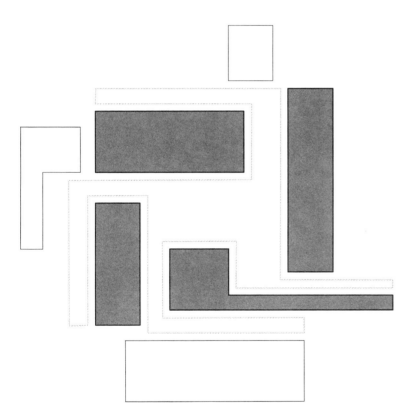

Figure 2.71. Radial, spiraling extensions from a centralized focal point.

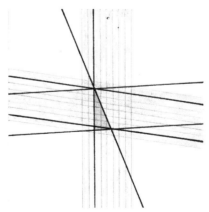

Figure 2.73. In this diagram, lines intersect at a central hub. The intersection outlines a small region that functions as the organizational focal point. Each line is of a different hierarchical value that determines ordering relationships between elements arranged by the pattern. STUDENT: DEREK JEROME—CRITIC: JAMES ECKLER—INSTITUTION: UNIVERSITY OF CINCINNATI

ORIENTATION

Position or direction in relation to a point of reference

Generative Possibilities in Directing Toward

The site had a street on only one side; the other sides were adjacent to neighboring properties. This street was the only point of access and the primary starting point for the approach to whatever building would eventually be constructed on this site. With that in mind, the architect oriented the project toward the street edge. That would be where the public face of the building was located; it was the front.

The street grid of this town was rotated several degrees off of the cardinal directions. Understanding the new project's orientation relative to north, south, east, and west was a starting point for figuring out strategies for environmental response. Orientation relative to the position of the sun determined the various qualities of light that would be achieved by placing windows in one place as opposed to another. This is just one of many implications of orientation relative to the position of the sun.

Orientation is an organizational principle that relates object to site. The basis of the relationship provided by orientation is direction. It requires an external reference to which an object toward which, or away from, it can be oriented. The directional relationship established is between the object and the directional reference. That reference can be physical—one object oriented toward another, for example—or it can be conceptual, as in orientation toward a cardinal direction. What roles does orientation play in organizing elements of a design? How can it impact process? The two modes of orientation listed above speak to compositional relationships among elements or a relationship to the environmental characteristics of site.

The cardinal directions provide a reference for the measurement of various environmental factors relating to architectural design. Orienting a design according to this directional convention allows the designer to have control over the impact those factors have on space. Issues of light, temperature, view, wind, and so on are governed by orientation. The implications of this are not purely performative; rather, there is also the potential to capitalize on strategies for environmental response in order to control experiential characteristics of space. For instance, issues in design that pertain to the quantity or direction of light in a space can be addressed through orientation. Desired spatial outcomes regarding the creation of an interior environment can be accomplished through iterative studies in orientation.

Orienting an object toward or away from another is a compositional gesture. It facilitates design intent for organizational structure; it also establishes specific relationships between elements of a composition. Doing so requires that the objects being related through orientation have a definitive front and back, a primary face, or some other reference to determine the direction in which they are oriented.

» *See also* Direction.

POSITION

The location of an element

To place an element purposefully or strategically

A single location within a larger network of possible locations

Generative Possibilities in Placement

The project called for much of the site to remain open as public gathering space. The size required by the project's program was small enough, so this wouldn't be a difficult requirement to meet. However, as one of the initial steps of the design process, a strategy for positioning the project on the site had to be developed.

Several analytical studies were conducted to address the influence of surrounding streets and buildings on any proposed position for the new building. It was decided to elongate the program in order to make a linear building positioned to one side of the site. This strategy was the first to be explored because it enabled the largest portion of the site to remain open for the function of gathering. It would also provide the possibility of future expansion. It was changed, however, because the new design would have been positioned too close to a neighboring structure, and this would limit any attempt to provide natural light to interior spaces. Eventually, the project was positioned along the street edge. This created a public face without limiting the open portion of the site very much.

To position something is the primary act of organization. It implies that within that act, there is intent that justifies placement. How is it that simply locating a design, or a component of one, can impact its function? A position is an organizational notion that relates one element to another or to its surroundings. The act of positioning an element within an organizational structure is a process involving both craft and decision making.

Location refers simply to a geographic point. A position, however, requires a resulting relationship to occur between the element that is placed and an aspect of its surroundings. This difference is not one of semantics. Positioning an element is a strategy for creating that organizational relationship. That strategy might define contextual response, the linking of spaces, or the

distribution of program. When that position is based upon certain design criteria, it becomes a strategy that is employed through iterative process to advance the design.

Position can also reference design intent. One can take a position regarding a particular topic, which is the statement of opinion or intent

Figure 2.74. This model is part of a series that studies the positioning of an intervention relative to the features of a site. As a part of the investigation, those features are connected to the construct with a network of paths. The topography is modified in order to receive the intervention and paths. STUDENT: BRITTANY DENNING—CRITIC: JAMES ECKLER—INSTITUTION: UNIVERSITY OF CINCINNATI

formulated from available information. It is the foundation of design conception. As it regards architecture, taking a position refers to the role of a design within a larger intellectual (social, cultural, or technological) context. It is a statement that a particular design should function in one way or another.

In order to take a position regarding a design topic, a trend must be identified. It is then the role of the designer to predict where that trend will be at some point in the future. The choice, then, is to respond to that predicted outcome, to respond to the current state, or to attempt to alter the trend's course. This logical model can be applied to many design related issues. In a sense, this aspect of positioning is an effort to organize oneself, or one's design, relative to other viewpoints in the discipline of architecture.

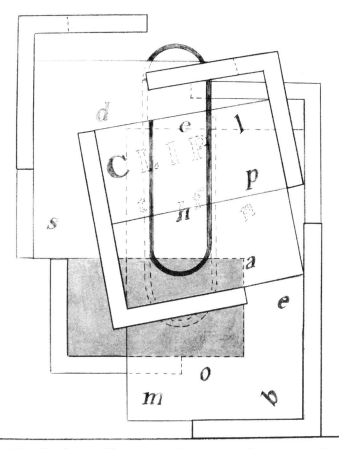

Figure 2.75. This drawing illustrates position at a smaller scale than the previous example. In it, components of an assembly are shown to operate in different ways as they are positioned and repositioned. The study focuses on understanding clipping as a strategy for connecting and relating parts. Using a clip, components can be arranged so that the containing brackets are brought together, or repositioned so they are fractured but the word clip is revealed between them.
STUDENT: JOE WAHY—CRITIC: MATTHEW MINDRUP—INSTITUTION: MARYWOOD UNIVERSITY

PROXIMITY

The relative nearness of parts

Generative Possibilities in Being Near or Far

The houses were close to one another in this part of the city. This block was no different: the houses were separated by a small strip that was used as a path from the street to the interior of the block. The residents shared the communal interior space. Technically, it was divided into small parcels attached to each house, but there were no fences or gates to define territory.

In this informal situation, ownership and responsibility were determined by proximity. People cared for and maintained the portion of the interior that immediately surrounded their house. Any items placed in the interior space were known to belong to one person or another based upon their proximity to one of the houses.

Proximity defines an organizational relationship of distance. More specifically, it is an associative relationship between elements that is established because of relative closeness. How can closeness be used to generate ideas for architecture? How can the simple act of positioning elements in proximity to one another be an organizational strategy?

Proximity can be an organizational structuring principle for a project. Positioning elements close to one another can be one method of associating them compositionally or programmatically. Because distance has direct implications on perception and experience, proximity can be used as a means of developing spatial ideas related to path, itinerary, or approach.

Proximity can be one contributing factor in a more complex relationship between spaces. Elements being placed close to one another can be a starting point for considering the materials, assemblies, and experiences that act as a link across that short distance. This can be done as a way of embedding a particular spatial operation within the design.

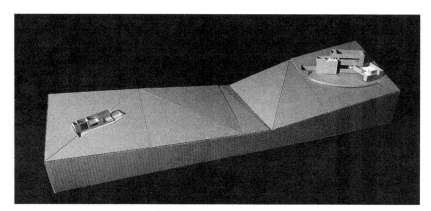

Figure 2.76. Components of this design are kept distant from one another. The relative positioning of the two moments describes a bound territory between them. However, because of the distance, they are less related to one another and more individually distinct. STUDENT: TREVOR HESS—CRITIC: PETER WONG—INSTITUTION: UNIVERSITY OF NORTH CAROLINA, CHARLOTTE

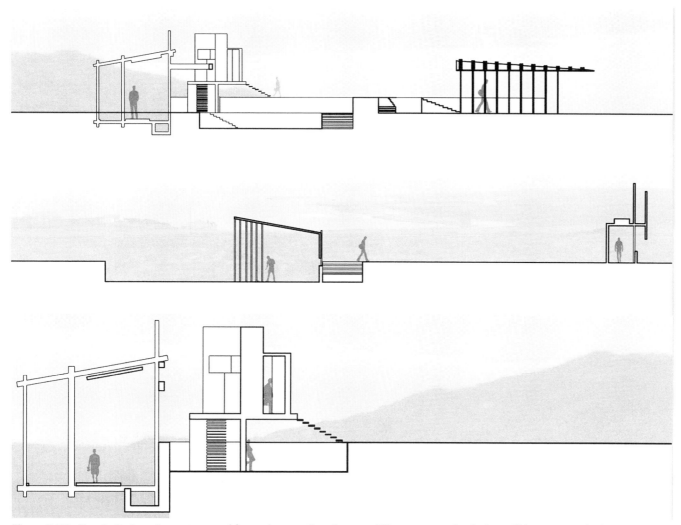

Figure 2.77. *Proximity is an important tool for understanding the way different parts of a design will function and relate. In this study, the student documents different parts of the design according to their distance from one another. The implications are not only organizational but also spatial and formal. Distance must be considered according to circulation, or the way one might occupy the area between parts. Additionally, that interstice must be defined through assembly.* STUDENT: UNKNOWN—CRITIC: JOHN MAZE—INSTITUTION: UNIVERSITY OF FLORIDA

RELATE

To connect or associate parts through a set of characteristics

Generative Possibilities in Association

When entering the building, guests first came into a small room, where they were greeted. In this space, introductions were made, and sometimes gifts exchanged. Guests arriving early could sit in chairs arranged so that they could converse while waiting for the main room to be prepared. Once all was made ready, they moved into the main room, where eating and socializing occurred at a larger scale.

The two spaces related to one another through arrangement and function. They were positioned adjacent to each another, with openings that permitted access from one to the other. The small space was a moment of pause on the way to the ultimate destination in the main room. It functioned as a way of preparing the guest for what came later in the sequence. The spaces defined a relationship that is both physical and programmatic.

Figuring out ways of relating pieces or functions of a design is one of the core motivations of an architect. It is something that is both a principle of organization and of process. It is a function of organization as spaces and forms are related through arrangement. The act of relating components of a design is a part of process. Design thinking carried through various stages of an iterative process drives it. The question then, is one of generation. Can an organizational relationship generate space? How does an act of relating elements generate or resolve a design concept?

The arrangement of forms within an organizational pattern creates designed relationships through a physical connection or the similarity of physical characteristics. This type of organizational relationship is compositional. It helps to define and represent the ordering logic used to distribute design components. Representing that logic can not only help communicate the design ideas inherent to it but also help communicate functions of space to an occupant. Spaces, on the other hand, can be related to one another within in an organizational pattern based upon many potential physical, experiential, or programmatic characteristics. Defining the way one

Figure 2.78. Language is one way in which spaces are related in this model. There are a few strategies for assembly and composition that are used consistently throughout, producing an awareness of relationship through similarity. Spaces are also related through the connections and disconnections between them. STUDENT: VICTORIA TRAINO—CRITIC: KATE O'CONNOR—INSTITUTION: MARYWOOD UNIVERSITY

space relates to another can do several things for a project. It can provide criteria for the formal assemblies that will contain the spaces. It can also help the designer determine the relative placement of those spaces within the building composition. In addressing spatial conditions of organization and arrangement, the designer can also consider issues of itinerary and the experience of an occupant as a way of distributing programs.

These considerations of relationship and organization engage process by providing a conceptual framework for decision making. They can help guide the evolution of a project by resolving generative ideas. Considering the various relationships between design elements becomes a way of associating and creating space, form, and organization simultaneously. They each contribute to relationships between design components and can therefore be understood to be interrelated and interdependent design attributes.

Figure 2.79. Relationship speaks to the manner in which elements are associated. That does not necessarily mean those elements are directly connected or allied in a common purpose. In this example, separation defines the relationship between two spaces. The division between spaces is established by the separating wall and reinforced by the gap between the wall and the lower plane of the space at the right of the image. The two are still associated through adjacency and proximity, despite being separated. STUDENT: CARI WILLIAMS—CRITIC: JAMES ECKLER—INSTITUTION: MARYWOOD UNIVERSITY

RHYTHM

The pattern of recurring or repeating elements

A measured sequence

Generative Possibilities in Sequential Patterning

The music hall sponsored a program for musicians in residence. While attending, they would be provided with opportunities to practice their craft, write, and perform. As the program developed and became more successful among young musicians, a new building had to be built to house it. In it there would be a large performance hall where the musicians in residence would present their work. Both practice studios and bedrooms would surround it.

Instead of grouping the different types of spaces together, it was decided to mix them. The design placed a practice studio after every two bedrooms. This way, each studio could be assigned to the residents closest to it. This rhythm of two for every one persisted around the periphery of the large performance hall. It was a way of ordering elements of the design to facilitate a programmatic function and relationship between residence and productivity.

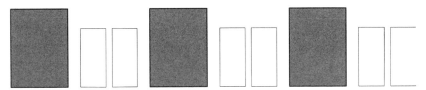

Figure 2.80. Rhythm is a sequential structure based upon order and repetition. In this example, an abbabb rhythm is described. The order is abb; the repetition is the continual copying of that grouping.

A rhythm is a serial logic. It defines a methodology for sequencing or ordering elements of a design. Rhythm is established through repetition in intervals or as a formula for arranging elements according to type. How can a rhythm be a tool for generating space? How does it facilitate design thinking or spatial conception? A rhythm is not just repetitious; it is a measure of repetition within an organizational pattern. Rhythm can be used as a logical standard by which spaces are generated or arranged. It can be used as a tool for measuring space. And in its role as a measuring device, it can be used as a way of identifying or quantifying the transformation of a formal type across an area.

A rhythm implies the use of a standard unit to measure repetition. It is a pattern to which repetition conforms. Just as a poem may use a structured rhyming scheme to provide a framework for its creation, space can use a rhythmic structure to dictate its composition. An *abab* scheme is one in which *a* types and *b* types are arranged in an every-other pattern. Those types may refer to components used to compose a space. If that is the case, the space will be characterized by a series of segments. The scheme may also refer to spatial types, in which case it may be a way of establishing a system by which spaces relate to one another within a larger composition.

Using rhythm as a standard of composition also raises the possibility for using it to read or analyze an existing space or arrangement—as a measuring device. So discovering the rhythmic logic applied to the original generation of a space or organizational pattern can provide information pertaining to the idea that generated it.

Rhythm is also a structure that can be made apparent. In making a rhythmic structure obvious or conspicuous as a space is experienced, variations are highlighted. Since the rhythm is a sequence, change or disruption within its order becomes even more evident to an observer, allowing rhythm to be used as a tool to measure transformation over an area. Subtle shifts in ordering or the manipulation of characteristics of a type can be understood in a serial pattern through the use of rhythm. Instead of defining an *a* type and then changing it within a composition, the designer might be able to define a series of transformative steps arranged in a rhythmic pattern. This enables an observer experiencing the transformation to understand the relationships or correlations between the result and the original.

» *See also* Sequence; Repetition.

Figure 2.82.   Rhythm is evident in the size and position of the overhead panels; they describe a relationship between the depression below and the plinth. They vary in width and the extent to which they protrude to one side. STUDENT: GRACE DAVIS—CRITIC: STEPHEN GARRISON—INSTITUTION: MARYWOOD UNIVERSITY

Figure 2.81.   Rhythm is evident in the material banding in this example. It is an a-b-a-b pattern and illustrates the role rhythm might play in material or assembly. STUDENT: OLEA DZILNO—CRITIC: VALERY AUGUSTIN—INSTITUTION: UNIVERSITY OF SOUTHERN CALIFORNIA

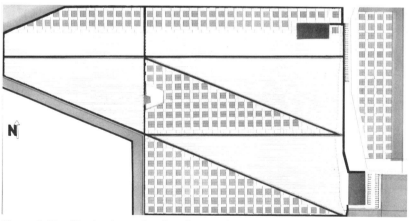

Figure 2.83.   Rhythm is used to distribute different site programs across a field. Each division is a result of topographic features that are favorable to the prescribed program. STUDENT: SETH TROYER—CRITIC: JAMES ECKLER—INSTITUTION: UNIVERSITY OF CINCINNATI

STRUCTURE

A construction

A system of support

A system or strategy for composing

Generative Possibilities in Organizational Patterning

Patterning of the civic building grounds made its organizational structure evident. Small hills formed in regular geometries, rows of trees, and pathways all contributed to a repetition of shapes stretched across the site. Elements placed on one side were aligned with elements on the other. Those alignments also correlated to the pattern of shapes that dominated the plan.

This strategy for arranging pieces of the design carried through into the design and construction of the civic building itself. The patterning of the site defined a set of rules for the building design to follow. The building was oriented along an axis determined by the patterned shapes. Elements of the interior aligned with elements of the exterior, continuing the structural strategy at the smaller scale of the building.

Structure is a reference to all things constructed. It has several obvious connections to architecture as a reference to built form. However, as it refers to other aspects of human manufacture, it can be associated both with process and organization. What is a procedural structure? What is an organizational structure?

Whether at the scale of assembly and building or at the scale of the contextual field, design is an act of structuring. That act may be in the conventional assembly of a wall or in the invention of a pattern of arrangement. Much of process is devoted to logic—the creation of systems and patterns. Providing structure where there use to be none, identifying and adapting to a structure that exists, or replacing one that is no longer useful is fundamental to architectural design at any scale. Additionally, structure can be an ordering device. As this applies to process, a structure may be an order to the application of techniques or methods, a staging of procedures, or any set of guidelines that governs the way a design is developed through process. It acts as a kind of choreographed creativity.

Figure 2.84. This drawing illustrates an organizational structure based upon dimension, proportion, and alignment. It is a structure of an object not seen. The logic of the framework provided enables the object to be drawn without having it present as an observed subject. Student: Carrey Givens—Critic: Jim Sullivan—Institution: Louisiana State University

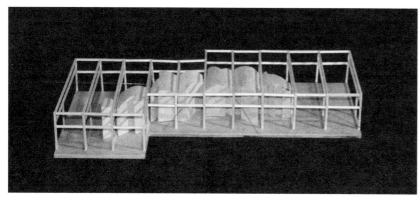

Figure 2.85. The module defines the organizational structure of this project. A series of bays outlines the project limits and divides it into segments corresponding to design criteria. Within this structure, designed elements are inserted corresponding to the bays. STUDENT: MARY DICKERSON—CRITIC: JOHN HUMPHRIES—INSTITUTION: MIAMI UNIVERSITY

Understanding structure as an ordering device speaks directly to organization. An organizational structure is physically manifest through the order of elements. It consists of any element or strategy that defines a pattern of arrangement.

SYSTEM

A group of interacting or interconnected elements

An organized method; a strategy

Generative Possibilities in Cooperative Function

The designer for the house developed an organizational strategy that called for the various programs to be separated into distinct groups. She created a series of diagrams that broke the house into three segments: sleeping, eating, and entertaining. Each segment held a group of programmatically allied spaces. For the sleeping portion she arranged three bedrooms along with bathrooms in a linear bar. For the eating group she placed dining and storing spaces adjacent to the kitchen and preparation spaces. The kitchen acted as a central hub, and the other spaces were distributed around it. Entertaining spaces were reduced to one large, irregularly shaped space. It acted as a bracket, linking the other two groups. By enacting this strategy she created three distinct spatial systems. To unify them she placed them under one uniform structural system and a single roof spanning all three groups.

System is a broadly applied term in architecture. It refers to a set of interrelated spaces, forms, or operations of design. Outside of the design process, building mechanics are referred to as systems. Mechanical systems in a building share a common characteristic with the more general application of system to other facets of design and design process; they are composed of multiple parts interrelated to perform a single function. This defining attribute affects our understanding of architectural organization. Any organizational pattern or strategy is, by definition, a system. How can a system be applied as a design principle? A system functions as an ordering device, whether it is applied to a set of spaces, forms, or operations. It presents an organizational logic that is based on use.

A spatial system consists of a set of allied spaces. Those spaces may be related through program or even physical attributes. For instance, a design scheme that uses a space housing the primary program as an anchor for surrounding, support programs forms a system. Likewise, a set of spaces combined in a sequence that begins with a compressed corridor and ends with an expansive volume forms a system. The first scenario is a system of arrangement and

event. The second is a system of spatial transition. Each is comprised of a set of spaces with a single purpose. Understanding the possibilities for spatial systems gives a designer another skill set in reading and inventing spatial relationships.

Formal systems are compositions that act in service to larger design ideas. They consist of interrelated objects. For instance, a series of markers used to delineate a region within a larger organizational pattern forms a system. A column grid in a building might also be understood as a formal system. The first example is a system of marking and communication wherein the

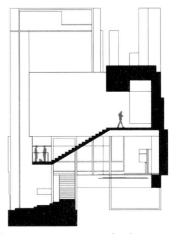

Figure 2.86. In this example, the use of systems to compose the design is evident in both space and form. The spatial system is one in which different volumes are stacked, differentiated, or connected according to configuration and program. Additionally, formal systems are made evident by the different assemblies, which are themselves compositions acting in service to space. It is the arrangement and configuration of form that facilitates the distribution of spaces in both the plan (left) and section (right). STUDENT: UNKNOWN—CRITIC: JOHN MAZE—INSTITUTION: UNIVERSITY OF FLORIDA

occupant is made aware of the boundary between areas. The second is a structural system intended to support the various loads of the building.

Operational systems can be mechanical or methodological. A mechanism (apart from the commonly referred to mechanical system of a building) consists of any operable component. A wall composed of movable louvers or a wall that slides to open a space are both systems of operation. They consist of many components assembled in a way that permits the physical function of movement. However, operational logic can be applied to process as well. Methods and techniques are systems of actions employed in the process of design. In this sense actions are ordered to produce a specific result. For instance, techniques for cutting, shaping, and assembling wood are predictable and have predictable outcomes. Those techniques form an operational system—a method of production.

» *See also* Organization; Order.

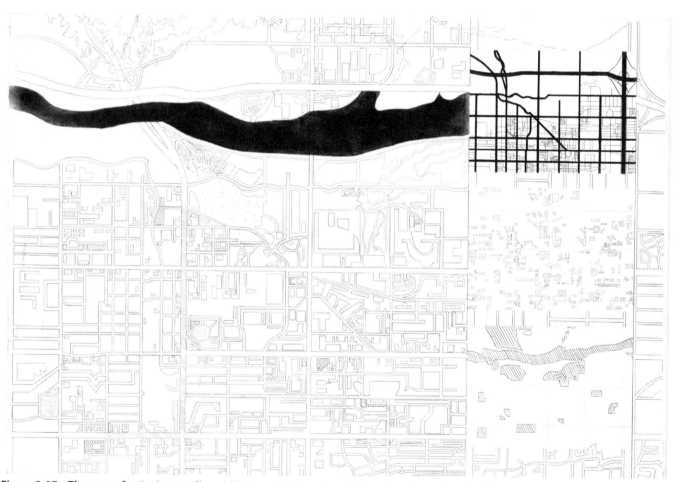

Figure 2.87. **The map of a city is actually a collection of different and interrelated organizational, spatial, and formal systems. In this drawing, the systems pertinent to the study are seen collectively and then isolated for analysis in the banner at the right of the image.**
STUDENT: JIHYE CHOI—CRITIC: MILAGROS ZINGONI—INSTITUTION: ARIZONA STATE UNIVERSITY

ZONE

An area distinguished by a particular characteristic

A region of space defined by a particular characteristic

A region established to serve a particular purpose; a programmed area

Generative Possibilities in the Division of Space

The museum was divided in several ways. Each floor was dedicated to a different era or artistic style. Each floor was then divided into individual displays. This zoning strategy helped us navigate the museum whenever we came.

The third floor is reserved for impressionist painting, a kind of territory for that style and time period. This is where we really wanted to go because the museum had just acquired several new impressionist pieces. When we get off the elevator we make our way into the first of several rooms. Each room is a zone within the larger territory that highlights the work of one artist. Occasionally, a gallery is shared by the work of several artists, but only in circumstances where there are noticeable similarities between them.

A zone generically refers to a region, or territory. Any organizational pattern is a composition of zones. The ways that different zones are divided or made distinct establish spatial and organizational relationships between them. Given the breadth of function and the definition of *zone*, does it have any specific application to design or design process? The answer to that question lies in the different types of zone.

A region represents a subset within a larger entity. This definition can apply at virtually any scale, from an area within a single space to an extensive field divided into smaller parts. It can be a product of mapping or construction. As a subdivision, it is typically defined subtly through delineation rather than dramatic surface shifts or assemblies. If a region is defined through large-scale construction, the larger entity can become indistinguishable. In this case, the region is isolated and not read as being a part of a larger whole; it instead becomes self-referential. The way the region is bound determines its relationship with neighboring zones. This is at the heart of its role in the

design process. It might indicate patterns of use within a space or distinguish one space from another within a larger composition. It might also be used to distinguish slight shifts in program or denote formidable changes in use or access at the scale of the contextual field. The way the region is bound and articulated determines its individual characteristics as well as its relationship to its surroundings.

Figure 2.88. A zone is an area, region, or territory. This diagram breaks up a field into zones based upon various compositional characteristics of that field. The goal is to determine opportunities for intervening within the existing condition. STUDENT: JOE GIBBS—CRITIC: JAMES ECKLER—INSTITUTION: UNIVERSITY OF CINCINNATI

A territory is similar to a region, except that it is a singular entity. It is a contextual condition defined by ownership or influence. This implies that the territory is dependent upon an anchor or focal point. That anchor might be cultural in the case of ownership, or it might be the physical definition of an area of influence surrounding a construct. The territory is the component of an organizational structure that determines which zone is associated with which element. This could be the immediate site around a building, or an area that a project will have some other design influence over. Like the region, the characteristics of the territory are largely dependent upon the composition of its boundaries. Different from the region, however, the territory might also be defined by grouping similar elements, in which case the characteristics of the territory are determined by commonalities in the group.

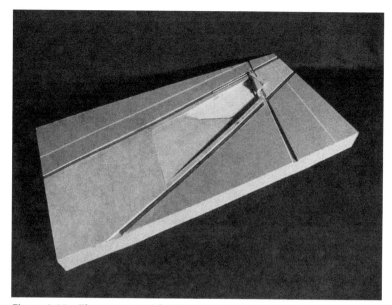

Figure 2.89. The contextual field is articulated with angular zones to determine areas of influence or relationships to the intervening architecture. STUDENT: NICK YOUNG—CRITIC: JASON TOWERS—INSTITUTION: VALENCIA COMMUNITY COLLEGE

3. TERMS OF OPERATION AND EXPERIENCE

Student: Nathan Simpson—Critic: James Eckler—Institution: University of Cincinnati

APERTURE

Generative Possibilities in Opening

A man stands in a dark room. The space is twice his height, and twice again as wide. It disappears into the darkness beyond, making its length indeterminate. A single sliver of bright light cuts into the space, dimly illuminating the area around the man but brightly illuminating a single band that stretches across the floor and up one wall, preventing him from seeing anything beyond. Within that linear pool of bright light sits a pedestal with a glass object resting upon it. The light refracts through the glass; fractured, colored light sparkles across nearby surfaces.

This space serves a function of display for that object and that object alone. The aperture is intended to admit light and nothing else. That light is intended to put the object on display and keep the rest of the space shrouded from view. The slit that cuts across the ceiling and through the wall opposite the pedestal stops just above the man's head, which makes seeing beyond impossible.

The slit is narrow, so the object will only be illuminated at a single point during the day. After marveling at the glass sculpture on display for a time, he steps farther into the dark parts of the space. His eyes adjust and he leaves, moving on to another space and another display.

What can an aperture do? What can it become in a space? A window is a type of aperture; so is a door. Apertures can be used to allow access, and to allow light, or sound, or air to enter a space. They can be used for views of something specific or to provide a vista of the horizon. Apertures can be fixed or operable; they can also be used to establish rhythm, measure, or some other compositional quality of a constructed surface. There are seemingly endless possible variations for apertures, raising certain questions: What is needed in the space you are about to create? What role does the aperture play in the creation of space?

The word *aperture* is useful, as it is stripped of most formal connotation or preconception. An aperture can be or become what the designer needs it to be. The word *window* implies a particular image of what a window is, based

Figure 3.1. An aperture provides access to space. In this instance, apertures are used to direct light into the space. They are positioned so that the light will create patterns of light and shadow that allow the configuration of space and form to be discerned. STUDENT: MCKINLEY MERTZ—CRITIC: JOHN HUMPHRIES—INSTITUTION: MIAMI UNIVERSITY

upon previous experience; it is the same with the word *door*. The designer can script the way that an opening informs a space by thinking of it as an aperture rather than referencing an image of a particular object (i.e., the single hung window, complete with drapes). This way, the aperture serves a space with a specific intention as defined by the designer.

Can one walk through the aperture? If so, it will have a definite scale relative to the human body. It can be short, forcing one to duck, or tall, drawing the eye upward. It can be narrow to compress an individual or expansive to create an extension of the space beyond. The barrier that is overcome by this aperture can also be considered: it can be thick or thin, light or massive. The surface within which the aperture is set contributes to the definition of a spatial characteristic of transition from one side to the other.

Does it allow light into a space? An aperture can manipulate light. It can be filtered or direct. It can be allowed access only at certain times of the day,

depending upon the orientation and thickness of the barrier the aperture penetrates. Such control of light can be accomplished through the specific design of the aperture.

Does it allow one to see into or out of a space? An opening might permit viewing from one side to the other; the occupant might be the observer or the observed. Or an opening might be meant for viewing a particular object or event—a framed view. Perhaps large, expansive transparency is used to give complete visual access into or out of a space.

Does it mark, announce, or impact some other aspect of spatial experience or formal composition? The aperture is also a function of spatial or formal composition, as it determines access or view; it also delimits where light pools and shadows are cast. These elements of an aperture have a direct correlation to the events in a space and can be used to articulate the way architecture is inhabited and encountered.

Figure 3.2. *An aperture intended to create a ray of light to illuminate a particular aspect of the forms that shape the space. The light itself becomes another tool in the articulation of the surface.* STUDENT: RYAN BOGEDIN—CRITIC: JAMES ECKLER—INSTITUTION: MARYWOOD UNIVERSITY

Figure 3.3. *Gaps formed between elements of an assembly create apertures that illuminate aspects of space as well as the assembly method for the forms that contain it.* STUDENT: JOHN CASEY—CRITIC: MATTHEW MINDRUP—INSTITUTION: MARYWOOD UNIVERSITY

APPROACH

To move closer to something

A path toward a destination

Generative Possibilities of Arrival

You look up the hill to see a large white structure at its peak. No other structure is built on this hill—at least that can be seen from this side. You stand at the base of the hill; a tall wall separates you from the gardens that extend down the hillside from the front of the white building. You can either go right or left. Either path will take you to your destination. The paths are divided symmetrically about the gardens in front of the building.

You walk to the right, and as you begin moving onto the path the building vanishes from view behind a stand of trees. The path becomes a compressed space with trees and plants on either side; all you see is the path ahead of you beginning its ascent. The path progresses a short way before angling back toward the center of the gardens, where the tree line breaks and the building is once again visible.

In order to continue, the path folds back into the vegetation, and the building is lost from sight once again. This is repeated several more times before your arrival. At each interval your goal becomes larger on the horizon, and you can see details of the worked facade more clearly. The approaching pathways become a ceremony of arrival that prepares you for your encounter with this structure.

What is the function of approach in design? An approach can accomplish several things. Fundamentally, it is the beginning of a circulation system, or an extension of the interior circulation system to the exterior. As a component of circulation, what possibilities does it present that can inform the creation of space? An approach is a sequence of encounter. It is a path that orders experiences as one moves toward a destination. An approach can be a complex sequence of exterior spaces or events that lead to the transition to interior space. It can also be a simple announcement of a building's presence on a site. Designing an approach is a tool for controlling the way one encounters the architecture. Whether it is short or long, simple or complex, it is a kind of ceremony of arrival.

The ceremony of arrival is, or can be, a preparation for inhabitation. What does it mean to prepare someone to enter or inhabit a space? The sequence of arrival—the approach—prepares an individual for entry or inhabitation by acting as a kind of buffer between an environment external to the design and the new environment of an interior space. Spatial character or program intent will determine the kind of approach that is warranted. The approach to a large civic building might be composed of a continuous, uninterrupted promenade from outside to in. In contrast, an approach to a back door might be secluded to provide exclusivity. Approach raises the following questions: How does one encounter architecture? How can the transition between exterior and interior be a designed event?

Figure 3.4. An approach is a component of a path or itinerary. It is a spatial event of encounter. In this example, approach focuses on destination. It marks a transition between one set of spatial characteristics and another. The path moves from an open, expansive space to one that is enclosed. Student: Nathan Simpson—Critic: James Eckler—Institution: University of Cincinnati

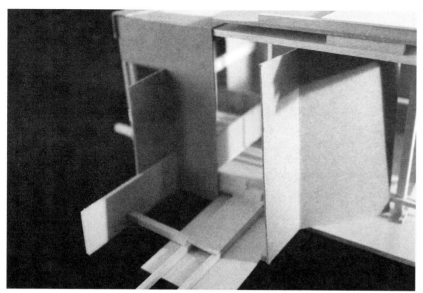

Figure 3.5. Approach can be limited to the moment of encounter. In this instance, it marks the short extension from the space that houses the threshold between inside and outside. That extension serves as an approach. It contains the event of transition across a boundary. STUDENT: NICK REUTHER—CRITIC: JAMES ECKLER—INSTITUTION: MARYWOOD UNIVERSITY

Figure 3.6. Approach is the moment of encounter. Here it is celebrated with a set of steps that ascend to a thick wall penetrated by a threshold. STUDENT: THOMAS HANCOCK—CRITIC: MILAGROS ZINGONI—INSTITUTION: ARIZONA STATE UNIVERSITY

BARRIER

An obstacle

A divider

Something that bars, limits, or regulates passage across

Generative Possibilities in Division

You walk along a path. It is lined on either side by a row of trees. The trees are of the same species, about the same size, and arranged at regular intervals. As the path turns a corner, you encounter a locked gate. You do not have the keys and cannot continue forward as you had expected. Instead you decide to seek an alternate route. You turn, walk off the path between two of the trees, and continue down a short slope to a well-worn patch of grass. Looking back up to the gate, you realize from the trampled vegetation and packed earth that this alternate route has been taken many times before. This new path was not paved as the other had been, but is well established through use.

You continue on just a short way from the paved trail, now with trees on only one side. The path descends down a slope. It is not long before the steep incline between the original paved trail and your current one prevents your return. Thinking that this newly discovered path would eventually lead you to your destination, you decide to continue along it.

The gate presented a physical barrier to your progress. And later, the relative position of the two paths presented a spatial barrier.

A barrier is any object or condition that stops or slows access from one side to the other. It is often an object or physical obstacle that obstructs movement. However, a barrier can also be considered an operation of space. A spatial arrangement can also act as a barrier if it limits or redirects movement—anything that functions as an obstacle to access can be regarded as a barrier. How can something that interrupts access motivate design process? How is a barrier different from any other form of spatial containment—from a wall or a partition, for example?

The act of interruption is an operation of space and composition. It might serve as a way of terminating a path while still providing visual access to the other side of it. A barrier might also be a kind of filter that limits access based upon some criteria or characteristic. Interruption can be a method for organizing or relating spaces to one another.

However, the primary role of the barrier in space is as an obstacle. It is something that interrupts access without blocking it entirely. This may be characterized by an intersection that diverts movement in multiple directions.

Figure 3.7. *The short elevated wall serves to divide the interior of a construct into distinct spaces. It does this as a barrier. It provides view and awareness to the other side, but blocks passage. Because either space might be habitable, there is a means of overcoming the barrier to get to the other side.* STUDENT: NICK REUTHER—CRITIC: JAMES ECKLER—INSTITUTION: MARYWOOD UNIVERSITY

It may be a form that forces one to move around it—to redirect toward an alternate route. This has experiential connotations for the itinerary through space. For instance, choice might be a function of a barrier. By eliminating the direct path, an occupant will be forced to decide upon another route.

A barrier might also serve as a moment of pause or a slowing of movement, as one is forced to find a way to overcome the obstacle. The placement of the barrier might correspond to another spatial element or program. The occupant might be made aware of some aspect of the design by being forced to transition more slowly from one side of the barrier to the other. Similarly, redirecting the route of an occupant might be a way of repositioning the individual relative to some other aspect of space or event. The barrier functions as a point along the itinerary, a spatial structure that links one path to another in a more complex route.

The barrier differs from a wall in that it implies temporality. The barrier is something that interrupts but that can ultimately be overcome. The wall is something that is meant to block movement or divide space; it is singular in this purpose. It is a permanent fixture of design. When it is moved or altered, the space is transformed. The barrier is an addition to space, one that can be overcome or removed.

» *See also* Edge; Boundary.

Figure 3.8. The ribbonlike structure in the foreground of the image functions as a barrier dividing interior and exterior spaces. STUDENT: JENNIFER HURST—CRITIC: JAMES ECKLER—INSTITUTION: MARYWOOD UNIVERSITY

Figure 3.9. In this example, there are several barriers that block or limit passage. The first is the ribbonlike structure that also appears in Figure 3.7. The second is the barrier composed of tightly packed linear elements that would impede, but not stop, passage. STUDENT: JENNIFER HURST—CRITIC: JAMES ECKLER—INSTITUTION: MARYWOOD UNIVERSITY

CONTAIN

To hold within a set of limits

Generative Possibilities in Holding and Inhabiting

I look at the glass jar on the table. It is half full of nails. Many of them are rusting; this has clouded the glass with reddish-orange dust. The nails have been untouched for years, held within the confines of the jar. Light from a high window shines through the jar, casting shadows and reflections across the workshop table. The tools remain hung in their proper place. The machines lie dormant.

I decide to begin the process of reopening the shop. I look around at the space, assessing the work that needs to be done in order to make the shop operational. The machines are half covered with dusty white sheets. Most of the walls are covered hand tools hanging from hooks. There are several tables each devoted to a piece of machinery. There is a short wall to one side of the space. It has no tools

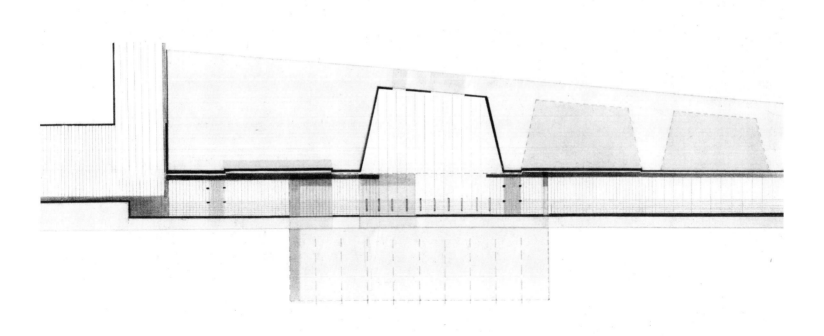

Figure 3.10. Spatial containment in a precedent building is examined in this drawing. The profile of the space is documented in conjunction with the tectonic elements that compose that profile. STUDENT: LIU LIU—CRITIC: JAMES ECKLER—INSTITUTION: UNIVERSITY OF CINCINNATI

hanging from it, it doesn't reach as high as the ceiling, and it is disconnected from the walls to either side of it.

In assessing the condition of the shop, I look at the extent of the space that I have to work with. I can sense the edges of the space and understand the reason that the equipment is placed where it is. Each machine is in a spot that receives light from the large windows. Tools are hung on walls surrounding the center workspace. Just as the jar contains nails, this space contains the equipment and workers required for its function as a shop. It is a specialized container providing light, view, storage, and entry in their proper places. But it is still a container.

The origin of the word *contain* can be traced back to the Latin word *continïre,* which means "to hold together." Similarly, the containment of space is made up of those elements that define its outer limits. Architecture contains space and event. How does containment differ from envelope? Does it address issues of design thinking?

Containment is the outer boundary of a space. It can be implied or constructed. Whereas the envelope is a physical assembly that holds space, containment refers more generally to the definition of its limit. The envelope is a seal that distinguishes inside from outside. A container is not limited to the exterior boundary. It might distinguish interior spaces from one another. Or the envelope can be used to contain space in which case it does distinguish inside from outside. The envelope is then a type of containment. The spatial container doesn't necessarily indicate a complete seal. It might be established by a protrusion or an articulation that marks the edge of a space or the boundary between spaces.

The physical character of the container determines various aspects of spatial composition and habitation. It is the assemblies of form that contain space, that determine its profile—and consequently, the manner in which occupants interact with their environment. The various assemblies involved in containing space determine its relationship to those around it. Materiality, tectonic form and proportion will determine experience, operation, function, and the interface between occupant and architecture.

» *See also* Space; Envelope.

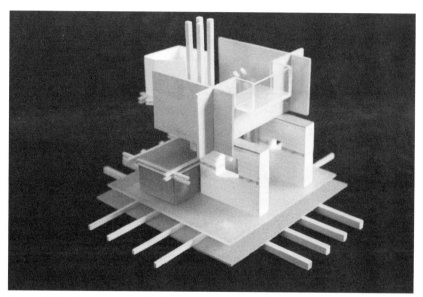

Figure 3.11. *Space is contained at several scales in this model. Larger spaces are centrally positioned with smaller niches that extend from them. The varying dimensions of space indicate a compositional hierarchy. Containment is achieved by marking the outer limits of a space without the need to fully enclose it.* STUDENT: KIM COMMISSO—CRITIC: STEPHEN GARRISON—INSTITUTION: MARYWOOD UNIVERSITY

DENSITY

Massive or thick; compacted material

The number of instances per unit of measure

152

3. TERMS OF OPERATION AND EXPERIENCE

Generative Possibilities in Thickening or Filling

The building itself is very large, and the gallery space extends from one end of it to the other. The room is empty except for the massive columns that divide the space. The exterior walls are made entirely of glass, making the city visible on all sides. The volume of this space is immense. Being inside it seems more like being in an open field than within a building.

An art exhibition is scheduled to take place in this space. As preparations are made, temporary partitions are erected to divide the space into sections. No longer can the city be seen all around; instead, glimpses of it are caught between white walls. Podiums are arranged throughout the space to display pieces of sculpture.

Throughout this process of arrangement, pieces of art arrive and wait to be displayed. When the space has been divided and enough room has been made for each piece of art, a group of people begins hanging paintings and placing sculptures. That evening, people begin to arrive. Gradually, the space fills up with artists, critics, and the interested public. What was once an immense empty volume is now a tightly compressed space. Views of the city are almost entirely lost now. People jostle past one another in the tight spaces between partitions. Density has transformed the gallery.

Density relates to architectural thought in two ways. As it refers to a relative number of objects in a given area, it has spatial implications. As it refers to the thickness or heaviness of an object, it has formal and material implications. How can the density of objects inform space? What impact can the heaviness of material or the thickness of form have on the development of a project?

People or objects inevitably occupy architectural space. Those objects serve to reconfigure the space and the way it is perceived. They interrupt the continuity of space. The view might be obscured, movement redirected or slowed, and the perceived scale and proportions of space altered. In a space filled with people or objects, patterns of movement wander around obstacles and weave between people. The space itself seems to be smaller, more compressed. These effects can be purposefully manipulated in order to achieve a particular spatial condition.

The population of objects in space also implies density's influence on organization. The placement of elements in proximity to one another in an organizational pattern can introduce density as a means of relating parts.

Material density is something that can often be perceived by an occupant. Based upon observation and intuition, an individual can realize the difference between a massive object and one that is hollow or framed. This introduces a formal hierarchy into a space. A wall might be read as a

Figure 3.12. The sketch documents the density of figures and objects in space. The density of these figures defines space by marking its edges. Student: Kyle Coburn—Critic: Humphries—Institution: Miami University

more formidable barrier as the occupant moves through an opening in it—an opening made deeper by virtue of its density. Or a space might continue past a partition that is read as being light or comparatively insubstantial.

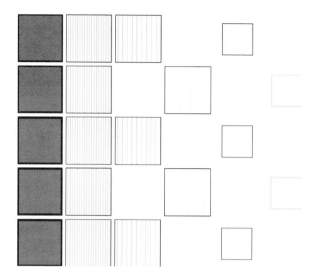

Figure 3.14. This illustration demonstrates density in two ways. First, it illustrates density in terms of amount or quantity: there is a large quantity of squares per unit of area to the left side that gradually diminishes toward the right side. Second, it speaks to density of form. The shading and hatching imply a gradually less dense material composition moving from left to right.

Figure 3.13. In this example, there is a contrast in the density between the two sides of the model. The higher density of elements provides for a means of intricately and precisely configuring spaces. The less dense left side remains open in one large space. The relationship between the two sides can be considered contextual in nature—the dense spatial construct positioned within the large open field.
STUDENT: DIANNA ROBERTSON—CRITIC: JOHN MAZE—INSTITUTION: UNIVERSITY OF FLORIDA

ENCOUNTER

To come to or meet

Generative Possibilities in Finding

A woman has been looking at the displays at the art show all day. She has been making her way from piece to piece, inspecting each of them. She has even found a few that she liked enough to buy. She is nearing the end. There were several pieces that she specifically came to see, and she wants to make sure she has had the opportunity to view each of them.

Satisfied with her progress and that she's seen everything she wants to, she turns away from the last painting. Heading toward the exit, she turns a corner and encounters a new room. It is surprising at first because of how much larger it is than the long, narrow galleries she had been in previously. It is positioned in a way that secludes it from the rest of the show; yet it is unavoidable: everyone will have to walk through it to leave.

At the center of the large room there is a single display case holding a sculpture. It was one she had heard about and wanted to see, but it had slipped her mind. She walked up to it. She looked at the sculpture for a long time before leaving. It turned out to be her favorite piece in the show.

An encounter is a meeting with something or someone, one in which the entity encountered has been found by design or happenstance. The meeting can be unexpected or even confrontational. An encounter can be a physical meeting, or it can be a more abstract notion of discovery—coming upon some unanticipated thing or environment. As a meeting typically describes a behavior or the interaction of people, how can this have an impact on design, design process, or design thinking? Can an encounter be an idea that governs the conception of space?

The physical encounter between individuals or elements is an event. It is a program that an architectural space might house. The characteristics of that meeting can then be used as criteria for the design of space. The type of interaction to occur within it can govern the process of making

space. The scale of the meeting—between two individuals or a large group of people—can dictate the size of the space in which the encounter is to take place. Likewise, an encounter can be informed by other events or purposes. The meeting might occur during a meal. It might take place standing up or sitting down. It might require that more or less light be permitted into a space. These characteristics of the meeting determine the requirements of the space that is to house it. The act of meeting is then a generative device for the design of spatial characteristics and experiences.

Understanding the encounter as an event that is not only responsive to the space around it but also one that has the potential to generate design ideas for the creation of space can be important in comprehending a narrative of architecture. An encounter can be thought of as a part of a larger, designed itinerary. It might constitute a single event among many that occurs in a space or along a route. An encounter could even be a destination unto itself—in which case an individual must navigate a path toward it. This line of thinking creates opportunities for design in that other events or spatial constructs can be incorporated into the path leading up to the intended meeting. Perhaps those events are specifically designed to prepare the individual for the interaction that is to occur. Or the possible confrontational connotation of the encounter might demand that there are obstacles set between the individual and the meeting point.

Often an encounter is a meeting of happenstance or the inclusion of some element or condition that is unexpected. The characteristics of a space itself might be the encounter. A path that suddenly and unexpectedly widens presents a moment for the inhabitant to pause and wonder at the sudden change in surroundings. This aspect of discovery presents itself as a tool that allows the designer to introduce some aspect of the design to the inhabitant. Creating opportunity for this designed element to be discovered is a strategy for informing itinerary and for revealing information. The itinerary is informed through process; the events leading up to the moment of revelation must be carefully choreographed in order to produce the desired response. This choreography, in turn, affects spatial and formal composition as well as the strategies for organizing the elements of a design.

The information that is revealed can be many things. It might be programmatic, encountering some sign or symbol that reflects the functions of space. It might also be novel—an experience that is unique or otherwise captivating. The information revealed can also be about the design itself. This may be one moment of clarity on the part of the occupant, when the goals and intent of the design is made clear, as is the way the design is to be used.

» *See also* Itinerary.

ENGAGE

To involve an element of design in the operation assigned to another

To relate parts through interlocking

Generative Possibilities in Interactive Function

The room is appointed with several chairs, a table, and a long sofa. It is an intimate gathering space of a scale that promotes long conversations between a few people. The ceilings are high, and light is filtered through a set of windows on one wall. It is separated from other spaces by two pairs of large wooden doors.

Normally, this space is the perfect size to accommodate the activities of daily life. It is a place where one sits, reads, or drinks a glass of wine. Today, however, it is too small. People will be arriving shortly. Their numbers will overwhelm the space. An ideal size for a single conversation is rendered useless by a press of people all talking at once.

In preparation for the guests' arrival the doors are opened. The heavy timber panels recede into the walls. Adjacent spaces are joined at that point. The openings left by the open doors reach almost to the ceiling and are nearly the width of the wall. The frame remains as a reminder of what the room used to be.

The two spaces become engaged in a single purpose. The crowd is dispersed across a larger area. Once again conversation is achieved—in several places throughout the conjoined spaces.

An engagement describes an interaction. This notion of interaction extends into design thinking because it describes an interlocking connection or a simple act of securing one piece to another. It might also describe the interface between occupant and surroundings—ways in which architecture might hold the attention of an occupant. What role does engagement play in spatial composition? How can it define an occupant's experience? There are three ways in which engagement might be a consideration in design. One is the way an occupant engages, or is engaged by, space or form. The second is through joinery. In the third, elements might engage one another through a common function or operation.

The interface between an occupant and architecture can be simple or complex. It can consist of a point where one touches or manipulates an element of design—a door handle or other mechanism. It might also consist of a range of mechanisms and spatial configurations that precisely control phenomenal experience. In these scenarios, engagement can be manifested in two ways. It can be the point at which an occupant grasps or touches a component of design. Spatial experience has the potential to engage the senses of the occupants and draw their attention toward a particular aspect of the design.

These types of engagement can drive design process and thinking. They might dictate the proportion and form of a detail meant to be grasped. Or they might result in a manipulation of light to enable the display of content, or to facilitate some social interaction.

Where one component engages another, there is a point of connection or interlock. This might not describe the joint specifically, but rather a logic or strategy for joining elements. Defining a point of engagement in an assembly is a way of determining where and how pieces are attached to one another. This has implications for the functions those pieces have in making space. It refers to a process of relating forms through a common function in containing architectural space.

Engagement can also enable a particular operation of space. Multiple elements might be engaged through a common operation. This relationship among parts facilitates program or habitation by defining spatial composition. For instance, the relative position of parts might alter the proportions of a space—an expansion or compression. Or the way they are organized relative to one another might provide an opportunity for a designed transition. There are many ways in which elements can collaboratively produce a spatial effect or operation that influences habitation. In these scenarios, those elements of a design are related to one another through the operation they facilitate: they are engaged in the function.

» *See also* Interface; Assembly; Operation.

ENVELOPE

A wrapping or container

A physical boundary defining the limits of a volume or space

Generative Possibilities in Bounding the Interior

A woman leans against the rail of a terrace that is an extension of her building. The entire site is sloped so that the terrace sits atop an earthwork on the upper portion of the hill. Access to it is gained from the second level of the building. Its floor is a concrete slab, an extension of the second floor. She turns to look back at the large glass doors that will take her back inside. She notices the furniture arranged on the terrace—tables, chairs, a small bar, and several planters that are also used as benches when it is crowded.

This place functions just as any other room inside the building. It is often used by the residents for a variety of activities that take them away from their apartments. Despite this, it is not an interior space. It exists entirely outside of the building envelope. The line that marks the division between inside and outside is the door, the wall the door is set within, and the various windows that complete the seal.

She walks to the doors and pulls the handle. The envelope is breached for a moment to grant her access. She notices that the floor material changes. This floor is protected from the elements. It is in a controlled environment. It is polished wood.

To envelop something is to wrap or cover it, and an envelope is such a covering. As it pertains to architecture, the envelope is the exterior limit of interior space; it provides the overall form of a piece of architecture. It consists of any shell, skin, or exterior wall assemblies that contain and enclose the composed spaces of the interior.

The envelope in architecture is a formal construct. How can it be used to inform spatial conditions as a part of design process or thinking? Usually, the envelope is referred to as a building system that seals interior space from the exterior environment. It does this to facilitate various controls over the relationship between interior conditioned space and the exterior environment.

Considering this function conceptually can allow the act of envelopment or even the physical qualities of the envelope to play a significant role in spatial conception. The envelope's principal role is in defining interior and exterior; as a function of that role, it acts as a filter that governs the experiential qualities of space and positions points of physical access by an occupant.

Figure 3.15. *The envelope is the outer assembly that seals or contains spaces within. The characteristics it possesses have a direct impact upon the configuration of space within them. In this example, the envelope is cut to permit light, view, and the revelation of structural components.* Student: Mary-Jo Minerich— Critic: Karl Wallick—Institution: University of Cincinnati

The formal assembly and material characteristics of the envelope enable it to act as a device for controlling environmental phenomena. It allows light to enter or casts the interior condition in shadow. The envelope determines what characteristics can be perceived from one side to another. These issues of phenomena and perception have a direct impact on habitation and program. The light that is permitted to enter will transform space depending upon solar orientation and the amount of transparency in the envelope. This dictates programs and activities that might take place within a space.

Other environmental conditions such as wind or rain are controlled by the composition of the envelope. These environmental conditions are manipulated to create sensory experiences for the occupant inside of the spaces contained. That perception also governs the activities and interactions that take place in a space. Light might cast patterns of illumination in a space highlighting particular characteristics, or it might facilitate view within the space. The transparent components of the envelope might also frame a view out. It controls what can be seen and heard of the outside. These sensory

filters might also incorporate operable parts of the envelope assembly, permitting more specific control over the qualities of interior space.

The envelope is also one of the constructs in architecture that greets and receives the individual that approaches. As a function of receiving those from outside, the envelope interfaces between occupant and form. The envelope's material might provide a texture or some other tactile sensation that causes it to be perceived as different from the divisions of interior space.

» *See also* Shell; Skin.

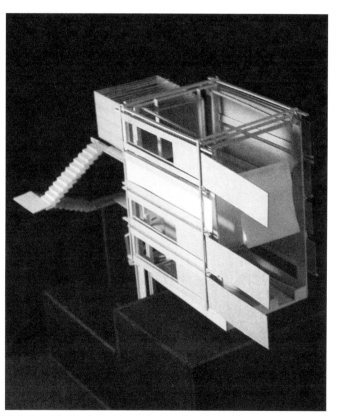

Figure 3.17. Intricate assembly evolves from the simple gesture as more decisions are made and design intent becomes clearer. In this example, the envelope consists of multiple details that have implications for the spaces it contains. The sliding panels permit control over the amount of light that can enter the space within. The envelope changes and defines a more compressed space to define the point of entry. It directly contributes to the characteristics of space. Student: Heinz Von Eckhartsberg—Critic: John Humphries—Institution: Miami University

Figure 3.16.   The envelope might begin as a simple gesture used to investigate various possibilities for configuring the spaces within. In this example, the investigation occurs through juxtaposing an opaque material with an open screen structure. Student: Ashley Cavellier—Critic: Kate O'Connor—Institution: Marywood University

EVENT

An occurrence or activity

Generative Possibilities in Program and Activity

An older man stands, looking at a statue. It is the focal point of a small park in the town square. The statue depicts several people standing triumphantly. The statue and the park are dedicated to the founders of the town.

One of the people depicted in bronze is the man's father. He remembers being a small child when his father worked to incorporate the scattered homesteads into a township. He recalls each of the people memorialized here. They visited often throughout his childhood. He remembers that after they founded the town, one of the first things they did was create this park. Around it, shops eventually opened, and it ultimately became the town square. Many years later the statue was built to honor the founding of the town and those that made it possible.

The garden with the central statue is programmed as a memorial: it is a place for remembering. Many activities occur here. People feed birds, eat their lunch, or just stop for a while to rest between visits to various shops. Its primary purpose, however, is the act of remembrance. As people stop and read the placard in front of the statue, as they consider the hardships encountered by that group of people, they are participating in an event orchestrated by the designer of the memorial park. This recollection is the designated activity of a space that is contained by trees' canopies and anchored by the statue.

Architecture is made with intent for habitation. The design of architectural space does not stop with composition. Instead, function and program define its purpose. They can drive the design process to compose space in specific response to this purpose. Taken together, the operations, functions, and programs of space comprise the events that take place within it. How can an understanding of events, as a broader understanding of operation,

function, and program, benefit the design process? If those other conditions that comprise the event in space are considered, what use is a more generic understanding?

A program indicates a resolved set of design criteria. Function indicates specific mechanisms at work in a space. Operations are compositional gestures that relate spaces to one another within a design that is gaining in specificity. Event, however, is a catalyst for these other considerations. It is a point of departure for testing spatial ideas and driving process and conception. It begins the process of crafting space and form to accommodate activity and behavior without the constraints of specific instances. This generality permits the event to be a generator of spatial design, whereas its more specific counterparts are the results of process.

For example, meeting is an event. It can take on many forms, but each has a set of common characteristics. It may be a meeting between individuals. It may be the meeting of a group. It could be centered around a table or over food. These other, more specific qualities describe an evolving program; the event is the basic act of meeting. It provides the starting point for imagining various possibilities that a space might accommodate. It is a point of departure for inventing space and scripting the activities that it holds.

Another advantage to beginning a program in more generic terms is that it anticipates the inevitable evolution of a design. Spaces that are made to accommodate program more flexibly can be inhabited in a more versatile way. The purpose of a design might change, and its composition will be better suited to evolve along with it.

» *See also* Program.

EXPERIENCE

The perception of an environment through the senses

Generative Possibilities in Sensory Perception

Light enters the space through open windows. Shadows flutter as light passes through the moving leaves of the tree outside. The breeze that causes those leaves to dance also flows through the windows. It is a quiet whisper as it moves around the window frame. The wood walls are a deep red and have been polished almost to the point of reflectivity. The texture of the grain can be seen but is difficult to feel through the finish.

These collective sensations create the experience of this place. Experience of space is in the light that comes through the leaves, the wind as it rustles past, the color of the wall, and the texture of its surface. All of these things provide sensory information that determines the way space is perceived.

In architectural thought, experience is the understanding gained through perception. It is a way of evaluating the functions of space based upon the way it is sensed by an occupant. Of the five senses, three are primary to architectural design and the perception of space. The built environment is perceived as a collection of impressions from each sense; however, it is the visual, tactile, and acoustic qualities of space that are most influenced by design. (Scent and taste are difficult to measure in architecture because there are few spatial consequences associated with them.) Can architecture determine perception? Can it control sensory information to a degree that can impact habitation, program, or behavior? Can experience be designed through the composition of space, form, and material?

Habitation is determined in large part by experience. The way individuals perceive an environment will determine what they are inclined to do in it, how they will use it, and the way they interact with others in it. The correlation between habitation and perception establishes experiential design as a critical facet of architectural consideration.

In architecture, experience is designed through the manipulation of phenomena. Phenomena such as light and sound behave in predictable and measurable ways in relation to material, orientation, and spatial proportion. A material might be reflective; its reflectivity can be used to control the way light behaves in a space. An assembly might act as a mechanism for filtering light, controlling the way it enters a space. Sound also reacts differently to various material characteristics and spatial compositions. It can be reflected off of hard surfaces and absorbed by soft ones. It can be baffled through the articulation of assembly. These characteristics of space and form serve as a way of controlling what an occupant hears. Echoes can be created or minimized and sound amplified or deadened depending upon spatial configuration, formal assembly, and materiality.

Haptic experience, however, is determined less by phenomena external to a design and more by the forms and materials themselves. The sense of touch assumes a direct interface with the physical qualities of an environment. Something can be rough or smooth, hard or soft. These characteristics are sensed as a result of the form and material itself. External forces such as temperature or moisture can only add to those basic tactile characteristics.

Visual experience is entirely based on light. Anything that is seen is an interpretation of patterns of light. The perception of depth, color, and texture is based upon light. Light can inform space depending on the way it enters. A light that rakes across a surface will illuminate various textures and characteristics of that surface, whereas a light that strikes it head on will serve only to hide those attributes. Depth and volume are perceived through the accumulation of shadows. The way light behaves in space can be precisely controlled. Openings in an assembly might be placed in order to direct light. The orientation of a space and the openings that permit the entry of light can be in direct response to the path of the sun overhead. The condition of light in space can be utterly controlled by the manipulation of form and the use of material.

In an acoustic environment, the forms that contain the space are arranged to manipulate sound. This might be used as a strategy for facilitating program. A space might require quiet, or sound might focus attention upon a speaker. The way sound is reflected, absorbed, softened, or reinforced creates an experiential condition of space that is a direct reflection of the event held within it. Formal composition and material characteristics determine the qualities of an acoustic environment.

The haptic experience involves touch. It is the direct interface between occupant and architecture. The way one might touch a surface or grasp a handle or rail is central to the design of haptic experience. The textures and surface manipulations of a floor might announce a change in program or spatial configuration. Texture might provide friction where one is to push or pull something. Temperature can influence the length of a pause in space or the frequency with which a surface is touched. Tactility plays a large role in the way we interpret information about our surroundings and can be used to influence habitation through the design of form and the implementation of material.

EXTERIOR

Outside of or beyond some limit

Generative Possibilities for Architecture Beyond the Envelope

A colonnade divides the building's facade into segments. Between each column there is a set of double doors leading onto the colonnade. On the second level, above the colonnade's roof, there is a large window for every door. The building and colonnade enclose a courtyard on three sides. The floor of the colonnade is concrete. It raises a single step from the courtyard, which is paved in loose white gravel.

The gravel extends out away from the building, and is eventually contained by a row of small trees. It narrows and continues as a path through the gardens. On either side of the gravel path there are spaces defined by trees and hedges. Each of them has a unique arrangement of benches and other furniture, as well as flowering plants. They are of different sizes but still governed by the module established by the colonnade. Each is a kind of room, an extension of the program of the building. The surrounding exterior is as much a designed component of the building as the interior spaces. The exterior contributes to the various functions of the building.

The exterior is the outside boundary of space as well as its surroundings. It can refer either to a contextual environment within which a design is placed or to the envelope as a physical, designed object. Is the exterior of a piece of architecture a considered component of the design, or is it just a result of the composition of interior space? Being outside, what relationship might it have with interior space?

There are several ways that the exterior can be considered in the design process. As a contextual environment, it can be used as a way of generating strategies for intervention in order to knit a new design into the larger built environment around it. Both the physical and contextual exterior of architecture can be viewed as a result of interior spatial design—the residual space left once the design criteria for a project are satisfied. It might also be used as the primary vehicle for design—a designed shell meant to receive various

programs and spatial attributes. The role the exterior plays in design conception should be determined by the nature of each project.

The exterior is a reflection of the interior. They are intrinsically linked. This relationship between inside and out can be designed. The character of the exterior can be used to inform interior space. The exterior shell might be used as a way of mapping or revealing the different programs held within. Likewise, the exterior might be used as a kind of veil or mask meant to

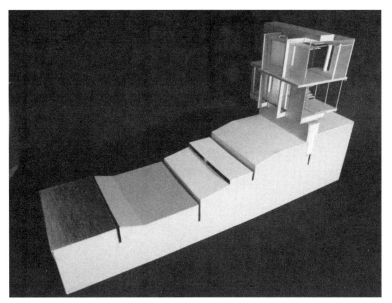

Figure 3.18. Architectural design considers not only interior space but also a relationship to aspects of the exterior environment. That consideration includes both exterior space and the response to natural conditions of site. In this example, the architectural intervention responds to topographic characteristics to define the relationship between inside and out. Student: Matthew Sundstrom— Critic: Jason Towers—Institution: Valencia Community College

obscure the specific purpose or arrangement of interior space. These are a few functions of many possible operative roles the exterior might play in relation to interior space. In either scenario, the exterior functions as a mediator between the needs of interior space and exterior contextual forces that act upon a project. The characteristics of composition in an exterior environment are an extension of the design intent used to generate the interior environment.

» *See also* Interior; Context.

Figure 3.19. In this example, the relationship between inside and out is created in the design of exterior spaces. Those spaces serve as extensions that link the architecture to its different aspects of its surroundings. The space beneath the main body of the structure provides a degree of shelter without being wholly enclosed. On the upper level. space extends to the exterior and wraps around the main body, providing immediate access between inside and out. STUDENT: CHRISSY SHORT—CRITIC: TIM HAYES—INSTITUTION: LOUISIANA TECH UNIVERSITY

INTERIOR

Generative Possibilities for Architecture Within the Envelope

The building stood abandoned. It was a monument to another time, to a purpose for which there was now little need. It also stood as a challenge. It was a building that, despite years of neglect, maintained some of its grandeur. It had stood for so long that it had become an important part of local identity. The challenge was to provide it with a new purpose.

With little work the exterior stood once again as an icon of the town. It framed the street, providing some shelter for those walking along the sidewalk. It also created the potential for new commerce to attract more people to this section of the town.

The scope of the renovation was limited to the interior. It had once been a department store. People would line the street to peer through the windows and see the latest innovations available. Now, though, there was no demand for a new department store in this area. Instead, the massive floors that were once dedicated to retail would be divided among many small shops, restaurants, and residential units. The project was to reconfigure the interior to accommodate new uses.

The interior is the collection of spaces that exists within the confines of the architectural envelope. Typically, it is the primary container of program—the habitable condition of architecture. Occasionally, an architectural design will center on programming a site or structuring an exterior environment to contain habitable space, but such projects are the exception. The interior environment is spatial, it is a product of form, and it manipulates experience through composition and material. It is therefore a primary aspect of the architectural discipline. With interior space being a primary component of nearly every piece of architecture, can it really be considered a strategy for design?

The question of interior space in the process of design, in craft and conception, is one of priority. Is the design going to emphasize external spaces

Figure 3.20. The interior environment is one of architecture's primary considerations. It addresses every issue of habitation and experience. Architectural design determines the way an interior space is perceived. This drawing studies the way proportion is perceived. The perspective is an analog for human perception and as such is a means of studying qualities of a space as an inhabitant would perceive them. STUDENT: MARY WATKINS—CRITIC: JIM SULLIVAN—INSTITUTION: LOUISIANA STATE UNIVERSITY

Figure 3.21. *Interior space can be configured to be a particular experiential environment according to its specific function. In this example, light is admitted through slats overhead. It washes the far wall, revealing material textures and producing patterns of light and shadow. Points of entry and exit are arranged so that an occupant moves entirely through the space. The floor plane is articulated to provide a focal point at one end of the space.* Student: Lauren Whitehurst—Critic: James Eckler—Institution: University of Cincinnati

and site conditions? Is the design going to highlight formal composition? Is it going to be programmatically based? These questions can drive the process of conception. If a project focuses solely on site design, any structure within it risks becoming an object within the field. On the part of the occupant, it may no longer be considered a habitable environment itself, but rather a landmark or folly. In a design based in formal composition, however, interior space becomes relegated to a secondary consideration. It is placed and composed where it will fit within the formal composition of a sculptural shell. Program, habitation, and experience are therefore held as secondary to form.

When the experience of space is designed to facilitate program, the interior environment is a primary consideration. This process moves from the inside out. Formal composition is then a result of spatial arrangement. This method causes a distinct relationship between interior spatial condition and exterior form to evolve. The exterior becomes a reflection of the interior, and vice versa. Through the placement of thresholds between interior and exterior space, it is possible to script experiential, programmatic, and formal relationships between inside and out.

» *See also* Exterior.

INTERSTITIAL

Space that exists between parts

Generative Possibilities for the In-Between

Turning a corner, I realized that I had deviated from my normal route. I was in an alley, a gap between buildings, a place made seemingly without purpose. It was a result of buildings that were created separately, without a definitive plan. I've seen places like this before. They are usually given purpose based upon the needs of the place. They become filled with refuse or a storage place for things people would rather forget.

This one, however, was somehow different. It had been given purpose in an unplanned way. It had been left to the whims of people that happened to occupy the adjacent buildings. But this particular alley was not used as a hiding place for all of those things that people regarded as unwanted or unsightly. It was a place programmed for meeting, for gathering, and for interacting.

The alley was too narrow to accommodate much pedestrian traffic; it could certainly not accommodate a vehicle. But it was wider than most others, which is perhaps the characteristic that made it suitable for the activities that took place within. Looking up, I could see row after row of clotheslines stretching between opposing windows of the two buildings. Neighbors shared them; perhaps they talked often as they hung their clothes to dry. The sun shone through the layers of multicolored cloth, and a slight breeze sent the lines into a flurry of light and color.

I continued to walk. At the far end of the alley there were several small tables and chairs arranged by the residents of the two buildings. Here people shared food and conversation. They invited me to join them, but I declined because I had to move on. I was content with discovering this small interstice of the city that was made over into a site for designed events.

An interstice is an intervening space, or the space between. It can be either a designed separation between elements of a composition or simply the leftover space between parts. In a hierarchy, the interstice is possibly the least important component of a composition. If interstitial spaces are the gaps between designed components, what role can they play in design thinking? How can they be used to inform the spaces that are primary to the intent of a design?

The designed interstice is purposefully placed between elements. This gap can serve a variety of functions relative to the components it separates. It may act as a buffer, isolating one or more spaces that it contacts from other portions of a composition. Or it may predict a future iteration that will see one of those spaces expanding into the empty area around it. More conventionally, the interstice might be considered a support space, one that is meant to hold equipment or other systems vital to the effective operation of the primary space.

The residual interstice results from the design and craft of design components that do not meet. It is a void or gap that occurs when specific design criteria dictate that portions of a design be formed without interlocking perfectly. Many times these slivers of space are covered or hidden within the assemblies that define the primary spaces, but they can also present new opportunities for design. They may become a site for an ad hoc or impromptu event or program—one not initially considered by the designer. They might be captured and reformed to become an integral part of the composition.

At the moment one of these interstices is made habitable, it will be charged with a program and a purpose. It may be used as a secondary means of circulation, or an obstacle as users move from one primary space to another on the other side of the interstice. It has the potential to serve a variety of secondary or tertiary roles in a design, and through investigation in process can become an interesting experiential environment.

Figure 3.22. Interstitial space occurs between habitable or designed spaces. In this example, the stair shows a primary portion of the circulatory path through the project. Beneath it, there are interstices: spaces that, because of the decreasing height beneath the stair, are not habitable or programmed. Similarly, the gaps and fissures of space between assemblies are interstices. STUDENT: UNKNOWN—CRITIC: JASON TOWERS—INSTITUTION: VALENCIA COMMUNITY COLLEGE

Figure 3.23. In this example, the programmed spaces are defined and contained within niches in the massive white volumes. Within these white volumes are also cuts and hollows not large enough to receive programmed space. These open volumes are interstices. STUDENT: STEPHANIE CHARTRAND—CRITIC: JOHN MAZE—INSTITUTION: UNIVERSITY OF FLORIDA

ITINERARY

A route

A series of connected paths; a path punctuated by other spaces or events

Something that pertains to the sequential movement from place to place

Generative Possibilities in Encounters along the Way

A child stands for a moment, staring with awe and excitement at the movement, people, and myriad lights of the carnival midway. This reaction lasts only briefly before she chooses her first destination and runs off, pulling at her parents' hands the entire way.

The midway functions as a large promenade, with groups of rides, games, sideshows, and concession stands arranged around and within an elliptical path. The path is paved and as wide as a four-lane street in order to accommodate the numbers of people visiting.

By the end of the night the little girl had taken a very complex route. She moved from one attraction to the next in the order they caught her interest. Rather than moving around the ellipse, she continually crossed back and forth, as lights and sounds caught her attention. She was mostly entranced by the rides; she even managed to convince her parents to join her on some. The family sat to eat for a short time—for as long as the little girl could bear to be still in this environment.

A map of the route the family had taken that evening would show a single itinerary punctuated by a diverse set of events, experiences, and spaces. It would continually wrap back upon itself. It would not be a single path but rather a network of paths connecting the various events along the way.

An itinerary is a schedule of visits—an order of movement or travel and the associated route. Spatially, this notion has direct correlations with path and space. Itinerary can be considered a path, or series of paths, punctuated by spatial moments. These spatial moments usually involve some operation that might cause an occupant to deviate from the path or pause along it. Formally, the itinerary consists of some structure or object that delineates the path: an element that is to be followed. Additionally, the itinerary must

consist of multiple spatial constructs that intersect that path. The manner of intersection will be determined by the action an individual is to take upon encountering that spatial construct. Does the encounter deviate from the path, alter the course, or cause one to pause or wait before moving on? These, among others, are all possible spatial operations in relation to the function of the path itself.

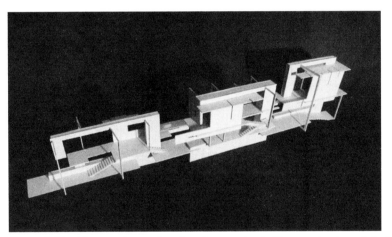

Figure 3.24. Itinerary is a series of paths punctuated by events along it. In this example, movement occurs from one end to the other. Stairs and walls provide moments where paths diverge. The events of redirection are coupled with enclosed spaces that open up farther along. The length of this model describes an itinerary of movement from one space to another. Student: Matthew Sundstrom—Critic: Jason Towers—Institution: Valencia Community College

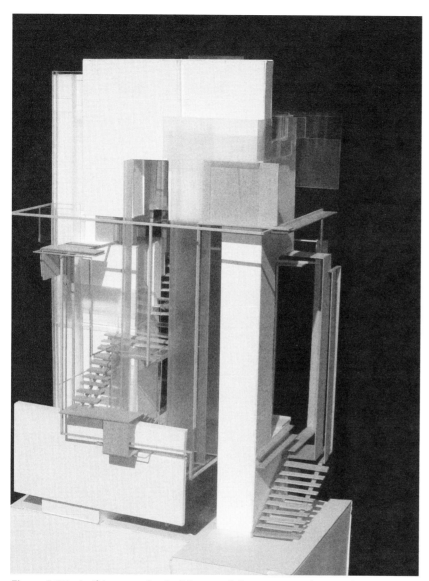

As a tool in the design process, itinerary can provide a structure for the narrative aspects of a space or site. It can provide the foundations of experiential design intent. It can direct design thinking in regard to movement, sequence, order, arrangement, approach, encounter, or discovery on the part of an occupant. It has the capacity to generate space, as it can be a tool for scripting the way an occupant inhabits, encounters, or moves through architecture. What spaces does one encounter within a project. In what order? How are they linked? Considering these experiential qualities of movement can inform the composition of spaces and the formal elements that contain them. Creating an architectural itinerary is an act of using elements of form and space to choreograph movement.

An itinerary functions similarly at both the scale of a building and the scale of the context. When thinking of an itinerary through a context, building takes on the role of one of the spatial moments along the path rather than the containment of the path. A slightly different set of considerations is presented in this instance. How is the building connected to context? In what way does one encounter the building? When responding to itinerary through a context, the new design may be placed along an existing itinerary. In this instance itinerary is not as much a tool for scripting the way space is encountered as it is a tool for defining larger-scale, experiential relationships among spaces.

» *See also* Sequence; Order; Path; Movement.

Figure 3.25. In this example, the itinerary follows a route that winds through hollows in the white bracket structure. It moves vertically to link spaces held above with those that are below. STUDENT: JOHN LEVI WEIGAND—CRITIC: JOHN MAZE— INSTITUTION: UNIVERSITY OF FLORIDA

MATERIALITY

The quality or characteristic of a material

Generative Possibilities in Material Characteristics

The substance is cold and rough to the touch. It is thick and opaque. Just by looking at it I can perceive its density and weight. Its mass demands that it be broken into smaller pieces before it can be used. It is stone.

The substance is rough, with a pattern of ridges that are both seen and felt. It closely mirrors the temperature of the space around it. It is light, malleable, and rigid. It is wood.

The substance is pliable; it can assume many forms. It relies on external structure for rigidity. It is an assembly of tiny elements and sometimes view or light is permitted to pass between them. It is fabric.

The substance is rigid, smooth, and cold. Light is both reflected off of it and permitted to pass through it. Its thinness and translucency gives me the impression that it is light, but a touch reveals its substantial weight. It is glass.

The substance is rigid, smooth, and cold. Light is reflected off of its surface. It is opaque. When well crafted and used properly, its strength overcomes its thinness. It can be shaped or molded into almost any form. It is metal.

I build up the base of stone so that I can be supported by its mass and not responsible for holding its weight. I will encircle the base with wood and place it above so I can take advantage of its rigidity for structure. Because it is light I am able to move and place it easily. Because it is malleable I can work it and fashion joints to assemble it in parts. I place glass within the wood structure because I demand light and view. I place fabric over the glass so that I can control light and view according to my needs. And I will bond all these things together with metal; it is strong even though it may be small. It can be formed to create many different joints between various materials.

Materiality drives the choices I make, the methods I use for craft, and the way I perceive and interact with the environment around me.

Materiality refers to material quality rather than the material itself. It usually encompasses those qualities of material that are perceived through interaction. Whereas a material is a named substance—wood, for instance—materiality is its opacity, texture, or warmth. It consists of those characteristics of material that are directly experienced. Materiality is constant; even if someone doesn't know that this substance is supposed to be called wood, the characteristics that determine the way it is touched and held, the way it looks, and how it is used remain the same.

In what ways can material experience shape design? Is it just a way of describing an environment, or can it be used to generate architectural ideas?

Figure 3.26.   Materiality references material characteristics. In the case of this image, the student constructs from glass marbles to take advantage of their reflectivity, their translucency, and their weight. The student experiments with ways in which they scatter or move to discover opportunities that might be exploited in design. Student: Troy Varner—Critic: Matthew Mindrup—Institution: Marywood University

Because materiality refers to characteristics of material, it can play an important compositional role, even at the preliminary stages of design. Because materiality is a principle that governs the interaction between occupant and form, it can be a valuable conceptual tool. These applications are in addition to its use in describing and analyzing an environment.

Choosing the appropriate materials to fulfill design needs is impossible prior to understanding what those needs are. Materiality can be used to test variations of a design in a way that incorporates habitation and the interface between occupant and form. A designer might be able to decide that a surface should be rough or an element transparent at an early stage of the design process. These decisions are made based upon compositional strategies to relate spaces to one another, or to facilitate a particular function of space. As ideas, however, they act as placeholders for material. They are defined by operation, by what the material has to do in a space. By determining the material's role in a space early in the process, it permits actual material to be chosen based upon its characteristics. It can be chosen for the way it functions to inform design. When something must be rough, porous, and opaque in order to function properly, the designer can then choose from materials and assemblies that meet those criteria.

Materiality can also be a powerful tool for identifying and describing the spatial operations in an existing environment. By understanding the his or her interaction with a particular material, an observer can make conclusions about the role that material plays in a design. Materiality is a way for reading and understanding relationships between spaces. It can be a way of determining the events that a space is suited to house. One can even study the materiality of a piece of architecture as a way of determining human behavior and interaction. A space might be secluded and therefore private. It may be open transparent, and therefore public. Observing the way material characteristics are distributed through an assembly that contains space can aid a designer in determining the social conditions promoted by the architecture.

» *See also* Material.

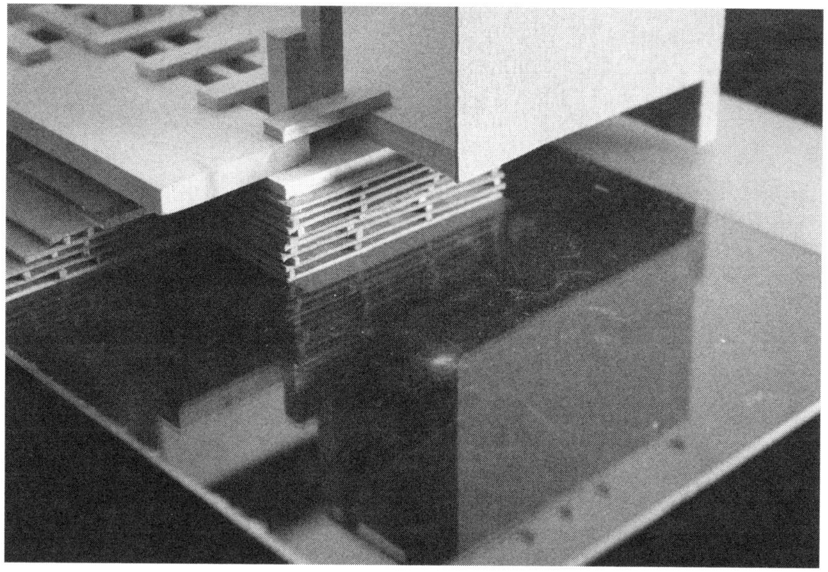

Figure 3.27. *Reflectivity and the control of light provide a visual register as the project is seen in the surface of the acrylic base.* Student: Kevin Utz—Critic: James Eckler—Institution: Marywood University

Figure 3.28. *Materiality dictates craft and technique. In this example, the sheets of paper bend and fold over on themselves. This is made possible by the paper's particular material characteristics. Methods for connecting and forming material are specific to their qualities.* Student: Kimberly Steele—Critic: Jim Sullivan—Institution: Louisiana State University

MOVEMENT

An act of changing place or position

Generative Possibilities in Circulation

The entire wall could pivot. With firm pressure it would rotate around a point one-third of the way from its left side. In one position it was a wall. It created two distinct rooms. There were doors on opposite sides of the moving panel to grant access to each individual room. In the other position it became a gateway. The two rooms were bound together as a single space. Two-thirds of the panel projected into the space to one side and one-third to the other. There was also a gap between the side wall and the pivoting wall just large enough to allow a few people to pass by each other. The placement of the pivot joint, which positioned the moving panel in the space rather than at the periphery, created a condition wherein the opened wall served to subdivide the open plan into sections. It provided a grain to the movement of occupants within the space. It was a physical tie that joined the rooms to one another.

Movement can inform architectural space in several ways. The movement of parts can be incorporated into the design, and the movement of an occupant through space should be considered during the design process. Time can also be a consideration of movement because pace is used as a device for measuring or evaluating spatial conditions and relationships.

Moving components in an assembly are typically very specialized details used to reconfigure a space with two or more possible options. Architecture relies on mechanisms for movement in many ways. The conventional door uses hinge to fold; spaces are sealed or linked. However, there are also possibilities for moving architecture that have a more direct impact on spatial configuration. Such operative components drastically reshape a design—as a wall that slides away to totally combine one space with another to create a single large volume, or, a portion of an envelope that is removed to extend interior space to the exterior and blur the boundary between inside and outside.

When these types of mechanisms are incorporated in a space, design occurs at several scales and in several variations. Each position of the movable component implies a different spatial configuration with a different function associated with it. Each position reflects a new design possibility that is separately, if not completely independently, considered. Furthermore, the mechanism itself must be designed in order to properly position the moving components. This act of detailing surpasses the typical detail: it is

Figure 3.29. Movement in architecture is not only the movement of components but composing space and form to facilitate movement of the occupant as well. The stair and corridor are spatial constructs capable of becoming experiential events. STUDENT: PAUL GEISE—CRITIC: ALLEN WATTERS—INSTITUTION: VALENCIA COMMUNITY COLLEGE

responsible for joining many different parts in ways that permit them to shift in an anticipated manner.

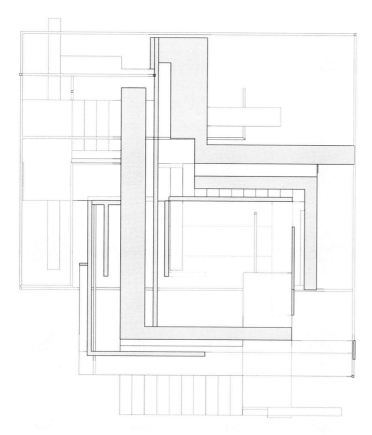

Figure 3.30. **The size and proportion of a space is determined by program. Movement is a programmed event of space. In this plan, circulatory paths are defined by bracketing structures that compress space and provide directionality to movement.** Student: John Levi Weigand—Critic: John Maze—Institution: University of Florida

Architecture might take on another strategy for incorporating movement: to create a simple space that can be reconfigured using movable objects. The goal is versatility. Design in this scenario is primarily focused on defining a system of organizing the movable parts. The challenge this poses in making and representation is to define a way of communicating the organizational system that is to govern the placement of objects in space.

Movement within and through space is a critical component of understanding habitation. It is something that can be choreographed through the composition of parts in a design. Spaces can be distributed according to an order of encounter; spaces will link to one another through a series of transitions. Organizational structures are made apparent through movement between related spaces. A path might be diverted to provide a choice of direction and destination. One of architecture's responsibilities is to guide an occupant through its spaces. This choreography of movement is accomplished through composition by providing places where movement is possible, denied, or redirected. Spaces can be linked by a variety of potential paths left up to the choice of the occupant, or it can be a singular, planned route.

A final consideration of movement is pace. Time of transition is important; it impacts an occupant's perception of an environment. An assembly might move at a slow pace, giving an individual time to pause and consider the transformation occurring. Or it might be a sudden transformation that does not hinder normal habitation or create a need to wait or decide. Its configuration and the programs that it houses can determine the rate at which an individual moves through space. A person might move quickly through a space that is long and confined: there are fewer stimuli there. That same individual might slow when entering a larger space where an activity is taking place. Using composition to encourage a pace for movement is one way of controlling what an occupant is made aware of and determining the relationship between parts of a design.

» *See also* Assembly; Itinerary; Path.

OPACITY

The degree to which a material will permit light to pass through it

Generative Possibilities in Blocking, Limiting, or Permitting View

A woman walks into a coffee shop. The service counter is immediately in front of her as she walks through the door. Behind this counter is a wall where menus and prices are posted and the machines sit on a shelf. To the right of the service counter, as well as behind the wall, seating is provided at small tables. The back wall is opaque and it creates opportunity for dividing space, keeping seating away from production.

She decides what she wants, pays, and searches for a place to sit. There is a small window over one table. It has been etched so that objects outside cannot be clearly seen. It does, however, permit enough light to spill onto the table to make reading easy. The window is translucent, and it creates opportunities to control sight and the direction of one's attention.

All of the tables in front of the counter are occupied, so she continues around to the back. There she sees that the outer terrace is open. Large sections of the outside wall are slid to the sides. The floor extends, uninterrupted, outside. The regular interval of columns clearly marks the point where the exterior environment ends and interior space begins. However, the open surface provides the opportunity for light, air, and the occasional fallen leaf to enter the shop. Tables are arranged as if there were no separation; the terrace is integrated with the rest of the café. The transparency of the wall is provided by the gaps between columns. It creates the opportunity for relating interior and exterior space, for extending the boundaries of program, and for providing visual access to the outside.

Opacity is a measure of visual access. Varying levels of opacity can be referred to as opaque, translucent, or transparent. Something that is opaque denies all visual access; it is a barrier to sight. Something that is translucent permits filtered or exaggerated visual access; it is a veil to sight. Something that is transparent permits complete, undistorted visual access; it is an opening to sight. Opacity is a function of materiality; it is a material characteristic without exclusively referring to a particular material. It speaks to solidity and

perception, not necessarily brick or wood, treated glass or rice paper, clear glass or the open frame.

Opaque

Impenetrable to light or view

The material quality of something that blocks sight

The spatial function of opaqueness is evident in its ability to divide, define, and contain. Something that is opaque separates without giving any

Figure 3.31. The opaque material does not permit view or the transmittance of light. It encloses and secludes spaces it defines. STUDENT: JOHN HOLLER—CRITIC: REAGAN KING—INSTITUTION: MARYWOOD UNIVERSITY

experiential access to, or awareness of, the other side. The opaque element clearly defines the parameters of a space. It creates a *sense* of containment, even if spatial containment is not actually achieved. The defined edge gives the occupant of a space a clear understanding of dimension, proportion, and the limit of the volume.

With these spatial functions in mind, how might an opaque element be deployed within a design? It can be used to define the limits of a space, its perimeter, or perhaps as an interruption within a space. The opaque element may be an obstacle to be overcome by the occupant, or an impenetrable wall. The relative scale of the opaque element may mean that it does not rise up to the height of the occupant, that the occupant can see over it. Nonetheless, it still differentiates between spaces, even while permitting the larger volume to be perceived.

Various spatial possibilities determine the way architecture is experienced. They can be responsive to intent for composition or program. They can drive decisions regarding the development of the design throughout the process. The opaque element might be a placeholder to guide the composition of space. However, as that element takes on more specific characteristics of material, dimension, and relationships, it will drive the evolution of the design. The device used for testing arrangement gradually transforms into an actuality of space and form through the design process.

At that stage of resolution there are other possible drivers for the inclusion of the opaque element into a design. How is something that is opaque assembled relative to other forms? Opaqueness might imply a density of material or thickness of form more often than translucency or transparency. This is not, however, a productive assumption: a very thin membrane can be just as opaque as a thick wall. Opaqueness does not necessarily imply structure, so its deployment in an assembly of formal elements must be considered. If the opaque piece is thin, how it is held by other components must be considered. If it is thick, it may have the potential to provide some structure. Opaqueness might be implied by the dense accumulation of smaller pieces, or it may be an actual quality of a material.

These issues of formal relationships have implications for the way space is perceived and inhabited; they contribute to an experiential interface between the occupant and the built form. Is it the intention of the design to cause an individual to move around the opaque piece, or to be blocked by it? Is sight the only sense that is inhibited by the opaque element? Perhaps awareness is a product of some other sense. These issues of assembly will follow speculative composition and drive decision making in the design process.

Translucent

Permitting the penetration of light or view in a filtered or diffused way

The material quality of something that clouds sight

The spatial function of translucency is evinced by its ability to separate and to filter. Something that is translucent separates while giving some experiential access or awareness of the other side. That limited visual access across a boundary defines an operative or spatial relationship between the spatial zones. They are linked in function or composition.

Figure 3.32. Translucent material veils sight. It permits the transmittance of light, but figures and scenes are reduced to silhouettes. In this example, the mask that screens light and makes the glass translucent also controls the quantity of light permitted to enter or leave the space. Student: Paul Geise—Critic: Allen Watters—Institution: Valencia Community College

Relating spaces through the use of translucency suggests that there is some reason that partial awareness of an event will direct the way space is occupied or the way an occupant engages form. How might a translucent element be deployed in a space? Translucency can be used as a filter in two ways: it can diffuse light coming into a space, or cloud view from a space. Perhaps the translucent element is intended to permit the access of light while limiting the distraction of view, maintaining focus toward the interior. Perhaps translucency permits the glimpse of a shape or silhouette; it doesn't tell a complete story, but compels the occupant toward another space, or to some discovery. A translucent element can define the limits of a space while it facilitates an association or linkage to another.

Various spatial possibilities determine the way architecture is experienced. They can be responsive to the intent of the composition or program. They can drive decisions regarding the development of the design throughout a process. The translucent element might be a speculative placeholder to guide the composition of space. However, as that element takes on more specific characteristics of material, dimension, and relationships, it will drive the evolution of the design. The device used for testing arrangement gradually transforms into an actuality of space and form through the design process.

At that stage of resolution there are other possible drivers for the inclusion of the translucent element in a design. How is something that is translucent assembled relative to other forms? Translucent may imply a lack of material density or a thinness of form. However, this is not a productive assumption: both a thick structural block and a thin membrane can be translucent. Translucency does not necessarily imply a lack of structure, so its deployment in an assembly of formal elements must be considered. If the translucent piece is thick, how it holds other components must be considered. But it may be thin and without structural potential as well.

These issues of formal relationships have implications for the way space is perceived and inhabited; they contribute to an experiential interface between the occupant and built form. Is it the intention of the design to cause an individual to move around or through the translucent piece, or to be blocked by it? Is one meant to glimpse something of the other side, or to be seen form the other side? Is the image a silhouette or a distortion? These

questions of material, assembly, and experience will follow speculative composition and drive decision making in the design process.

Figure 3.33. Translucency can provide a limited awareness of the other side. Just enough of the space beyond this translucent volume can be seen to perceive its composition, but any detail is lost. Student: Stephen Williams—Critic: Jason Towers—Institution: Valencia Community College

Transparent

Permitting the penetration of light or view fully or without distortion or interruption

The material quality of something that permits unimpeded sight

The spatial function of transparency is evinced by its ability to link spaces and mark the edge of a space. Something that is transparent delineates an edge or boundary by virtue of its existence. However, that edge or boundary is simultaneously overcome visually. Transparency permits view across that edge or boundary and develops experiential links or spatial joints. The transparent element is a tool for defining volumetric parameters without compromising the relationships between spaces.

Figure 3.34. Translucency can also be used to provide a selective view. Those elements closest to the translucent material are clearer than those farther away. The stair is in direct contact with the translucent material, making it plainly visible while its surroundings are unclear. STUDENT: CASEY O'NEIL—CRITIC: REAGAN KING—INSTITUTION: MARYWOOD UNIVERSITY

Figure 3.35. Transparency permits the complete transmittance of light and view as if no material were present. STUDENT: NATHAN SIMPSON—CRITIC: JAMES ECKLER—INSTITUTION: UNIVERSITY OF CINCINNATI

Figure 3.36. The absence of material is used to represent transparency in this example. The frame outlines the limits of space, and transparency is understood as contrasting to the opaque material composing other parts of the model. Student: John Holler—Critic: Reagan King—Institution: Marywood University

Figure 3.37. Transparency allows visual access to a space. It also permits direct light. The quantity of light coming through a transparent material is greater than that coming through a translucent material. However, the ability to control, limit, or direct light entering a space is greatly diminished with transparency. Student: James Chadwick Knight—Critic: John Maze—Institution: University of Florida

How might a transparent element be deployed in a space? Transparency can extend one space into another perceptually. Transparency can facilitate the unfiltered entry of light into space. It can be used as a tool to make an occupant explicitly aware of a spatial condition, object, or event occurring in another space. Transparency, unlike either opaqueness or translucency, is an inherently outwardly focused material condition: it extends the perception of an occupant beyond the limits of the space, whether that extension is directed out, adjacent, or through.

Various spatial possibilities determine the way architecture is experienced. They can be responsive to the intent of the composition or program. They can drive decisions regarding the development of the design throughout a process. The transparent element might be a speculative placeholder to guide the composition of space. However, as that element takes on more specific characteristics of material, dimension, and relationships, it will drive the evolution of the design. The device used for testing arrangement gradually transforms into an actuality of space and form through the design process.

At that stage of resolution there are other possible drivers for the inclusion of the transparent element into a design. How is something that is transparent assembled relative to other forms? Transparent implies either a lack of material clarity and thinness of form or a void in a formal assembly. This differs from either opaqueness or translucency in that material properties and methods of assembly are more limited. A transparent element can be composed of very few materials and is almost always a thin plane or membrane. Variation comes in the alternative to a material understanding of transparency. Transparency can be implied with nonmaterial voids in an assembly. Frames can delineate an edge or even a barrier while being mostly empty. Or materials can be carved or opened to create a transparency of void.

These issues of formal relationships have implications for the way space is perceived and inhabited; they contribute to an experiential interface between the occupant and the built form. Is it the intention of the design to cause an individual to see something in particular, or to provide a vista? Is one meant to see something of, or to be seen from, the other side? Does the transparent piece separate spaces or link them? These issues of assembly will follow speculative composition and drive decision making in the design process.

» *See also* Materiality.

OPERATION

A function that is performed

The functional purpose of an object, space, component, or assembly

Generative Possibilities of Function

A man leaves the crowded sidewalk and enters through the main door to the building. He emerges into the foyer. It is relatively small, considering the building's public nature. He gives his eyes a moment to adjust to the dim light of the hall. Leading from the foyer there is a grand stair that takes him to the main hall, which is very large compared to the space he just came from. Upon reaching the top of the stair, the man notices that the ceiling soars above him and the hall extends a great distance in front of him. There are rows of columns in this hall that subdivide the space. A lounge and brochure stand is behind one row of columns, a restaurant and bar behind another. Tables and plants are placed between the columns, barring passage except in specific locations. Most of the surfaces of the main hall are stone or wood. The place echoes.

The hard stone gives way to carpet as he makes his way past a plant and into the restaurant. He is taken in and seated in a small booth tucked behind a low wall. The wall does not extend the full height of the space, which remains large, and for the most part, uninterrupted. Instead it provides a pocket of seclusion and privacy within the larger room.

He likes coming here, and as he waits for his friend to arrive he thinks back on his journey from the sidewalk. He begins by recalling the transition between the entry and the main hall provided by the stairs. The sudden expansion of space that he experienced when he first entered the room served as an announcement that he had arrived someplace new, someplace different. He considers the way the barriers and columns divide the space and filter those that want to stop and eat away from the bustling crowd. He also appreciates that the booth he chose is somewhat small and secluded despite being near the middle of such a large space. It will make for easier conversation. Perhaps it is that journey was so simply scripted, using the arrangement and variation of rooms, that warms him to the atmosphere of this place.

Spatial operation refers to those characteristics of space that determine the ways it is experienced or inhabited. Operation is a kind of mechanical function, and architecture can be considered a set of parts (spaces) acting

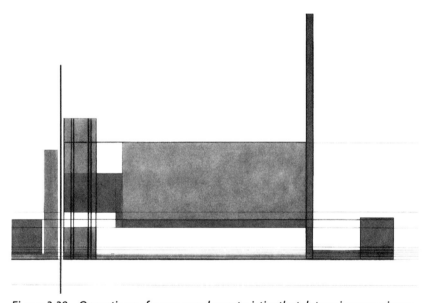

Figure 3.38. Operations of space are characteristics that determine experience and use. They are the ways spaces and forms work to produce particular effects. There are a vast number of potential operations that might be employed in the design of a space, and those listed in this section are only a select few. This diagram is a mapping of spatial operation. It documents all of the moments of transition from one characteristic to another. It marks places where space becomes compressed or expanded. It maps the characteristics of space that impact both experience and the program that space is to hold. Student: George Faber—Critic: James Eckler—Institution: University of Cincinnati

in concert to serve a particular purpose (program). An operation of space is a single, small task that contributes to the larger purpose of architecture. It can be an experiential operation, a compositional operation, or it can literally refer to mechanical operability.

Creating and controlling an occupant's experience in space is one primary function of operation—spatial operation is a narrative function rather than a programmatic one. What relation is there between narrative and architecture? Architecture is a collection of opportunities for events to unfold before an inhabitant. They depend on the experiential quality of a space. Its physical proportion or orientation can become an operation of space in the way it facilitates a means of habitation. Program, in a more conventional sense, can be facilitated by directing the way in which space is to be inhabited, the way one moves or pauses within it, a general sense of enclosure, or the nature of the interface between the occupant and the forms that contain space. Together, these events and characteristics define a kind of story created by the designer, for the inhabitant.

Instead of facilitating an architectural program, the spatial operation might engage habitation compositionally. A compositional operation of space occurs when the relationship between spaces is made apparent to an occupant. This relationship might exist in the way one space extends beyond another, or it may be in the ordering of spaces along a programmed path. This type of operation determines experiential relationships between spaces, the transition from one portion of a design to another, a place where visual access from one space to another is given, and whether a space is isolated or removed, or integrated.

Composition and experience are often correlated through operation. It is rare that a spatial operation will be strictly a designed experience independent of composition, or vice versa. Therefore, it is often helpful to the design process to consider ways that a compositional gesture might influence experience and to use both as tools to script the way one might inhabit space and the way programs are distributed through the architecture.

Mechanical operation facilitates the previous two operational categories by a mechanism used to manipulate space. A wall might move aside; an element might shift up or down; parts of an assembly might open or close. These mechanical functions become spatial operators when they are used to define an experience or establish a compositional relationship between

Figure 3.39. *This model illustrates one of the many potential architectural operations that are not listed in this chapter. In it the student investigates the characteristics of a clip by addressing the material qualities of the clip as well as the act of clipping. The end result is a model where the joint, characterized by the act of clipping, facilitates perception. The panels can be positioned and clipped in place to reveal the word* clip. *The implications of this study speak to a strategy for composing and assembling space based in the material qualities of tension and flexibility, and the spatial qualities of transformation.* STUDENT: JOE WAHY—CRITIC: MATTHEW MINDRUP—INSTITUTION: MARYWOOD UNIVERSITY

spaces. The interaction between occupant and mechanism is another consideration. The use of the mechanism by the occupant has both experiential and compositional consequences. Someone might grasp and move a handle or stand in a specific spot, and as a result, experience the space in a specific way.

Just as there is a range of potential individual experience, there may be an infinite number of possible spatial operations that can be employed in design. Listed in this section are several examples of the operative conditions of space. They do not encompass a full range of design solutions, nor are they necessarily present in every architectural design. They are included as exemplars of operative types. They demonstrate ways in which the different kinds of spatial operation can be applied toward generating and realizing design intent.

Expansion

Being made larger

The act of moving into a larger contained space

A spatial condition in which the volume of a space is increased to facilitate a desired effect

Compression

Being made smaller or compact

The act of moving into a smaller contained space

A spatial condition in which the volume of a space is reduced to facilitate a desired effect

Expansion and compression are compositional spatial operations. They describe the transformation of space by altering volumetric proportions. Expansion is a general increase in size, whereas compression is a decrease. How can the transformation of a space be an operation or influence program? Is it an exercise of the design process, or is it apparent to an occupant?

Figure 3.40. *The expansion or compression of space is an operation that can facilitate different programs or create different experiential conditions for the occupant. In this illustration, the space between the two bars is expanded to the left side and gradually becomes more compressed to the right.*

As compositional operations these ideas are used to relate multiple spaces to one another. They might inform another operation, such as a transition from space to space. Imagine that a person is in a large room socializing with a group of people; that individual then moves through a small, compressed space as he or she enters another large room. The two are similar in program and proportion but made distinct by the compression used to inform the transition between them.

Either expansion or compression might operate as a signifier of arrival. Consider the experiential effect as someone walking along a narrow, confined path that suddenly expands into a great open space. That sense of confinement coupled with release indicates the person's arrival at an important place. The suddenness of the discovery might instill an understanding of that importance by virtue of the contrasting spatial types.

These two ideas might also be used as a way of mapping different programs in a space. A space that is divided into regions of where the profile undulates to create areas of expansion and areas of compression can be used as a tool for positioning different functions or events. An open plan might be broken down using variations in ceiling height. In this application, expansion and contraction are used to delineate regions of space. The compressed areas might be used to promote an intimacy or separation, whereas the expansive volume is used as place for public interaction.

In all of these scenarios, composition is directly tied to program. It is the operation of expansion or compression that relates those programmatic situations or events to one another. There are also experiential consequences, especially what it would be like to move from the compressed to the expanded is considered.

Figure 3.42. Expansion and compression are used to mark progression through space and create an opportunity for discovery. The outer expanded spaces are gradually reduced in size as one progresses further into the project. At a certain point in the advancement, the space expands once more to reveal an entirely different environment. STUDENT: KIM COMMISSO—CRITIC: STEPHEN GARRISON—INSTITUTION: MARYWOOD UNIVERSITY

Figure 3.41. In this example, a smaller volume is inserted into a larger one. The result differentiates between the enclosed and compressed space of the smaller volume and the expanded, open space of the larger one. STUDENT: MIRANDA LASOTA—CRITIC: KATE O'CONNOR—INSTITUTION: MARYWOOD UNIVERSITY

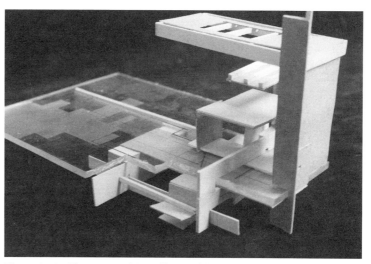

Figure 3.43. The compositional logic of this project is to contain a series of compressed spaces within a larger, expansive one. The compressed spaces are specifically configured, and the expansive one defines a relationship to a surrounding context. STUDENT: MARY-KATE HART—CRITIC: JAMES ECKLER—INSTITUTION: MARYWOOD UNIVERSITY

Extension

A shortened element

An element or part that references but does not physically meet a boundary or other physical limit

Contraction

An elongated element

An element or part that continues beyond a boundary or other physical limits

A reference to movement and/or time beyond a set of parameters

Like expansion and compression, extension and contraction are operators that transform space by altering its proportions. However, this transformation occurs in a particular direction. A volume might be extended past another or contracted within a set of limits. As with expansion and compression, the role these operators play in process versus habitation must be differentiated. To do so, the difference between the act of extending something and

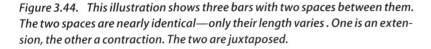

Figure 3.44. This illustration shows three bars with two spaces between them. The two spaces are nearly identical—only their length varies. One is an extension, the other a contraction. The two are juxtaposed.

a physical extension must be identified. The differences between expansion and extension seem to be minimal; are the differences between them enough to affect design process in a significant way? The various correlations between these operations and program are similar to those discussed above. However, the compositional differences can be used to inform the design of spatial relationships, which can vary dramatically from those that result from an expansion or compression.

To extend or contract a space is a process-related exercise in which decisions are being made with regard to the relationship between spaces. A

Figure 3.45. A space is formed by a formal contraction. A portion of one side of the stacked component is pulled back to define a volume in the niche. This is juxtaposed against an extension from the component on the opposite side. Student: Elizabeth Schwab—Critic: Kate O'Connor—Institution: Marywood University

space may be extended beyond another; this increases its size and alters its proportions in relation to the other space. This can have impact on hierarchy and program. The space is larger and more elongated, enabling it to contain a different event or scale of activity. Its size can also establish prominence in a composition relative to other spaces around it. This describes a compositional relationship between spaces that can also influence habitation. The extending portion might be visible from other parts of a building. Its prominence might be regarded as a destination or primary program. Its characteristics that contrast with those of neighboring spaces might be used as a tool for finding one's way in space, a marker, or a reference point.

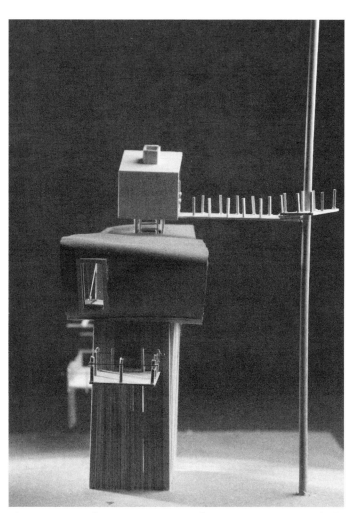

Figure 3.46. An linear extension reaches out to incorporate the lone vertical element in the surrounding context. It extends the space of the project out into its surroundings. STUDENT: STEVEN HONORA—CRITIC: TIM HAYES—INSTITUTION: LOUISIANA TECH UNIVERSITY

Figure 3.47. Linear elements extend from a spatial moment and connect to another. They form linkages and associations between parts. STUDENT: ARI PESCOVITZ—CRITIC: JAMES ECKLER—INSTITUTION: UNIVERSITY OF CINCINNATI

An extension or contraction might also define a more direct relationship between spaces in a design. Consider the implications of extending a space into another. An overlap is generated. It might operate as transition or as a means of linking programs both spatially and perceptually. A contraction of one space away from another inevitably generates an interstice between them. That division might act as a buffer to isolate or separate programs and control an occupant's access to them.

The physicality of extension and contraction are the formal results of spatial thinking. An extension is a physical manifestation of the act of extending a space. It is the element that is seen. It provides clues about the process and conception of the space it contains.

Filter

A device or material used to select what is to pass through it

A porous material or assembly that controls passage from one side to the other

---

The previous two examples are of compositional operations of space. The following sections address experiential operations of space that are facilitated by spatial and formal assembly.

A filter is any object, assembly, or space that acts as a selective transition. It is something that controls movement by limiting what crosses it based upon quantity or characteristic.

The object and assembly function as physical filters. They literally control movement from one side to the other. In this sense the filter can inform the character of a space by controlling the entry of environmental conditions. For example, a louver system might act as a filter for light. Or it might act directly on habitation by selectively permitting individuals to move across it. Consider the way a turnstile slows the flow of people; only those that pay a fare or present a ticket are allowed to cross.

In a more conceptual sense, the filter describes a narrative or programmatic condition of space as a control point for movement or access. It is a spatial mechanism used to determine if something is able to continue along a path or gain entry to a space. It is a tool for pacing flow. In this instance

it is anything that interrupts movement and provides an alternative route. The bench that causes some to pause while permitting others to continue on behaves as a filter in relation to habitation and program. To use this in a design requires an alternative pattern of movement to provided. When there is a choice between routes, that choice becomes the mechanism of selection. The individual can choose to stop and sit on the bench or continue forward.

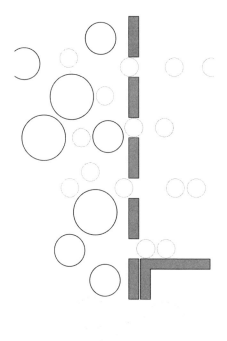

Figure 3.48.   A filter is an operation of selection or control. It is achieved in design by configuring spatial or formal systems to limit access or passage based upon particular characteristics.

What relevance does this have for design? Can a filter be a generative component of process? The role of a filter in every instance described above is that of interruption and divergence along a route. This characteristic can be exploited by the designer as a way of influencing human behavior within a space or controlling access to different parts of a project. Compositionally, the placement of a filter along a path can help generate strategies for relating different spaces to one another. It can also impact the design process by

Figure 3.49.   Formal assemblies are used to filter light entering a space. It is only permitted access between the slats in the assembly. STUDENT: NATHAN SIMPSON— CRITIC: JAMES ECKLER—INSTITUTION: UNIVERSITY OF CINCINNATI

Figure 3.50.   Formal assemblies are used to filter light in several progressive stages. The control and patterning of light contribute to the composition and configuration of spaces. STUDENT: J.D. FAJARDO—CRITIC: REAGAN KING—INSTITUTION: MARYWOOD UNIVERSITY

introducing a new compositional variable that might cause drive decisions or reconsiderations. In its role as a device to control various environmental conditions, it can be used to define the way a space is experienced. It can change the amount and direction of light, sound, or water. These conditions affect perception. Introducing filters in an assembly can be a method of informing space through phenomenal experience.

Transition

A means of passage from one form, place, or state to another

A transition indicates a change over time or distance. As an operation of space the transition functions as a way of experientially relating spaces together. The transition can be abrupt or gradual, and the characteristics of the transition play a large role in relating or differentiating the spaces, components, or forms that it links.

Spatial transitions, or those joints between habitable spaces, are the moments when one space becomes another. The transition might be manifest as an overlap—an area that can be considered a portion of two distinct spaces. It can also serve as a separation between spaces—an interceding volume that one must enter before moving on to the next area of a design. These types speak to the relationship between the spaces they connect. The first example might imply a similarity in character or function by virtue of the simultaneously used overlap. The second example is a separation: one must leave the first space completely before entering the next. This might imply that these two spaces contain very different functions, are accessible by different groups of people, or are distinctly composed. These characteristics can exist both as a brief moment of connection or a drawn-out series of events. A threshold is a spatial transition; so is a corridor.

A formal transition relates to assembly. Multiple components come together to create varying qualities, characteristics, and functions. The point of separation between parts of an assembly is a transition from one formal logic to another. This condition is a direct result of craft and making. The way one joins parts of an assembly or works a material determines that assembly's characteristics and the way it can be used in a spatial application.

A transition in state influences architecture at two scales. It can refer to material states and craft or to a more general condition of a building or the

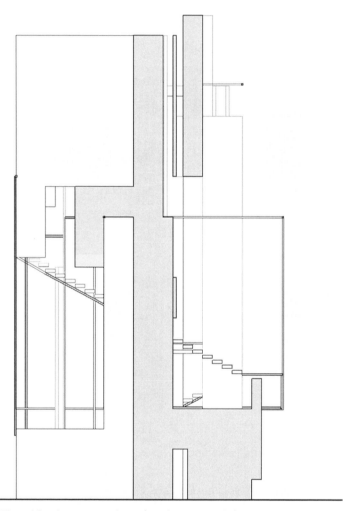

Figure 3.51. Transition is an operation wherein one spatial environment gives way to another. It is an experiential event facilitated by the composition and configuration of space. In this example, a series of transitions links different spaces together within a larger compositional system. Most notably, the transition from one side of the thick central wall to the other determines the relationships between the spaces on either side. STUDENT: UNKNOWN—CRITIC: JOHN MAZE—INSTITUTION: UNIVERSITY OF FLORIDA

Figure 3.52. *This example shows a spatial transition to a more contained and secluded interior space. The formal assemblies that describe the transition also facilitate the shift in spatial character. As one crosses that threshold, the containing forms become more enclosing.* STUDENT: UNKNOWN, TEAM PROJECT—CRITIC: TIM HAYES—INSTITUTION: LOUISIANA TECH UNIVERSITY

discipline. In terms of craft and material, transition is a transformative process. A material might weather over time, thereby defining time as a transition from one material condition to another. Decay redefines the material attributes of form, eliminating some possibilities for use in making while creating others. This kind of transition might also refer more broadly to the state a building, or even to architecture as a discipline. These general uses of the term focus more on social understandings than design. A building might transition from one program to another through adaptive reuse. The discipline might evolve through innovation and technology, or the role that it plays in the larger social environment might change.

» *See also* Narrative; Composition.

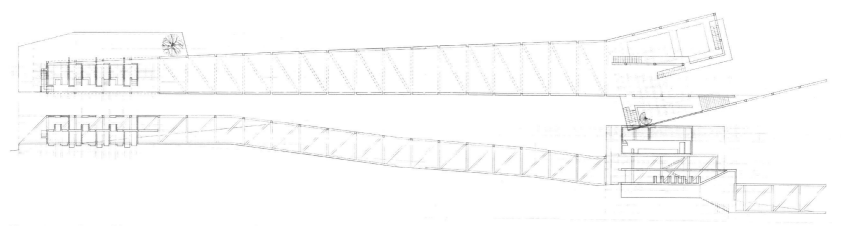

Figure 3.53. *A transition prepares an occupant for an encounter with a new spatial environment. That process is not necessarily immediate. This example illustrates an extended transition that gradually shifts from one space to the next over a distance.* STUDENT: HOUSTON BURNETTE—CRITIC: PETER WONG—INSTITUTION: UNIVERSITY OF NORTH CAROLINA, CHARLOTTE

PATH

A route from one place to another

Something that is built to denote the route from one place to another

Generative Possibilities in a Designed Route

A woman steps out of the door and onto the elevated walkway. It is made of closely bound wooden slats. The walkway hovers a few feet above the ground, which maintains its irregular surface; it had not been disturbed during the construction of the walkway.

She considers her destination and the shortest route to get there. She turns to her right and begins walking. The path itself is not simply a means of transportation. It connects her starting point with her ending point, but it also presents a variety of experiences to be had along the way. If she had more time, she'd be content to take a longer route.

As it is, the short distance she does have to travel is marked by several transformations of the walkway. Its edges are not uniform or parallel. Instead they undulate in response to the topography and other features of the landscape. The resulting narrowing and widening of the path provide opportunities for other events to take place. In one of the widened regions there is a bench that folds up from the surface of the walkway. If she were not in a rush, and were so inclined, she could stop and rest.

A portion of the path becomes more enclosed. Walls rise up on either side. After a while an overhead completes the enclosure. The path is now darker and punctuated by regularly placed skylights. On either side there are apertures strategically placed to provide a view of different elements of the surrounding landscape. This is one of her favorite spots because the way the light comes through these opening makes beautiful patterns all around her. But her destination is immediately beyond this enclosed portion of the walkway and she must hurry. She arrives at the door, opens it, and leaves the path behind her.

A path is a spatial construct programmed for movement. It links one space to another. Path speaks to habitation, to the movement of an individual from one space or event to another. And as a function of habitation it

is an experiential event in itself, a point of transition from one environment to another. The path can be manifest in several ways. It can be an explicit path, one that is constructed and distinct from the spaces it connects. It can also be implied through organization: a path that is defined by its endpoints rather than its own character.

Everyone has had experiences with paths in one form or another. Those paths were not always even recognized for what they were. With such a common purpose, does a path bear on design innovation, or is it merely a pragmatic necessity of architecture? A path might be a nearly universal

Figure 3.54. A path wraps around a central space. Student: James Chadwick Knight—Critic: John Maze—Institution: University of Florida

necessity of architecture, but it can also be a designed component that serves other purposes besides movement.

Consider the path. It is an occupied linkage between spaces. It might have a single direction, or it might be used back and forth. Either way, it is a spatial transition from one environment to another. Functioning as a transition, it can also be used as a way of preparing an occupant to enter a new place. It is a way of controlling how that transition is experienced. It may be a long extension that fully removes individuals from the place where they began prior to introducing them to something new. It might also be short or overlapping as a way of blending one space with another. The characteristics of a path determine much of the organizational, experiential, and operative qualities of the spaces it links.

The explicit path exists as a spatial component of a design. It is conceived and made similarly to any other programmed component of architecture. Its own spatial, formal, and material characteristics define relationships to other aspects of the design. An implied path, however, is dependent upon the destinations that define it. Its character is determined by the way those destinations are designed to receive movement. It might occur within a constructed space, serving to link different areas within it. Or it might exist as a condition external to a space, one that connects disparate components of a design.

In any manifestation, the path is a portion of a design that determines the way one encounters and approaches architecture. It can prepare an occupant through experience for what is to come. It can also be a compositional

tool to define organizational relationships. In most cases, the path will do all of these things, whether the designer considers them or not.

» *See also* Itinerary.

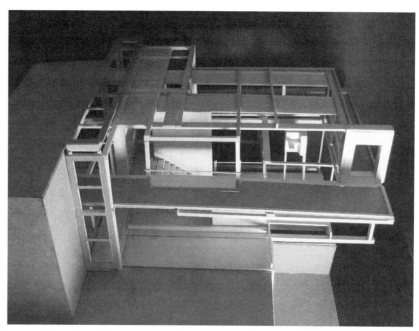

Figure 3.55. A path wraps around one space and separates it from another.
STUDENT: RACHEL MOMENEE—CRITIC: JOHN HUMPHRIES—INSTITUTION: MIAMI UNIVERSITY

POROUS

Permeable or penetrable by way of cavities or holes

Generative Possibilities in Filtering

The hotel lobby has a long edge fronting the street. The wall that defines it is thick. Entrances occur at regular intervals along its length. There are many small apertures distributed across its surface. The openings are densely arranged, causing patterns of mass and void to emerge in the composition of the wall. Light filters through those tiny windows, casting those patterns onto the floor of the lobby space. There is a constant flow of people in and out of this place as a result of the array of entry doors.

The space itself serves several public functions. In it there is a restaurant, a gift shop, and the hotel's concierge. The porous street front wall provides the consistent flow of pedestrian traffic necessary for these programs. It also presents a means of promoting the hotel. It is unique to this city and instills curiosity in passersby.

Porosity is a degree of permeability resulting from holes or cavities. Its physical and spatial characteristics cause it to filter that which passes through the pores. Porosity, as it is discussed here, is primarily a spatial attribute, one in which access to a space is given at many points along its perimeter. It is a spatial attribute in that it defines the outer edge as a constantly permeable

Figure 3.56. Material porosity provides opportunities for permitting light or air into a space. It can also be used as a means of creating texture on a surface. Student: Kirk Bairian—Critic: Lauren Matchison—Institution: University of Southern California

Figure 3.57. Porosity is used as a strategy for making apertures in a wall. Some grant access to an occupant; others are for light, air, and view. They are all created with consistent language adapted to their specific purpose. The overall effect of the strategy is the creation of a porous wall. Student: Nathan Simpson—Critic: James Eckler—Institution: University of Cincinnati

construct. But in addition to this application of the term, porosity can also be a material or compositional characteristic. The porous assembly is one way of defining a spatial and compositional relationship from one side to the other.

How can a space be porous? Isn't porosity more commonly an attribute of objects? Objects, forms, or assemblies can be porous; spaces themselves cannot. Space is intangible and therefore has no substance within which a pore can exist. However, the porous nature of the forms and assemblies that define space affect its function, the way it is perceived, and its relationship to its surroundings. Porosity can therefore be discussed for its influence over spatial conditioning. A space can be defined by a porous boundary. Or a porous element might be held within that space.

In considering the impact of porosity on space, the designer must first ascertain the substance that is being filtered through the pores. A space might be composed of screens—a kind of porous assembly intended to filter light. A space might also be considered porous if it provides a multitude of access points around its perimeter. Transparency might imply a kind of porosity because it provides visual access across a boundary. The frequency of transparent components in an assembly can impact spatial operation, experiential condition, or program.

Material porosity is a characteristic that impacts craft. How does one construct something using a porous material? What roles in an assembly can be filled using a porous material? A porous material might be absorptive, rough, or textured. These issues impact performance, perception, and general structural stability. These material characteristics can be taken advantage of

in order to facilitate particular design intent, but if they are not considered they have the potential to compromise the function or performance of an assembly.

Figure 3.58. The screen implemented along the outside is porous, like any other screen, but portions of it have larger opaque panels than others. The selective placement of these panels relative to the functions of the interior space facilitate the control of access. STUDENT: CHRIS HOLMES—CRITIC: KARL WALLICK—INSTITUTION: UNIVERSITY OF CINCINNATI

PORTAL

An entrance or means of passage

A constructed moment along a path or itinerary that creates a transition

Generative Possibilities in Transitioning

In front of you, standing on a manicured lawn, is a concrete structure with only one square opening. Leading up to that opening is a set of steps that lift you from the grass into the dark space inside. At the moment of entry your entire environment changes. You move from a bright, open place where grass softens your footsteps to an dark, enclosed hallway. The entire space is concrete, and light is only visible at the very end of the passage. No matter how softly you step, your footfalls echo off the hard surfaces.

Moving toward the other end of the tunnel you encounter a glass door that slides out of the way as you push it. You move beyond it and it snaps back into place behind you. It makes a loud noise that reverberates through the passage. Once again you are emerging into an entirely new environment, marked by the resetting of the glass door. The end of the tunnel is in sight, and you can make out pools of water just outside.

You traveled through two portals to gain access to this new place. The first took you away from the comfort of sun and grass and confined you in the dark space of the concrete structure. The second announced your entry into this new garden of pools.

In Latin the *portale* was the gate to the city. It was a point where inside and outside were differentiated. It was simultaneously a place of greeting and a protective barrier. Currently, a portal is, more generically, any kind of gate or gateway. It does, however, share some experiential and operative characteristics with its predecessor. It consists of the objects and assemblies of an opening. To different degrees, the scale of the opening is designed to be appropriate for the object or individual passing through it. It can also consist of spaces and events directly associated with the transition from one side to the other.

Figure 3.59. The portal is a physical construction that facilitates passage across a barrier. In this example, it is a moment along a path or itinerary that marks a transition. STUDENT: DIANA ROBERTSON—CRITIC: JOHN MAZE—INSTITUTION: UNIVERSITY OF FLORIDA

Every habitable space requires a means of entry. How can the inclusion of a portal contribute to design process or conception? The portal is a moment along an itinerary; it is a transition where one path ends and another begins. As a gateway it celebrates entry and creates a programmed event of it. And since it is a disruption in a surface—an opening of a particular dimension—its scale proscribes the object or individual that is intended to pass through it, making it operate as a kind of filter in addition to its other purposes.

The portal, as a moment along an itinerary, is a point at which within and without are defined. It is a point of designed control over who or what is permitted admittance. This function presents several opportunities for design. In addition to providing entry to a space or place, a gateway can also function as a sign or marker. It is a reference that can be read from positions along an itinerary that are still far away. The spatial and formal characteristics of the portal can indicate qualities of space, experience, or program to the other side of it. The gateway becomes a design tool used to announce what is to be expected of the other side. That expectation might be fulfilled, or it may be a purposeful misleading, resulting in surprise or discovery.

The plane that it penetrates might be thick or thin, thereby extending or contracting the transition between without and within. The opening itself might be of a scale to admit only one at a time, or large enough to admit crowds of individuals seeking entry. The portal is a gateway; it may hold a gate to be operated before crossing from one side to the other, or it may be an uninterrupted passage. These issues dictate the degree of awareness the occupant has of the conditions on the other side. The physical gate may be porous to permit glimpses, or it may be solid. The length of the transition may limit perception by tightly framing a view and holding it at a distance. The degree of awareness, the spatial and formal characteristics, and the events that characterize the approach up to the portal can be a programmed sequence of events—a set of experiences that makes a ceremony out of transition. This is the potential of the portal, the gate, or the door.

» *See also* Path; Itinerary; Operation; Transition; Threshold.

Figure 3.60. In this example, the portal links a small spatial extension to a larger interior volume through a vertical plane. STUDENT: CARI WILLIAMS—CRITIC: JAMES ECKLER—INSTITUTION: MARYWOOD UNIVERSITY

Figure 3.61. A portal is sometimes the physical assembly of a threshold. It determines a point of access or entry. In this instance the portal is also marked by a compression of space, as the thick overhead is suspended over an occupant. STUDENT: JEFF BADGER—CRITIC: JAMES ECKLER—INSTITUTION: UNIVERSITY OF CINCINNATI

PROGRESSION

Movement onward

A continuous sequence of movement or events

Generative Possibilities in Advancing

The room is large and rectangular in plan. In it there are rows of display cases housing myriad artifacts and sculptural objects. Both of the walls on the long sides of the room have a centrally positioned opening. These doorways are large and have no actual door in them—they are just an empty frame. They provide entry to the many people that frequent the museum each day.

They perform other functions as well. They provide a glimpse into both the next room in the sequence as well as the room that came before. They also define an orientation for the space. Each opening aligns with others along the intended route through displays.

The museum organizes its displays based upon chronology. Each room is designated to a particular span of time in history. The goal for most visitors is to move forward through historical periods toward the present. This last room—the one dedicated to artifacts of the current age—is the destination. It is positioned at the end of the building near the exit. The different types and sizes of artifacts demand different spatial configuration for their display. So although each room is similar, they are uniquely configured to house particular types of objects. The objects being displayed, as well as the characteristics of the galleries, establish the progression of spaces as one travels from room to room.

As they pertain to spatial composition, progression and sequence are similar. However, where a spatial sequence implies an ordering of spaces, a progression implies order in a particular direction. It is an incremental series of spatial characteristics that encourages movement in that direction. How can space encourage movement? What bearing would this principle have on design process?

A spatial progression can occur in the ordering of multiple spaces or in the variation of elements used to define a single space. In either case, progress must be measurable in some way. The incremental change in space establishes the unit by which measurement can occur.

That change might occur from one space to another. The increment might be defined by location or proximity. For instance, with each successive space through which one travels, that person might become closer to a destination. Here each individual space defines an incremental measure. The progression is then based upon proximity to the destination. Transformation

Figure 3.62. *This image shows a spatial composition and formal assembly that demarcates a progression toward the interior of the project. It passes through a series of spaces that vary in scale and configuration.* Student: Kim Commisso— Critic: Stephen Garrison—Institution: Marywood University

of spatial characteristics from one space to the next can also define an incremental measure. For instance, spaces might become smaller as an individual progresses from one to the next. In this case, progression is marked and measured based upon an ordering of physical attributes.

A sense of progression can also be manifest in a single space. This might be based upon orientation—on configuring a space so an occupant is compelled to move to a specific area within it. Progression then measures distance to the desired location. The progressive increment can be defined through the articulation of assemblies meant to contain the space. It might also be in the movement through defined regions of space. Assemblies can register the incremental stages of a progression through the repletion of elements: identical columns arranged in a row oriented in the direction of progress, or markings used to delineate regions of space. Those various regions might also measure progress through space. Each might hold a program or event that occupies the time, or changes the pattern of movement, of the occupant.

Understanding progression can impact design process in several ways. Progression influences the composition of assemblies meant to house space. It gives the assembly of objects a responsibility for demarcating these incremental shifts or changes in addition to its primary responsibility of defining space. Progression can also be a narrative of habitation. Ultimately, it is up to the designer to decide why an occupant should move in a particular direction and the role that these incremental stages of space play in the program of the design. These decisions have the potential to generate ideas for the way the occupant interacts with each incremental stage. Finally, progression might be used as a device for determining a design's organizational criteria.

And composition can be directed by the criteria generated by the inclusion of a progression of movement.

» *See also* Sequence.

Figure 3.63. This progression is defined through formal assembly. It is a sequence of progressively taller structures that create ascension. STUDENT: ELIZABETH SYDNOR—CRITIC: MILAGROS ZINGONI—INSTITUTION: ARIZONA STATE UNIVERSITY

PROJECT

To extend forward

Generative Possibilities of Pushing Outward

It's raining, and you run down the sidewalk holding a newspaper over your head. It keeps the drops out of your face, but does little else. A lit marquis marks your destination. The show is starting soon.

You see the glow in the distance and know you are close. As you get nearer you see the marquis. It is hung below a portion of the building that protrudes over the sidewalk. It has many tall windows that let you see inside. Groups of people with drinks and hors d'oeuvres are gathering before the show. You run beneath the marquis and the protruding, windowed box.

You wait a moment, brushing beads of water from your jacket. You present your ticket and make your way to the group of people you saw from the street. From this vantage point you can see along the sidewalk some distance—you could probably see farther if it weren't raining. A few people continue to arrive after you. The projecting space provides a framed view of the street to those in the building but is more important to those outside of it. To those approaching the playhouse, it acts as a marker. It is a place to take refuge from the weather. It also gives passersby a hint of the activities that are taking place inside.

Project is a word with two connotations in architecture. Its Latin origin is *prÿjectum*, meaning "something that has been thrown forth." It evolved into the English form *projecte*, meaning "to plan." It has since adopted both of these meanings, especially as it pertains to design. To project something is to extend it outward, away from a baseline or plane. A project has also come to mean a work in progress. It is a design that is still evolving through process. Because the form that refers to the incomplete or evolving work does not present multiple opportunities for consideration, this text will focus on the projection as a spatial or formal construct.

If a projection is nothing more than a protrusion, how can it influence design thinking? How is projection a spatial principle rather than just a

Figure 3.64. *This spatial construct behaves as a projection from a vertical surface. The narrow structure holds the construction aloft while providing spaces for entry and circulation up into the project.* STUDENT: WENDELL MONTGOMERY—CRITIC: JASON TOWERS—INSTITUTION: VALENCIA COMMUNITY COLLEGE

compositional act? To project something is to push it forward or outward. This can be a product or action of formal composition. An element or a fragment can be extended outward and become a projection. However, there are several spatial implications of this action as well. A space might be projected outward. Or a formal projection might cause a new space to be formed. In either case, investigating the potential spatial consequences of projection is warranted.

A space that is projected beyond some limit presents itself as an anomaly within a composition. This might be done to define a hierarchy of spaces. Because it will distinguish itself from other elements in a composition, the

projection will be read as being primary—a moment that is chiefly important to the design.

Additionally, projection implies orientation. It is a way of directing, or redirecting, the events in a space. For instance, a projection that runs perpendicular to the general proportions of a volume might establish a new organizational axis along which program can be distributed.

Projecting a portion of a space can also be a way of constructing a relationship between it and an adjacent space. This might create a kind of interlock formation that correlates space or programs. This requires that spatial boundaries be apparent and that the projection read as a deformation of that boundary. It is a way of sculpting the space in order to precisely accommodate a program and to link that program with an adjoining one.

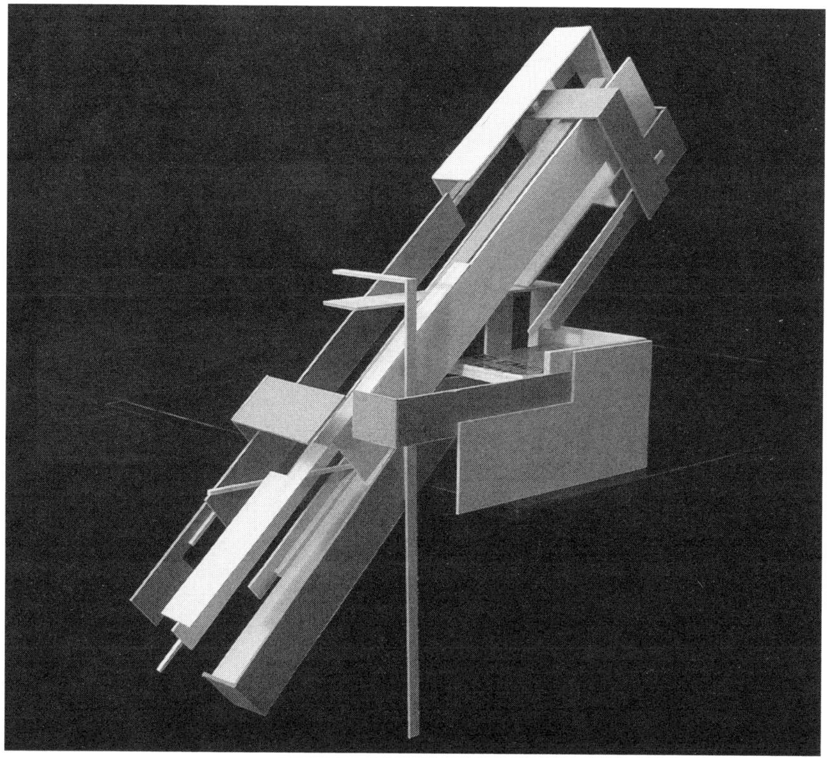

Figure 3.65. This container uses a small projection (coming from the diagonal bar and projecting toward the right) from the diagonal main body to act as a tray for holding and displaying a book. STUDENT: ASHLEY ELDRINGHOFF—CRITIC: MICHAEL HAMILTON—INSTITUTION: LOUISIANA STATE UNIVERSITY

Figure 3.66. The compositional strategy for forming and organizing space involves creating projections from the main body. The projection at the right of the image defines approach and point of entry; the projection toward the left is a secluded and bound space. STUDENT: NICK REUTHER—CRITIC: JAMES ECKLER—INSTITUTION: MARYWOOD UNIVERSITY

SEQUENCE

An ordered series

A succession of spaces or events

An ordered movement from on space or event to another

Generative Possibilities in Serial Encounters

A man returns to his home from work. He is a person driven by routine. Each day he returns to his house, places his briefcase in the office, and changes clothes before preparing dinner. Later he returns to the office to complete any work he wasn't able to get to that day. This order of events has become a daily ritual.

When renovating his house, this sequence of events drove a reconsideration of spaces and the way they are encountered. The front entry provides a small place to leave his coat. The office is placed adjacent to the front door to provide easy access to leave his work and to pick it up again in the morning on his way out. The bedroom is placed behind the office. A place secluded from the rest, its isolation makes it seem far away, but the hall used to access it is encountered immediately after the door to the office. The kitchen and dining areas are immediately across from the hall leading to the bedroom. The architecture is organized along a sequence derived from the events that it contains.

Sequence is important to design because it relates elements, events, or processes to one another through ordering. A sequence is a pattern based upon succession. This can relate to the order in which spaces are encountered in architecture, the order or rhythm of components in an assembly, or the order of techniques applied in process. A sequence is similar to a progression. However, a progression describes a shift or transformation in a given direction; a sequence is more a descriptor of the relationships between its parts. In a sequence there is a successive relationship of elements: elements lead to others that follow. How can an ordering of spaces or elements in a composition influence design process? What relation is there between an ordering of procedures and design thinking?

A sequence of space is a specifically designed order of encounter. It represents one way the architect can choreograph habitation. The programs, events, and experiences of architecture can all be tied to the way one moves through its spaces. A sequence implies that there is a specific order, that one space necessarily follows another along a complex itinerary.

This can have several effects on habitation. If spaces are configured such that they can only be occupied in a prescribed order, one space will inevitably prepare the occupant to enter the next. That preparation or anticipation of the successive components of the sequence might be in the form of

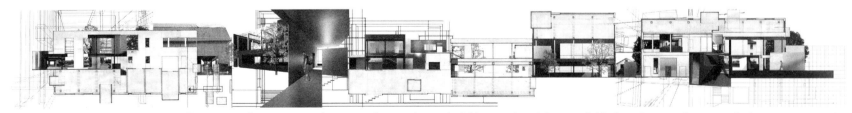

Figure 3.67.   This hybrid section collage maps the sequence of space and events housed within a project. It is an unfolded section cut along a path that an occupant is expected to take. It explores the spatial, organizational, and experiential factors of the design.   STUDENT: NOAH BERGMAN—CRITIC: JAMES ECKLER—INSTITUTION: UNIVERSITY OF CINCINNATI

spatial character, or program. Spaces might get progressively larger along a sequence. This shift in character is measurable; it can be anticipated by moving from one to the next. Similarly, in advancing along a spatial sequence one might find that they become more private in nature. The various programs inform an organizational structure and a pattern of movement.

A sequential assembly relies on repletion or rhythm as a strategy for construction. Based upon material, formal, or functional characteristics, objects are positioned relative to one another in a larger assembly. For example, the sequence in an assembly might be the repetition of similar tectonic elements that differ only in a small shift in proportion or size from one to the next.

Sequence applied to process refers to the order of applied techniques. This order directly influences the way information is generated and processed. As a result, the techniques used to craft pieces of a design reflect the way that design develops, both conceptually and actually. New discoveries are made as a result of working one particular way as opposed to another. Those discoveries can then lead to another successive stage in the act of making. The design process is not a predefined method that is directed by arriving at a particular final outcome. Instead it relies on one stage generating the next in sequence.

» *See also* Progression.

Figure 3.68. This project sequences spaces in a linear organizational pattern. A single path that runs the length of the structure links the spaces of the elongated construct. The path also serves to sequence the order in which the spaces are to be encountered. STUDENT: MATTHEW SUNDSTROM—CRITIC: JASON TOWERS—INSTITUTION: VALENCIA COMMUNITY COLLEGE

SPACE

A three dimensional volume that can be occupied by a person or object

A void given defined parameters, limits, or containment through the assembly of form

Generative Possibilities for Habitation

The space is composed of elements that are assembled as a container. A mass creates a base upon which the space is positioned; it also protrudes upward to define one edge of the space. Framing pieces are erected as ribs. They are joined to the mass along two opposing edges, while another spans framing piece spans between them. The frames define the limits of the space, its scale, and its proportion. Planes are attached to the frames to envelop the space and to define access to it.

The space is formed of material. The act of making space is directed by the attributes of the materials used. The density, weight, and texture of the stone determine the way the mass is made and connected to other elements. The lightness and rigidity of framing elements create new opportunities for spatial configuration. The opacity of planar elements control access and environmental response.

The space is experienced through sensed phenomena. Light and texture define the way space is perceived. Form is understood visually through the presence of shadows. Material is understood tactilely and visually.

The space is inhabited, which makes it architecture.

Space is architecture's primary characteristic. Architecture is motivated by habitation—the function of space. With this understanding, form and material act in service to space. They provide definition and containment. They serve as a medium in which space is crafted and composed. But throughout the design process, space is the single defining attribute of architecture. If architecture is unequivocally rooted in space, does it present variables or possibilities that can be exploited through the design process?

Space is any volume able to be occupied. The occupant can be an individual, a group, or even an object. Habitation is the defining attribute of architectural space. Form is deployed to define the parameters of space and its configuration, proportion, and scale. Material is deployed to define the

experiential characteristics of space. Craft and techniques for construction are applied according to material properties.

Space is central to a design process in which craft and technique are applied to configure it. Space can be crafted, manipulated, and tested through process in order to conform it to various criteria for design. Designing according spatial characteristic, as opposed to formal composition, means viewing purpose or experience as primary and form as a result. Using this approach to design, the architect is able to craft spaces according to

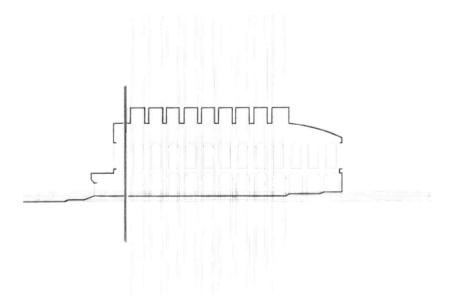

Figure 3.69. Space is empty volume with the potential to be occupied. This drawing documents the profile of space and the tectonic elements that make up that profile. Student: George Faber—Critic: James Eckler—Institution: University of Cincinnati

very specific needs and discover the resultant formal attributes derived. This stands in opposition to the view that architecture can begin as a formal gesture to which space and program are forced to adapt.

» *See also* Form.

Figure 3.70. This example is a single space contained on all sides. Scale is beginning to be made evident through the diversity of element sizes. STUDENT: LIU LIU—CRITIC: JAMES ECKLER—INSTITUTION: UNIVERSITY OF CINCINNATI

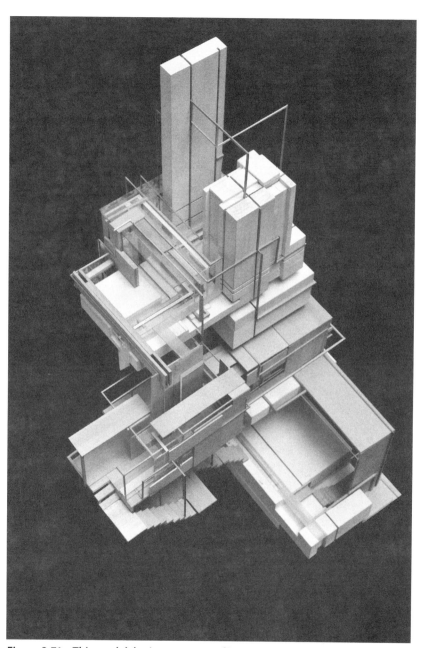

Figure 3.71. This model depicts a system of interconnected spaces; formal assembly and composition determine the operations that are possible within. STUDENT: JONATHON SILVA—CRITIC: JOHN MAZE—INSTITUTION: UNIVERSITY OF FLORIDA

THRESHOLD

An object such as a doorsill, a doorframe, or a doorway

A physical mark at the beginning of a space or pattern of movement; also, an ending to the preceding space or movement pattern

A moment of transition from on space to another

Generative Possibilities of Entrance or Transition

A person walks along a gravel path with grass on either side of it; he can hear the crunching of his footfalls upon the stones. The path changes; it becomes a hard slab of concrete polished to reflect a little bit of light. His footfalls are now muted whispers. He continues his approach to a structure, and a few steps later he is behind a tall wall to his left. Soon a wall to the right joins the first, along with a thick overhead that spans between them. Here there is shelter from the rain, but also little light. What was once expansive exterior space is now compressed into a small volume. He reaches out, grasps the metal door handle, and pulls it open. He steps inside.

Threshold originates from the Old English *threscold* or *thaerscwold*, meaning "a point of entrance." The first portion of the term, *thresh*–, meant "to tread." This is significant to design, as it implies a function of movement rather than the identification of an object.

A threshold can be a space—or part of a space—that performs a function of transition. Spatially, the threshold is all of those elements that contribute to a transition from one space to another. In this example, the threshold can be considered the concrete slab, the wall that extends out to guide the passage of the individual, the containing overhead with the right side wall, and the door. These elements perform two functions: they provide a structure for the movement of the individual, and they mark the passage of that individual from outside to inside by creating a compressed space. In this instance the threshold performs the operation of compression as a means of crafting the transition from outside to inside.

Considering the threshold in this way opens a multitude of possibilities to the designer. The act of passing from one space to another can be an event in itself, its own self-contained spatial experience. Perhaps the threshold

functions as a way stopping, redirecting, or revealing something new. How might one or all of those occurrences be orchestrated in built form? Perhaps a wall might block a straight path, forcing someone to turn and see something previously hidden. This is just one of many possibilities.

When designing the threshold, consider the function it has to serve. Is it a transition from an exterior space to an interior space, or between two interior spaces? What is the character of the two spaces it is linking, and does the threshold act as a tool for making them distinct or blurring the boundary

Figure 3.72. The threshold is a specialized transition that marks the end of one condition and the beginning of the next. Often used to describe the transitions between exterior and interior, the threshold can also be used to mark the transition between spaces within a project. STUDENT: LAILA AMMAR—CRITIC: JAMES ECKLER—INSTITUTION: UNIVERSITY OF CINCINNATI

between them? Is it to be something static, or does it transform one or more spaces? Each decision will direct an act of making and encourage the invention of forms to contain space in a way that creates an experience of the transition. The threshold thereby becomes a product of intent for spatial operation and experience.

The role of the threshold in the development of a design is intrinsically linked with other larger spatial systems. In addition to being its own subset of sequenced experiential events, it is also a part of a sequence of events choreographed through space. Understanding the implications that the threshold might have on other aspects of a project can bring cohesive organization to the conception of space.

A threshold can be an object, a function/operation, and/or an experience/event. The process of design becomes a means of inventing the placement and size of the object, the operation that needs to be performed, or the nature of the experience to be had by the occupant.

Figure 3.74. This is an open threshold. The point of entry is marked by a single framing piece. It delineates the point at which one side ends and the other begins. Student: Matthew Sundstrom—Critic: Jason Towers—Institution: Valencia Community College

Figure 3.73. This is an enclosed threshold. The point of entry is contained between a planar structure and the volume to which the threshold grants access. Student: Dave Perry—Critic: James Eckler—Institution: Marywood University

Figure 3.75. This image shows a compound threshold in which there is a point of entry between the exterior and an intermediate space. At the right of the image, there is another threshold between the intermediary space and the interior space. Student: Seth Troyer—Critic: James Eckler—Institution: University of Cincinnati

VIEW

A field of vision

A way of looking or seeing, especially from a controlled position or angle

Generative Possibilities in Display and Visual Access

There is a very special window in this room. Whereas the other windows in the building provide light and a vista of the gardens outside, this particular window does little of either. It is a tall and narrow opening limiting the scope of what can be seen. Around it, the wall thickens substantially. It is set so deeply within the thickened wall that looking through it is almost like peering into a small cave. Little light can actually make it through that long opening carved through the wall.

Pausing to look through the narrow aperture yields a view of the only thing in the field of vision that it offers. There is an oak tree in the center of the gardens. It was planted there decades ago in honor of a previous owner of this property. The window seems to have approximately the same proportions of the tree. The frame that holds the glass is sunk back into the stone where it can't be seen. There are no distractions to the view that is presented. The tree is perfectly framed within the narrow opening.

The importance of the monument is emphasized here in this space. The narrow window defines a relationship between this space and the exterior environment. The memorial tree is made a part of the functions of the interior space. It is the specific view that links the functions of the interior with those of the exterior.

View is visual access. It is the means by which something is seen. It can be an experiential operation of space, in that it determines what an occupant is made aware of. Spatial attributes, such as orientation and proportion, position the viewer relative to the subject that is seen. Formal assemblies that contain space are composed to provide the view, to determine its parameters. How can a view generate design ideas? How does it inform process and design thinking?

View is often used in place of *vista*. There is an important difference, however, that has implications on spatial composition as well as on the generative ideas that drive process. Whereas vista refers to a visual survey of a broad range of subjects, view is specific. It is a way of seeing a select few portions or conditions of an environment. It can, perhaps, even refer to a narrowing of vision down to a single subject.

This understanding of view can influence the design of space in two ways: by relating interior elements, or by referencing exterior elements. Designing visual access to elements of an interior is necessary for functions of display or way-finding. In referencing elements of an exterior environment, view is used as a design tool for relating interior and exterior space. When view is designed to give access to a particular object outside, it is a way of incorporating that object into the spatial composition.

The composition of elements that provide the view will determine the position that an occupant takes in order to see the object. There might be a direct association between that object and some characteristic of space or formal assembly. It might be a spatial protrusion directed toward the object or a detail that aligns the object with some feature of the architecture. View is a tool for selectively providing awareness to the occupants of an environment external to the space they inhabit. It is also a tool for relating elements within a space to one another or for linking internal and external conditions through line of sight.

The formal assemblies that provide view can be specifically designed to frame it, and framing a view has a direct impact on composition. View is a visual extension of space that incorporates the object of study. Framing that view can determine the role the object will play in the conception, experience, or function of space. Framing a view also creates an experiential relationship between architecture and its surroundings. It also influences organizational logic. View might be a tool for integrating new design into an existing context by controlling the aspects of context that are visible or not. That selective visibility might then be used to highlight a characteristic or detail that is pertinent to the architecture within the place. Organizationally, view is a linking device between designed elements.

» *See also* Perception.

4. TERMS OF OBJECTS AND ASSEMBLIES

ASSEMBLY

A single object, system, or enclosure that is composed of multiple fragments joined together

The act of joining components to create a larger whole

Generative Possibilities in Tectonic Making

Two walls meet and create a corner. Overhead there is a ceiling, and above that, and a roof. This is not, however, a typical corner. At the point where they would have touched, both walls are cut away. Between them, a sliver of clear glass in inserted, sealing the opening left behind.

Light streams through the glass and rakes across the smooth surface of one of those walls. The structural ribs that hold the ceiling and roof are embedded into the tops of both walls; those structural pieces seem to extend directly from the walls. The ceiling seems to be a solid mass suspended from the underside of those structural ribs. The mass ends without touching the wall, leaving a small gap that reveals the embedded structure. Here, the corner can be occupied. Where the intersecting walls meet the floor there is a concrete mass, perfectly sized for sitting. One is able to see—and read by—the light coming through the gap where the two walls intersect, and to see the joint where frame, plane, and mass meet through the gap between ceiling and wall.

This assembly serves to tell a spatial story, a script that defines a method of occupation, and a program of event. It determines the way a space is enclosed, inhabited, and used. The assembly of these different components creates a comfortable spot, with just the right amount of light to read by.

The manner in which components meet determines the character of a space. Assembled objects, assembled spaces—even arrangements of objects—constitute assemblies meant to determine the occupants' interaction with their environment. There is a direct correlation between the assembly of objects and spatial enclosures and events. The assemblies that compose a space determine its character.

What is a space to be? What is to happen in it? These questions will guide the crafting of joints that determine the physical qualities of a space, as well as the manner in which people move through or inhabit that space.

Positioning objects could be an assembly that defines where an occupant is to move or pause. The assembly of spatial enclosure can determine an individual's access inside or out. The assembly of parts can be a direct result of, or a guide to, the way a space is used.

The act of assembly is the predominant function of much of the design process. Designing the intersection between elements can define a language that can be manipulated and applied to other connections between physical pieces or spaces as they meet one another. When assembly is

Figure 4.1. Assembly is the joining of elements to form components that contain space. Here linear elements are joined to masses in a way that configures several spaces of different sizes and proportions. This model is a single assembly that houses space. However, assembly can also occur at the scale of the individual component. The repeated linear frames that form a screen over the top of the model is an assembled component of the larger construction. Student: George Faber—Critic: James Eckler—Institution: University of Cincinnati

viewed as a generative device, the act of making becomes an outline of spatial conception and a vehicle for discovery. As in the narrative, joining two elements to imply a volume can begin a design. Possibilities for space will be discovered in that simple act, and new iterations—or a continuation of construction—will follow. Program could emerge from the proportion and spatial conditions that arise. What is a space supposed to be? What is the event that it is to hold? How can a joint, or series of joined objects that make space, facilitate the event?

Figure 4.2. *Here multiple assemblies are used to delineate space as well as construct a layered overhead. Within that layered overhead there are apertures that are also created through the assembly of small parts that frame the openings. In this assembly, the joints where whole components come together also demarcate zones within the project.* STUDENT: RACHEL MOMENEE—CRITIC: JOHN HUMPHRIES—INSTITUTION: MIAMI UNIVERSITY

Figure 4.3. *Complex assemblies are joined to create space for a stair. They define the limits of the space without fully enclosing it. They also communicate the scale of the space through the relative proportion of elements to one another within each assembly.* STUDENT: JONATHON SILVA—CRITIC: JOHN MAZE—INSTITUTION: UNIVERSITY OF FLORIDA

CONNECTION

A tangible link between two objects or elements; a joint

An intangible or conceptual relationship between two or more parts

A step in the act of making that can be either physical or conceptual; a compositional decision

Generative Possibilities in Contact or Association

A circular fountain sits at the center of a plaza paved in marble. It is large, flat, and barren. The fountain is the center of a radial pattern in the stone pavement. The plaza is elevated from the street by just a few steps that provide defini- tion to its edge and a grand entry for those who arrive in formal attire to see a performance.

There are two performance halls on either side of the plaza. Their front facades are turned away from the street, and they face one another. Each looks at the other over the top of the fountain positioned between them. The columns of each rise the full height of the imposing structures. It is as if they are mirror images of each other. The columns are aligned across the plaza. The general dimensions are similar. The reflections in the damp pavement show them as if they were extend- ing out to one another in perfect alignment. Sometimes it is difficult to tell which building is seen in the reflection.

Each will have a different show. When people arrive they will either turn left or right to find the performance they intend to see. But the association between these two auditoriums will be constantly maintained through the plaza that con- nects them.

A connection is any physical point of contact between objects. It can be characterized by a joint within an assembly, a moment where objects touch, or linked spaces. Besides the obvious implications of assembly, what other applications to design or design process can a connection have? *Connection* is a generic term with different connotations at different scales of design. This provides a multitude of design applications that can refer to physical joinery. It can also refer to an interpreted connection through organizational refer- ence or function.

As a part of an assembly a connection is the location of the constructed joint. It may characterize a type of joint or a strategy for detailing the joint. Similarly, at the scale of spatial composition a connection is a point of

Figure 4.4. A connection can be a physical point of contact, reference, or asso- ciation between elements. In this image physical contact is apparent in the joints between pieces. There is also an associative connection made through the consistency of joint making. In the foreground of the image one element passes through another, leaving a gap between them. That same strategy is used on joints in the background, creating an association through formal language.
Student: Michael Rogovin—Critic: James Eckler—Institution: University of Cincinnati

intersection between spaces. It is a smaller unit of the larger composition that may be characterized by a transition or some other spatial or experiential operation.

Connection might also be used to describe organizational or programmatic aspects of design. The components of a system might be understood as connected through a common function rather than through physical contact. In this instance the connection becomes a way of grouping or associating the components of a composition. Or the organization of a composition itself might define connections between components through principles such as registration or proximity. In this case components are connected through common organizational roles.

In any of these applications, a connection is used as a tool for joining elements, either physically or associatively. Prescribing the ways that connections will function at the various scales of a design can be a strategy for defining and making formal relationships between parts.

» *See also* Detail; Joint.

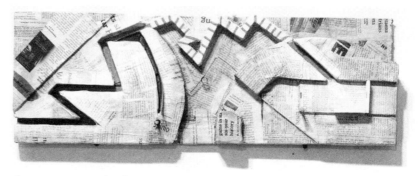

Figure 4.5. Consider the angular, ribbonlike component at the center of this relief model. It links the constructed areas of the two far sides. The connection between the elevated ribbon and the depressed groove stops short of physical contact. There are also no characteristic similarities by which a connection could be defined. Instead, it is a connection through reference. The dimension of the ribbon and the groove being the same, and the alignment of the two, allows one to act as a reference and extension of the other. STUDENT: UNKNOWN—CRITIC: TIM HAYES—INSTITUTION: LOUISIANA TECH UNIVERSITY

DEFORMATION

An act of distorting, transforming, or rearranging established formal or geometric patterns

A manipulated portion of an established formal or geometric pattern; a mark, scar, or anomaly

Generative Possibilities in Distorting

A sheet of metal is etched with a regular grid. You bend the sheet, and the lines of the grid stretch. You press it over a form that you constructed earlier. It makes a depression in the metal sheet that stretches the grid along the contours of the formwork.

Choosing an undistorted gridline as a guide, you cut the sheet. The metal plane is then bent to create a gap with the cut segment. You continue to fold, bend, cut, and contort the metal plane. By using these techniques for manipulating and deforming the sheet, you are able to create a variety of spaces within the folds and depressions of the metal. The grid that was once regular remains as a measure of that deformation.

A deformation is any alteration to the physical characteristics of an object. More specifically, a deformation is a reconfiguration that is significant enough to alter the way in which that object functions. Additionally, a deformed object retains some qualities of its preexisting state; this usually makes the deformed portions plainly visible relative to the previous state of the object, which can to some extent still be inferred from preserved characteristics.

Is deformation a principle of design? If designing architecture is rooted in making space and form, how is deformation not counterproductive to this process? Deformation can be the unintentional result of external forces acting on a design. However, it can also be an intentional and controlled strategy for reinventing an existing object toward a new purpose: it can be a process of making.

Deformation requires an existing object to become the subject of manipulation. That object can be changed in order to take on a new function in a design. It might facilitate program or composition. For instance, the flat surface of a wall might be deformed in order to provide opportunities to hold objects or vary a spatial profile. Deformation becomes the vehicle for charging form with added purpose.

A deformation is different from completely reinventing the object. It implies the previous state of the object and makes it apparent that the new formal characteristics of the object are actually a modification. In this respect deformation becomes a communicative device acting as a record of the design's evolution.

The act of deforming an object is a process that consists of any modification significant enough to alter function without going so far as to completely reinvent. It might be the marking or building up of a surface, or an alteration of an object's shape or proportions. Deformation impacts design thinking in presenting a comparative study. Through deforming an object, the designer will be able to juxtapose the characteristics of the original with those of the new, and the original function with the new.

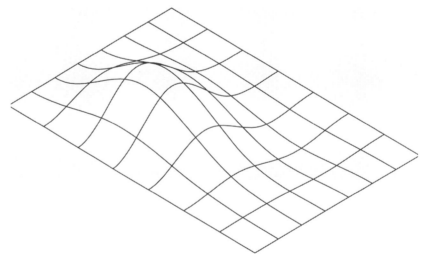

Figure 4.6. This illustration shows a surface deformed. The grid drawn across the surface is distorted along the contour of the deformation.

Figure 4.7. The stacked pieces of material come together to form a striated surface. Irregularities in the cut of each piece create hollows and depressions in the resulting surface. Each is a deformation of the baseline flat surface, which remains intact toward the upper portions of the model. STUDENT: DAVID GUZMAN—CRITIC: TIM HAYES—INSTITUTION: LOUISIANA TECH UNIVERSITY

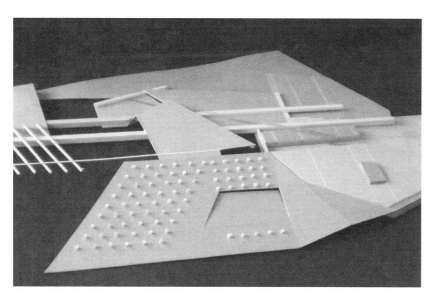

Figure 4.8. In this example, folding achieves a deformation of the flat surface as a means of representing regions within a field. STUDENT: LAILA AMMAR—CRITIC: JAMES ECKLER—INSTITUTION: UNIVERSITY OF CINCINNATI

Figure 4.9. This example shows a plane constructed of banded elements deformed through folding. It is made in a way that permits spatial constructions to occupy the gaps formed between the folds. STUDENT: DAN MOJSA—CRITIC: REAGAN KING—INSTITUTION: MARYWOOD UNIVERSITY

DETAIL

Minute aspects of a form that speak to its assembly, function, or role in a larger compositional order

An act of designing the minutia of a form

Generative Possibilities in Articulation

You reached your hand out to grasp the front door handle and felt the way it was contoured to precisely interlock with the human hand. And the door itself was made to reveal its construction: panels of wood were positioned so that their opposing grain structures would make them contrast with one another; a tiny gap was left between segments to exaggerate the joint between them. Beyond the door, the spaces in this building were just as extensively detailed.

In the walls, materials are separated by a tiny gap that reveals the different components contributing to the assembly. Joints between members are exposed. Rails are not bolted to the surface of the wall. Instead, a length of the concrete seamlessly protrudes to provided something that you can grasp as you walk down the stairs.

There are many other examples of the way details communicate the function of space and the methods of crafting form, but these are most notable to you because you came in direct physical contact with them. In this building, details are used to convey information regarding the purpose of elements, or to reveal the methods by which they were made. Nothing is hidden or covered up in the assembly of form; rather, those connections and joints are celebrated through the detail.

The detail is the smallest designed component of architecture. Detail refers to the way elements join and how that connection occurs. It is also the small-scale articulation of objects. The act of detailing is the process of design devoted to these minute considerations of a project. How can something that is so small contribute to the larger aspirations of an architectural design? How can a detail be significant to a building? Many of the structural and experiential responsibilities of architecture rest on the detail.

Pragmatically, the detail is the mechanism that joins elements. It is not just that they do connect, but *how* they connect, that drives the design of the architectural detail. It consists of the elements that join as well as the

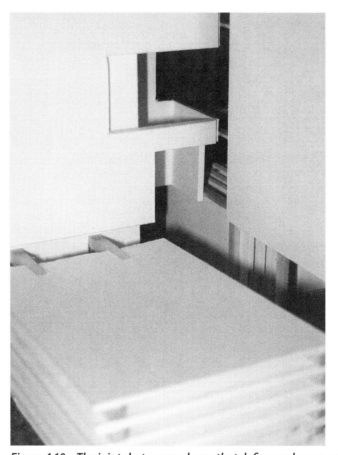

Figure 4.10. The joints betweens planes that define enclosure are detailed in several ways. Where the lower plane meets the back wall, the surface is pulled back so that the two are separated by a small groove. That separation is a detail meant to reveal the structure of the connection. The gap between the two sidewalls is a detail meant to permit access to light. It is articulated to shape and direct the light that enters the space. STUDENT: MICHELLE MAHONEY—CRITIC: JAMES ECKLER—INSTITUTION: UNIVERSITY OF CINCINNATI

hardware that joins them. It will determine the structural integrity of a joint. Additionally, the way a connection is detailed can determine other aspects of performance, such as environmental factors or operable components of an assembly. The act of detailing consists of designing (or in some cases choosing) the correct components to facilitate the proper function of a joint or system.

The detail can accomplish more in a design than just completing a connection. It can be an interactive device that determines the way an occupant engages space. It might also be a communicative device that is exposed,

or even embellished upon, in order to make an occupant aware of some structural logic, or to insinuate the function of the elements it joins. Aesthetically, the detail has the potential to represent a strategy of craft. It relies on a consistency of design language in order to unify or associate elements of a design. For instance, a particular type of detail might be used to articulate a system and differentiate it from another. Or a project might be minimally or intensively detailed as a way of establishing a consistency of language throughout.

» *See also* Connection.

Figure 4.11. A detail can be simple. In this example, it is a minimal expression of a joint. The notches used to receive a plane and join it to a perpendicular piece continue past the connection. It illustrates a strategy of joint-making. STUDENT: VICTORIA TRAINO—CRITIC: KATE O'CONNOR—INSTITUTION: MARYWOOD UNIVERSITY

Figure 4.12. A detail can also be complex. In this example, details express and contribute to the intricacy of the assembly. Small reveals expose various methods of joinery. Linear elements are connected in complex joints used to frame space. STUDENT: JOHN LEVI WEIGAND—CRITIC: JOHN MAZE—INSTITUTION: UNIVERSITY OF FLORIDA

FORM

The characteristics of an object

To design, craft, or manipulate objects

The physical, rather than the spatial, aspects of design

Generative Possibilities of the Object

Form is tangible; it can be touched and seen. It is comprised of material. It has mass, density, and weight. Form is three-dimensional and can be manipulated or reconfigured through techniques of construction.

Formal objects are joined to create assemblies. Space is a product of the arrangement of assemblies. Form acts in service to space. It is the vehicle by which space and its characteristics are defined.

Form contains space that is inhabitable, which makes it architecture.

Form is the physical character of architectural design. Architecture is a composition of form and space. Space is used to define habitation, and form is the primary vehicle in design for creating space. Form can refer to anything from the gestural mass of a building to the subsets of assemblies and components. With such a ubiquitous role in architecture, what specific opportunities for design, conception, or investigation does form present?

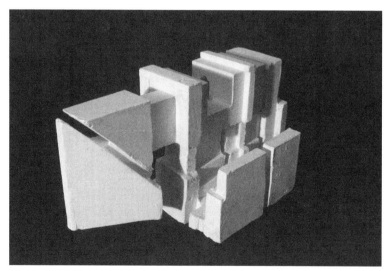

Figure 4.13. *Form, absent of material consideration, refers to the three-dimensional, geometric characteristics of an object. In this example, those characteristics are manipulated and configured to establish hierarchy and to differentiate between volumes.* Student: Unknown—Critic: Jason Towers—Institution: Valencia Community College

Figure 4.14. *Form, as it is precisely configured, acts in service to space. It is carved or assembled to define and contain space. In this example, the articulated object is made to contain volumes that begin to imply a scale of habitation.* Student: Robert White—Critic: Jason Towers—Institution: Valencia Community College

Form is ever-present in architecture; however, it provides different ways of understanding design at various stages of process. Building form as a gestural massing can be a starting point for developing a strategy for organization. It can also indicate contextual relationships. Formal qualities of assembly can be used to compose space as well as articulate spatial profile. Characteristics of form that are inherent to a single object can direct the way that it is joined to another, or the function it might serve on its own.

Additionally, formalism is a design position that prioritizes the composition of form over space—where formal manipulations or sculpting become the primary motivation of architecture. These formal manipulations can be executed in a way that searches for spatial opportunities within a shaped mass. They might also be the result of formulaic process: form-making becomes a manifestation of an organizational logic, or a scripted method of production. Creating form as the primary driver for architectural design carries with it some danger because it can also become driven by the novelty of a shape. And when considered independently from other responsibilities of architecture, shape can lead to a design that does not satisfy criteria rooted in program, experience, or performance.

» *See also* Space; Object.

Figure 4.15. Combining material implication with formal logic and assembly defines the attributes of space contained within the construction. In this example, a formal gesture is composed of multiple parts in an assembly that frames the space and permits light and view to penetrate it. Material sensibility determines the structural logic required to hold the construct in position; at the same time, structural members contribute to the configuration of the contained space.
Student: Zachary Culpepper—Critic: Tim Hayes—Institution: Louisiana Tech University

GESTURE

A simple motion or position used to express an idea

A simple form or graphic used to articulate some basic characteristic of a design

Generative Possibilities in Simplified Form

The architect begins with a gesture of space—a piece of folded paper. Eventually it will become her next building, but currently it exists only as a set of desires and parameters. She uses many more pieces of paper and takes many more steps before creating a simple compositional gesture that embodies some of those desires, one that holds the potential to satisfy those parameters.

The folded slip of paper provides general information about space and form: proportion, orientation, and profile shape. As she works, more desires for the configuration of space lead to intent. Pieces are cut away to provide additional access points or to create an opportunity for light to enter or view to be framed. More material is added to thicken the paper in places to satisfy parameters of structure.

The program is more complex than the single, folded paper would suggest. But it indicates the compositional strategies she will use to respond to those programmatic complexities. Through this gesture, her very first decisions are made; it represents a point at which her desire for a particular designed condition transforms into an intent for architecture to house function and experience. It allows her to generate ideas for future iterations.

When we speak, many of us augment our language with hand motions: we gesture in a way that represents the idea we are trying to convey. The gesture is a simplified representation of that idea. This understanding of gesture translates into design in several ways. As it pertains to architecture, the gesture is a simplified representation of space or form. Considering design in a broader sense, the gesture can also refer to representational techniques that capitalize on the motion of the body, or more specifically, the motion of the hand. Given that the gesture is largely representational, what qualifies it as a formal idea in architecture? And how can the simplification of form facilitate the development or evolution of architectural ideas?

For the purposes of understanding the principles of formal composition and assembly, this text will focus on those aspects of a gesture that speak to the simplification of form. Just as tectonic characteristics describe form in terms of composition and assembly, gestural characteristics describe form

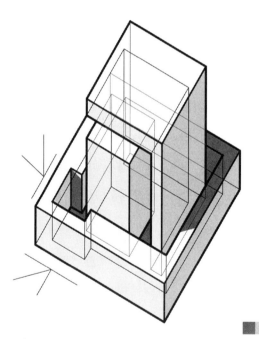

Figure 4.16.   The gesture provides minimal information. It is a generic scheme or formal strategy. It is useful in the beginning stages of design as a vehicle for resolving compositional issues. It is also useful as an analogue to test various aspects of a design. In this example, the simplified forms are being used to test the behavior of light upon, around, and through the gestural configuration.
Student: Mary Dickerson—Critic: John Humphries—Institution: Miami University

in terms of basic qualities of shape, proportion, and orientation. Horizontality and verticality are gestural qualities of form that address proportion and orientation. Orthogonal, diagonal, or curvilinear characteristics of a gesture address shape. These descriptors of a form provide a simple framework for the articulation of an architectural idea. This framework exists from concept to resolution of the final building. These simple formal characteristics can provide a starting point to a design—a generic shape to act as a vehicle to test progressively more complex spatial ideas. Or they can be a valuable tool for communicating the principal compositional ideas that generated a project.

Movement is an ever-present consideration of the gesture, as the simplified forms often reflect the motion of the hand that created them. At the beginning stages of a process, it is possible that an intuitive mark can be translated into a formal gesture. Dragging the hand from one side to another is a simple act, but in it there are already decisions about horizontal proportion and orientation, prominence and hierarchy (evinced by the thickness of the line), and the shape of the line. Each of these aspects of that initial gesture has consequences that may impact the final outcome of the design. Visualizing different ways this gesture can be manifest as architecture can generate many ideas for space, structure, and use.

Ultimately, the gesture is a basic framework for design that evolves through iteration; through process, the gesture can be incrementally translated into architecture. It helps generate new ideas through testing and visualizing various alternatives. In the end the resulting design may have deviated so much that the initial gesture is no longer recognizable. It may also be lost as the designer discovers a better alternative and modifies the gesture accordingly. But there is also the potential for that first form to be recognizable within the architectural result—a signifier of the process that the project has undergone.

It is that signifier that allows the gesture to be a tool of analysis. Analyzing architecture requires that it be broken down into separate information sets. The gesture might be one of those that aid the study of an existing spatial construction. Taking the gesture as a layer of information might yield an understanding of the logic for the composition or organization. It might yield recognition for the way programs are distributed through the building.

It might also provide insight into the intention the original designer had with regard to various relationships established through formal composition. Similarly, the simplification of information can be a valuable communicative tool that enables individuals outside the design process to more easily understand the ideas and objectives of the design.

Curvilinear

A formal gesture defined by curves

Curvilinear is a descriptor of form. It refers to any pattern, shape, volume, or assembly that is composed of arcing lines or curved surfaces. A curvilinear form is a volumetric gesture characterized by organic shape. How does an idea as simple as a curved surface influence design? How can it generate space?

In the same way as other gestural properties, the curvilinear form presents a strategy for composing volume. It begins as a strategy at the initial

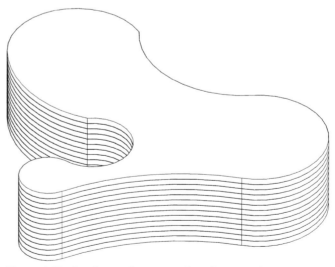

Figure 4.17. Curving surfaces or arcing elements characterizes curvilinear form.

stages of process and evolves through iteration as a characteristic of space. It impacts issues of formal relationships at the scale of context and composition as well as spatial profile and tectonic assembly at the scale of habitation. It can be introduced as an aesthetic position in process.

As an aesthetic position, curvilinear forms can be a way of providing complexity to the composition of space. It might be a space in which the form is put on display—a way of calling attention to a particular spatial characteristic. The emphasis that can be drawn through the integration of curvilinear

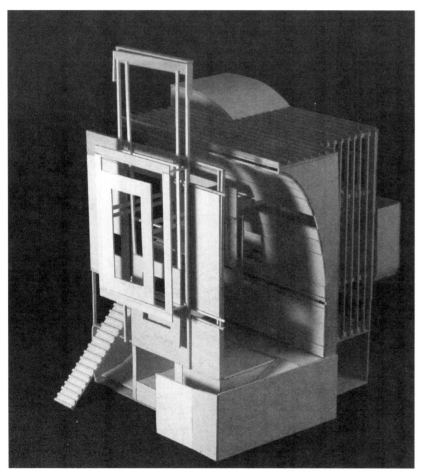

Figure 4.18. Curvilinear form defines the back surface of the space. Compared to the composition's other elements it is unique, causing it to be emphasized
STUDENT: MATTHEW NAYLOR—CRITIC: JOHN HUMPHRIES—INSTITUTION: MIAMI UNIVERSITY

form into a composition also presents a risk of novelty: the risk that the curving shapes contribute to the space in no other way than attracting temporary interest from an occupant.

The curvilinear form may also be the result of a strategy for responding to a program or event in space that is better served by a curving container. The curvilinear aesthetic is a strategy for interlocking spaces in a composition toward the design of specific spatial relationships or for the use of a particular material or crafting technique.

Resolving details, connections, and relationships in a curvilinear design is more difficult than doing so in an orthogonal or diagonal scheme. Irregular geometries often lead to unoccupied interstitial spaces or to awkward connections. Avoiding these design problems requires proficiency and a disciplined approach to design. Techniques for both craft and conceiving space should be developed with simpler geometries before attempting to integrate curvilinear forms into the composition of the formal gesture.

Diagonal

A formal composition consisting of slanted elements or oblique angles

Diagonal is a descriptor of form. It refers to any pattern, shape, volume, or assembly that is composed of nonperpendicular lines, obtuse angles, or acute angles. A diagonal form is a volumetric gesture characterized by

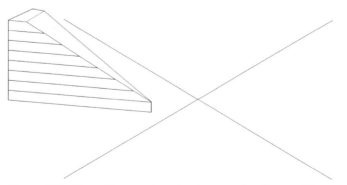

Figure 4.19. Nonorthogonal angles characterize diagonal form.

intersections of varying degrees. How does an idea as simple as an angle influence design? How can it generate space?

In the same way as other gestural properties, the diagonal form presents a strategy for composing volume. It begins as a strategy at the initial stages of process and evolves through iteration as a characteristic of space. It impacts issues of formal relationships at the scale of context and composition, as well as spatial profile and tectonic assembly at the scale of habitation. It can be introduced as a strategy for gestural composition as either an ordering system or an aesthetic position.

The diagonal ordering system is a strategy for composing and arranging elements. It provides a method for organizing various facets of a design project using irregular grids or registration lines. As an aesthetic position, diagonal forms can be a way of providing an approach of subtle variation to the composition of space. It might be a space in which form is used as a reflection of an event in a space, or a design objective that generated it. Or it could be a strategy applied for reasons of operation or performance, as it often is

to control various environmental factors such as daylighting. The diagonal aesthetic is a strategy for interlocking spaces in a composition toward the design of specific spatial relationships or for the use of a particular material or crafting technique.

Formal compositions, assemblies, and spatial relationships are somewhat more difficult to resolve in a design governed by diagonal strategies than one that is orthogonal. Irregular connections can yield to unstable joinery or awkward interstitial spaces. The irregular geometries introduced by a diagonal form also impact craft, as most materials and building techniques are more effective in orthogonal compositions. Crafting proficiency is important in avoiding these potential problems of a diagonal composition. Beginning design students should hone their crafting and space-making skills within an orthogonal composition and begin to introduce diagonal or curvilinear forms only as they become more proficient.

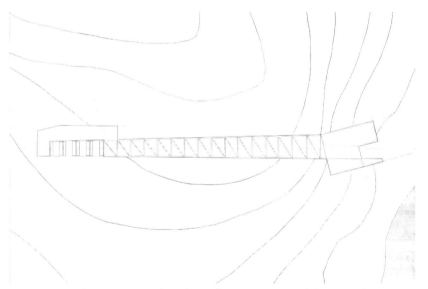

Figure 4.20. *The interior members are arranged diagonally relative to the upright elements in the foreground of the image. The diagonal components define an angular space between the two assemblies.* Student: Josh Frank— Critic: Reagan King—Institution: Marywood University

Figure 4.21. *There are several angles in the composition of this spatial construct. They are used to facilitate various operations of space. The box at the right of the image is angled relative to the extension that reaches across the page. This marks a point of transition between the space in the box and the corridor of the extension. The extension itself tapers to a narrow volume at the left. This gradual reduction in the size of the space prepares an occupant to encounter a compressed volume at the end.* Student: Houston Burnette—Critic: Peter Wong—Institution: University of North Carolina, Charlotte

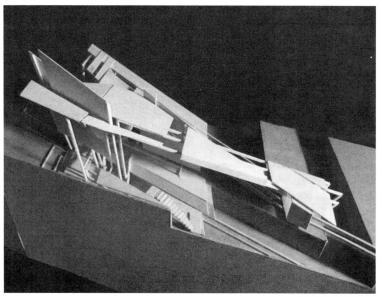

Figure 4.22. Acute angles define both formal assemblies and spatial composition in this project. The result is a linear organization of spaces that gradual taper outward as one progresses from the right side of the image to the left. This effect might be used to direct movement or to distribute programs of space sequentially along a path. Student: Unknown—Critic: Jason Towers—Institution: Valencia Community College

Orthogonal

A formal composition consisting of parallel and perpendicular arrangements; a composition of right angles

Orthogonal is a descriptor of form. It refers to any pattern, shape, volume, or assembly that is composed of perpendicular lines or right angles. An orthogonal form is a volumetric gesture characterized by intersecting right angles. How does an idea as simple as a right angle influence design? How can it generate space?

In the same way as other gestural properties, the orthogonal form presents a strategy for composing volume. It begins as a strategy at the initial stages of process and evolves through iteration as a characteristic of space. It impacts issues of formal relationships at the scale of context and composition, as well as spatial profile and tectonic assembly at the scale of habitation. It can be introduced as a strategy for gestural composition as either an ordering system or an aesthetic position.

The orthogonal ordering system is a strategy for composing and arranging elements. It provides a method for organizing various facets of a design project. As an aesthetic position, orthogonal forms can be a way of providing a simple approach to composing space. It might be a space in which form does not distract from an objective that the designer has for it. Or it could be strategy applied to increase the efficiency of construction. The orthogonal aesthetic is a strategy for interlocking spaces in a composition toward the design of specific spatial relationships or for the use of a particular material or crafting technique.

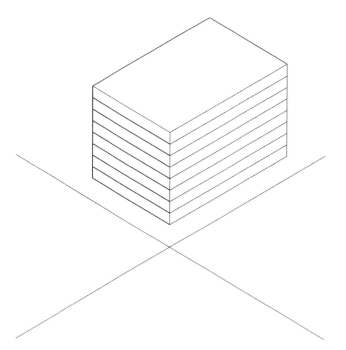

Figure 4.23. Ninety-degree angles characterize orthogonal form.

Formal compositions, assemblies, and spatial relationships are more easily resolved in a design governed by orthogonal strategies. More time can be devoted to developing ideas for space—instead of devoting time to figuring out how to make the irregular connections necessitated by both diagonal and curvilinear forms. Beginning students of design should hone their crafting and space-making skills within an orthogonal composition and begin to introduce diagonal or curvilinear forms only as they become more proficient.

Horizontal

Pertaining to or referencing the horizon

An orientation perpendicular to vertical

Horizontality is a gestural proportion or orientation of space or form that is parallel to the horizon. It is a gestural quality of form because it does not rely

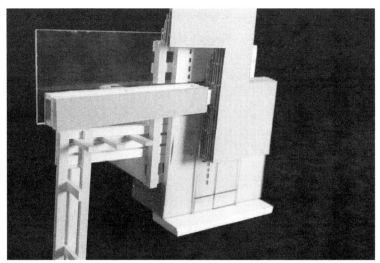

Figure 4.24. The organization of tectonic elements in this example is determined by an orthogonal pattern. The orthogonal regulating lines can be seen marked on the surface of a piece of acrylic embedded within the construction. STUDENT: KEVIN UTZ—CRITIC: JAMES ECKLER—INSTITUTION: MARYWOOD UNIVERSITY

Figure 4.25. In this example, space is made entirely of orthogonal forms. There is a regularity that comes from the orthogonal construction. However, spatial diversity is still achieved; spaces are different sizes and are of different configurations. Some are horizontal, some vertical, some central and wrapping, some enclosed and open. STUDENT: KENNER CARMODY—CRITIC: JIM SULLIVAN—INSTITUTION: LOUISIANA STATE UNIVERSITY

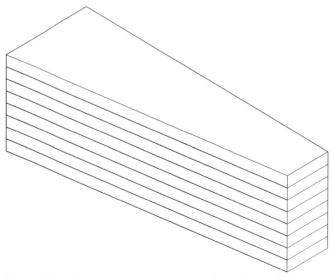

Figure 4.26. Elements that are elongated parallel to the horizon characterize horizontal form.

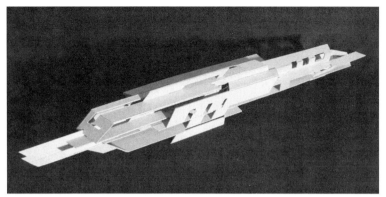

Figure 4.27. Horizontality describes this formal gesture. It is also linear, although that is not a requirement of the horizontality. In this example, the student has begun to make decisions regarding the spaces it is to contain. Apertures and hollows have been opened up in it. A diversity of proportions begins to establish relationships, scale, and an organized spatial system. Student: Wendell Montgomery—Critic: Jason Towers—Institution: Valencia Community College

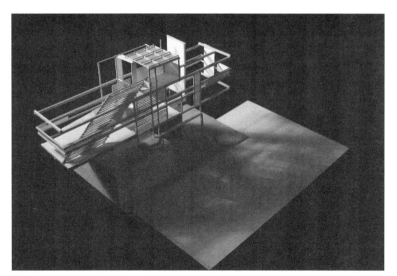

Figure 4.28. In this example, horizontality describes the orientation of volumes of space. They are stacked vertically, but each volume is itself horizontal, creating a kind of horizontal grain in the overall composition. There is also a definition in the design of space. It is no longer gestural, but has become more specific. However, if a generic, gestural form were based on this project, it would be a horizontally banded volume. Student: Katherine Cormeau—Critic: John Humphries—Institution: Miami University

on specific architectural information; rather, it refers to generic characteristics. So how is this gestural quality relevant to design? The horizontal gesture can be deployed throughout process in a variety of ways. It can be a generative principle—a starting point for developing ideas. It can be an analytical tool. It can also be a way communicating design intent.

The generative potential of the horizontal gesture lies in intuition. The horizontal gesture can begin as a simple formal rendition that indicates a desire to elongate across rather than upward. It reflects a preliminary design decision. From that moment, new responsibilities can be added to that first basic form. More specific tectonic and spatial information can be integrated. It can be sculpted and manipulated to reflect more design decisions.

Vertical

Pertaining to an upright position or orientation

An orientation perpendicular to horizontal

Verticality is a gestural proportion or orientation of space or form that is perpendicular to the horizon. It is a gestural quality of form because it does not

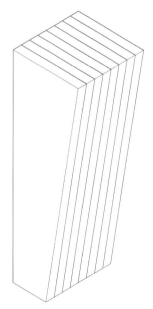

Figure 4.29. Elements that are elongated perpendicular to the horizon characterize vertical form.

rely on specific architectural information; rather, it refers to generic characteristics. So how is this gestural quality relevant to design? The vertical gesture can be deployed throughout process in a variety of ways. It can be a generative principle—a starting point for developing ideas. It can be an analytical tool. It can also be a way communicating design intent.

The generative potential of the vertical gesture lies in intuition. The vertical gesture can begin as a simple formal rendition that indicates a desire to elongate upward rather than across. It reflects a preliminary design decision. From that moment, new responsibilities can be added to that first basic form. More specific tectonic and spatial information can be integrated. It can be sculpted and manipulated to reflect more design decisions.

Figure 4.30.   Verticality determines the distribution of spaces and their relationship to one another. It can be described as an upper volume and a lower volume. Proportionally, this project has a small footprint compared to its height. Reducing this project to a simple formal gesture would result in a series of interlocked forms rising upward. Student: Unknown—Critic: John Humphries—Institution: Miami University

MATERIAL

The substance of which an object is made

Generative Possibilities for Craft

A woman stands in her studio looking at a pile of wood she has collected. The various tools of her trade surround her. She is a sculptor, and she has been gathering discarded fragments and remainders of wood from work sites all over town. She wants to use these items to make a mold, and cast a piece for her latest work. She contemplates ways the pieces can be composed and the forms she might be able to produce from them. She strategizes ways they can go together, how the plaster will fill the mold, and the way she will make the joints in order to remove it.

The mold will be intricate, so the plaster mixture will have to be looser than normal. This way, the wet plaster will be able to flow into the small creases and crevices she plans to build into the mold. Once cured, the plaster will be brittle, especially in the thinner portions of the cast. She will need to reinforce it with steel. She incorporates other materials into the mold in order to create different surface textures. Glass polishes the surface of the plaster. Gouging the wood makes it rough.

She will also need to treat each piece of wood differently. Some will be able to hold more weight than others. Some have prominent grain patterns, a coarse surface, or knots. All of these will be imparted to the surface of the plaster, so each characteristic must be considered as she begins making the mold. She categorizes each piece of wood depending on its characteristics. She knows that different species will be manipulated differently. She carefully decides if she must cut across or with the grain of each piece of wood, considering its structure and the texture she wants in the plaster. Knots are used as points of intersection between pieces; in this way, they will become an intended feature of the sculpture. When complete, she is satisfied with the outcome, and incorporates it into the ongoing work.

Material is the substance of an object. It is anything from which something is made—as opposed to materiality, which speaks to the characteristics of material. Does material have a significant impact on design? With the difference between material and materiality being so small, is their effect on design very different? Both material and materiality should be taken into consideration throughout the design process. Where material will influence decisions regarding construction and joinery, materiality will influence decisions made regarding the experience of a space and craft in representation. Although their roles in design often overlap, they can sometimes guide design thinking and making in distinct ways.

Material affects craft and assembly. Certain materials require different techniques for making to be applied. And certain design decisions are better represented in one material than another. Craft is an overlapping consideration of both material and materiality. The characteristics of a material will determine the techniques that can be used to manipulate it, as well as forms that it can successfully achieve. For instance, some materials are better suited to creating certain geometries. This is a function of the material, but it also impacts considerations of materiality. The material characteristics that determine crafting technique and the potential for achieving form are the same characteristics that determine how a material is experienced. Characteristics such as rigidity, opacity, and thickness are determining factors for both construction and interaction. Identifying material attributes, understanding the techniques that can shape it, and comparing those to the conceptual demands of a project will aid in making specific material choices.

» *See also* Materiality.

MEMBRANE

In biological usage, a thin layer of tissue

In relation to space and form, a thin material stretched within a frame in order to cover or seal

Generative Possibilities of Thinness or Making Skin

Light bathed the entire space. There were no shadows, just uniform illumination throughout the length of the gallery. The ceiling was the source of the light. It was made of white cloth stretched taut across the entire the space. It was seamless, and the light filtered through it, making the cloth seem to glow.

Above the cloth membrane and hidden from view by it, the roof was glass. It allowed natural light to enter the space and hit the cloth scrim, which distributed it evenly to all corners of the room. When the sun went down, artificial lights would shine on the cloth in an effort to take its place. The condition of the light allowed the art on the walls to be ideally displayed, no matter the time of day.

Membrane is a term borrowed from biology. It is any thin layer of tissue. Architecturally, it has come to refer to a thin layer of material, usually without any structural qualities of its own. This layer is typically used as a way of laminating another material that provides the necessary structure. Or it can be a material that is given the appearance of being stretched within a structural frame. As an object in an assembly, what roles can the membrane play in architecture? Membranes can be divided into two types: those meant to influence material performance, and those meant to sculpt the spatial profile.

A material's performance can be any measurable result of including it in an assembly. In architecture, performance often pertains to environmental response, and laminating membranes can play a key role. For instance, a membrane might be used as a watertight seal, or to insulate. A framed membrane might be used to filter light into a space. These membranes play a very specific role in an assembly, and their contribution to the purpose of the assembly can be measured precisely.

Spatial profiles can be manipulated in several ways by introducing membranes into the assembly of containment. Membranes that are laminated upon a structured surface can be a form of articulation; they can alter color or provide texture. Framed membranes can be used to sculpt space despite being thin. Because of a membrane's relative plasticity, it can take on any contour that can be built into the frame, providing more possibilities for the manipulation of spatial profile.

Figure 4.31. *The membrane is composed of many orthogonal panels stitched together and suspended to create an undulating surface. The construction has little structural integrity itself and instead relies on the suspending supports for its rigidity and configuration. Changing even one support could cause a dramatic alteration and the reconfiguration of the surface.* STUDENT: UNKNOWN, TEAM PROJECT—CRITIC: TIM HAYES—INSTITUTION: LOUISIANA TECH UNIVERSITY

There are also experiential considerations for a space that is contained by membrane assemblies. Moving through a membrane to gain access is a very different kind of transition than that provided by a thick, structured wall. Spatial distinction is minimal, given the abrupt transition from one to the other. This may cause the membrane to read as a partition dividing areas within a single space rather than one that separates spaces. However, a membrane that wraps its frame rather than being stretched within it can give the illusion of thickness; it effectively creates a hollow cavity between surfaces. Those surfaces can, as in other applications, be shaped and contoured in any number of ways. Another consideration is materiality. The membrane might be opaque, translucent, or transparent, giving it the ability to control the way light enters a space.

A membrane has an almost limitless number of ways that it can be applied to craft and construction in order to facilitate design intent. The single most limiting factor is structure. Its qualities of thinness and relative pliability make it dependent upon a separate structural system.

» *See also* Skin.

Figure 4.32. This example shows a membrane supported within a rigid frame. The thinness of the membrane causes it to rely on the frame around it for its structural integrity. STUDENT: AXEL FORSTER—CRITIC: JOHN MAZE—INSTITUTION: UNIVERSITY OF FLORIDA

Figure 4.33. The thinness of a membrane, made possible by a structure that lends rigidity and formal configuration, presents new possibilities for form and space. In this example, membranes define intricate geometries that would be difficult in other materials and crafting techniques. They also act as screens that admit light in quantities possible only because of the membranes' thinness. STUDENT: HECTOR GARCIA—CRITIC: ALLEN WATTERS—INSTITUTION: VALENCIA COMMUNITY COLLEGE

OBJECT

A physical form that can be perceived and with which one can interact

A single, tangible element or part

Generative Possibilities in Making and Placing Form

The building stands close to the water. It is taller than the buildings that surround it, and it rises to that height as if it were twisted all the way to a sharp point at its top. Its surface is intensively articulated, with overlapping grids and vertical slices that function as windows. The base of the building is cut to afford entry and intricately sculpted to provide some shelter to the exterior. The building's form is reflected on the surface of the water.

The building has little engagement with its context. It is a novel anomaly within the older urban fabric that surrounds it, and in some places is completely disconnected from that fabric by the placement of a wall or the arrangement of walking paths. This building is a formal composition, and as such is entirely self-referential. The intent is for the building to be viewed as an object placed within a landscape. It is a sculptural creation that provides opportunity for space and program to exist within it. Their placement, scale, and configuration are determined by the formal composition of the object-building. The attributes of the object that differ to such a degree from its surroundings define it as a landmark. It prioritizes visibility and authorship above use; it can be seen and recognized from all around, including the nearby interstate highway.

An object is a single, physical element that is inherently nonspatial. It can be a piece of a larger assembly or stand on its own as a self-referential element. In what ways can an object that is not spatial contribute to the design of space? Are there any ways that an object might contribute to a design other than as a part of a larger construction?

An object is the basic formal unit of architecture. Every space is defined through the assembly of pieces. The way objects are joined or distributed throughout an organizational arrangement determines function and experience. The characteristics of an object will determine the way it relates to other components, and ultimately the role it will play in containing or

delineating space. With that understanding, there is potential to design the single object through craft in order to define methods for joining and ultimately, the way it will define habitable space.

The design of the object might also play a role in the design of an organizational field. The self-referential object that does not contribute to the definition of space might serve some other function in the distribution of program. For instance, the marker might be a means of communicating

Figure 4.34. *An object is form that does not act in service to space; instead, it acts as occupant. In this example, the stacked boxes are positioned within a larger volume but do not contribute to its configuration: they are self-referential.*
STUDENT: VICTORIA TRAINO—CRITIC: KATE O'CONNOR—INSTITUTION: MARYWOOD UNIVERSITY

program, measuring space, or announcing boundaries. Or an object might be a reference point marking a place for gathering or serving as a landmark.

These uses necessitate the design of the object itself as a component of the larger design. However, the role of the object in architecture might also be as a priority for design. In architecture that places the sculpture of form over the composition of space, the entirety of the building might be thought of as an object set within the landscape of context. With this mindset, the designer seeks to create the building as an object, and the spaces it contains result from opportunities provided by form.

» *See also* Form.

Figure 4.35. Architecture, when not considered spatially, can be understood as an object within a larger environment. In this example, that understanding facilitates a study of the behavior of light around and within the object-architecture.
STUDENT: JIHYE CHOI—CRITIC: MILAGROS ZINGONI—INSTITUTION: ARIZONA STATE UNIVERSITY

PALIMPSEST

A physical reflection of a history or evolution

Built-up layers that reveal the state or condition of something through time

Generative Possibilities in Accumulating Layers

Cracks often form in the asphalt on this street. They always occur in pairs strad-dling the center. They are always the same distance apart and often run for great lengths. When the street is repaved, the cracks usually reappear within a month. The cracks are one of the many curiosities of this place.

Keen observation will reveal the source of these cracks whenever road con-struction takes place. When the workers scrape away layers of asphalt paving, older roads are uncovered. They are made of granite cobbles. In a past life, this city had extensive trolley cars running day and night. They plied up and down the streets, providing transit to a much larger population of citizens than currently live here.

The trolleys gradually faded from memory as the population declined and vehicular traffic became more convenient. The granite cobbles were covered up to make the ride smoother. The tracks remained embedded in the surface of the stones, hidden by layers of asphalt. But when they rust, they expand just a little— just enough to make their presence known through the layers of pavement that try to hide them. The palimpsest is evinced in the subtle memories of the past, brought to the surface in the form of cracks in the street.

Palimpsest is used in reference to writing on parchment, when sheets were routinely erased and reused, leaving slight visible traces of previous text. Palimpsest is also used, in a more generic way, to refer to anything that displays its origins or history. This idea of erasure and residue is relevant to architecture as a way of describing the subtle changes and transformations that buildings and built environments undergo throughout their lifespan. How can subtle changes, remnants from previous versions of built form, influence new design? The palimpsest is a record of evolution. It can provide information about a place or a building as it pertains to use, construction,

or events. These layers of history provide information that can guide design decisions. They can be the subject of research or architectural inquiry that leads to the generation of new ideas and strategies for making space.

Figure 4.36. This drawing is a palimpsest in its most literal form. It has been cre-ated with the subtle memory of other drawings layered onto the surface of the paper. In some cases, related content within a palimpsest might illustrate connec-tions or relationships that were previously unobserved. In others, unrelated content might create accidental relationships that do not actually exist. These accidental constructions, never the less, have the potential to inspire new ideas for new design.
Student: Mary Risley—Critic: Jim Sullivan—Institution: Louisiana State University

As buildings and places change they leave behind subtle traces of what they once were. Those layers are often covered or otherwise concealed. The palimpsest might refer to a wall that has been continuously reconstructed by laminating new layers of material upon its surface. A street might be composed of layers of different types of paving that correlate with different historical periods. A city itself is constantly changing, as new buildings replace old ones and as existing buildings are modified to serve new purposes. These changes become evident in the way different building types are joined or grouped. Context becomes a densely layered construct—a palimpsest.

Design inherently adds layers to the palimpsest. The new building characterizes a cultural, technological, or demographic change in a city. However, that change is recorded in the juxtaposition of the new building with the older ones that surround it. The history of a building itself is manifest when new design conforms to the limits established by a preceding iteration.

Often the design dilemma lies in discovering different ways of concealing those layers, of making the new ideas prominent. This aspect of architecture correlates to the process of erasure that is central to the making of the palimpsest. However, design also has the potential to reveal the evolution. Providing a glimpse into the origins of a design can be a communicative strategy for depicting a building's use, its connection to a place, or the design intent that drove its creation. This can impact the experience of space, with the various material layers providing different ways of interacting with one's surroundings. Identifying and responding to the layers of a palimpsest is a contextual strategy for design. In addition to the experiential possibilities, it can also be a way of designing relationships between architecture and place.

» *See also* Residue.

Figure 4.37. The palimpsest can present a way to drive process. The continuous overlay of information allows for a gradual resolution to be achieved. In this instance, the design is generated from a series of drawings overlaid onto their predecessors. Eventually the layers of the palimpsest become expanded into a relief model, as form and space emerge from ideas documented graphically. Student: Tamika Kramer—Critic: James Eckler—Institution: University of Cincinnati

Figure 4.38. In this example, the palimpsest is a more integrated aspect of the design. Layers of information are compiled, stacked, and arranged. Moments of overlap or alignment provide opportunities for the invention of space. Student: Dave Perry—Critic: James Eckler—Institution: Marywood University

PATTERN

A model or example used for imitation

A repetitive graphic composition of elements

A logic or ordering strategy for the arrangement of elements

Generative Possibilities for Making from a Template

A carpenter works in his shop, building an elaborate bench made of many interlocking pieces of wood. He carefully makes the pieces one at a time. He fits them together, decides if they are working as he would like, and modifies them accordingly. Through this process he has come up with several new ideas he hadn't thought of prior to beginning. He implements those ideas as he goes, and as a result the bench looks fairly different from the original sketches he created. He barely refers to them anymore.

He has taken a lot of time in creating this bench. It is one of a kind, and may seem to be an isolated work of creative ambition. But the carpenter has other plans for it. As carefully as he has built it, he begins taking it apart. He categorizes and documents each part and writes instructions for its reassembly. This first bench will probably never be used for sitting. It is a template to be used to create a pattern for the future production of many identical benches.

Over the next weeks the carpenter makes many components identical to those he used to create the original bench, which still lies disassembled, but organized, on a worktable to one side of the room. Before long he has created a dozen replicas of the original. They are to be arranged within another kind of pattern: the organizational grid used to guide the construction of his client's new garden.

A pattern can be useful to design and design thinking in several ways. It can be an organizational construct or a surface articulation. It can also be a model, template, or example used in a crafting process. Each of these applications of pattern relies on repetition. Pattern as organizational structure uses repetition as a way of defining areas for the placement of design elements. Pattern as surface articulation relies on a repetition of surface treatment to create an aesthetic or graphic communicative logic. Patterning

in production uses repetition in a different way: as opposed to distributing similar elements, as in the first two examples, a production pattern exists so that an element can be replicated consistently over time. Patterning in

Figure 4.39. *Patterning through repletion can be a tool for simultaneous analysis or the comparison of various aspects or characteristics of a subject. It is also useful for documentation. This example shows a figure ground pattern.* Student: Matthew Huffman—Critic: Tim Hayes—Institution: Louisiana Tech University

organization and graphics is inherent to those facets of design, but how might it be used toward the crafting of elements?

The pattern is a process-related tool, one that can ensure that multiple objects are crafted in an identical way. Identical components are often crucial to an assembly. A set of stairs might require that each tread be the same as the one before it. Or a wall might require the use of multiple identical structural components. A pattern can be used to ensure that each of these pieces is crafted with precision. In this application, design occurs in the creation of the pattern itself. The pieces produced are just the offspring of the template.

A pattern can also be used to influence an assembly by ensuring the crafted precision of a joint between objects. If a specific joint requires that two elements interlock in a specific way, it might be designed using a pattern from which the elements can be fashioned. In this use, the pattern is not guiding the creation of the entire object, but only those portions that are involved in joining it with another.

The various parts used in the production of an object might be stipulated in the design of a single pattern. Those parts can then be used in a way that allows an object or assembly to be reproduced many times. Consider the mold for a plaster cast. The various parts of the mold must interlock tightly to ensure there are no leaks. They might have to come apart so that the mold can be reused. A pattern is a product of a design process. It is the subject of iteration and tests that ensure the cast form that emerges from the mold is correctly fashioned. The pattern enables the designer to anticipate a set of production outcomes.

Figure 4.41. *This example shows the potential of patterning to influence spatial character. The patterning of screening elements presents a tool for controlling the admittance of light into a space.* STUDENT: ELIZABETH SCHWAB—CRITIC: KATE O'CONNOR—INSTITUTION: MARYWOOD UNIVERSITY

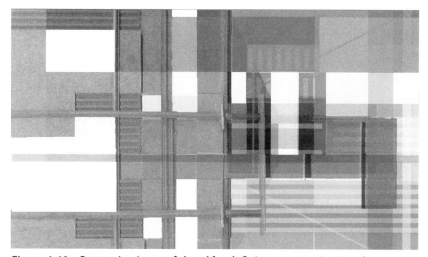

Figure 4.40. *Patterning is a useful tool for defining an organizational structure—and designing elements within it. This drawing shows an overlaid organizational diagram and a corresponding model derived from it.* STUDENT: RACHEL MOMENEE—CRITIC: JOHN HUMPHRIES—INSTITUTION: MIAMI UNIVERSITY

REPETITION

An act or instance in which something is replicated

An assembly or arrangement characterized by multiple identical or similar objects

Generative Possibilities in Replication

The workshop was a single large, rectangular space. In it, more than a dozen artisans used a variety of tools and techniques in the manufacture of furniture. The space was divided by a series of partitions. Each of these was identical. They were composed of rows of shelves stacked to a height that still permitted the workers to see over top of them. They were regularly spaced through the workshop, dividing it into equal bays.

Within these bays, different power tools were set up. The shelves of the partition walls held hand tools or maintenance equipment associated with each machine. The workers referred to each of these bays as a shop. Particular techniques were employed in each. Different kinds of furniture resulted.

The repetition of form within the workshop facilitated the function of the space by distributing storage throughout the larger space. It was used as an organizational strategy by dividing the larger space into zones associated with the various facets of the workshop program.

Repetition is a series of elements with similar characteristics. Repetition can be manifest in the arrangement of objects, spaces, or assemblies. It can also be a repeated articulation of form. How can the repetition of elements further the design goals of a project? Every element in a design cannot be unique, so is it even possible to avoid the use of repetition? Repetition can be a conscious decision to replicate parts toward a particular design goal. However, it can also be a result of a strategy for consistency in design language.

When repetition is consciously used as a design tool, it can be a vehicle in architecture for establishing and communicating many ideas. It can be used as a standard measure, module, or meter for a project. It can also be used to communicate an organizational logic for the arrangement of parts in a composition. Additionally, elements that are repeated within a design must have at least one characteristic that relates them. Repetition in this sense is a means of communicating that similarity. For instance, spaces with identical programs might share similar formal characteristics. As they are arranged in a pattern of repetition, their similar function is communicated to an occupant.

Figure 4.42. The repetition of elements defines a larger assembly. In this example, repetition is used to create the formal components used to contain space. Taking advantage of characteristics particular to repeating elements permits view and light to pass between elements. Gaps reveal design strategies and construction techniques. STUDENT: UNKNOWN, TEAM PROJECT—CRITIC: TIM HAYES—INSTITUTION: LOUISIANA TECH UNIVERSITY

Repetition can also be a tool for extending a function of built form over an area or along a line. Individual spaces or programs can be repeated in a composition, but so can the forms that house them. If a formal construct is extended through the use of repetition, it is reasonable to expect that its purpose will be extended as well. For instance, a marker that denotes a boundary might be repeated along a line. This extends the physical boundary along the length of the repetition. Or assemblies that define a space might be replicated in a way that expands that space. The purpose of that space can be understood to expand along with its container.

Despite its potency as a design tool, the overuse of repetition can result in needless or confusing redundancy. A repeated module that is not correlated with use or construction logic may serve only to complicate a space. Similarly, the repetition of elements that serves only compositional purposes rather than spatial or functional ones can be tedious to experience.

» *See also* Rhythm; Sequence.

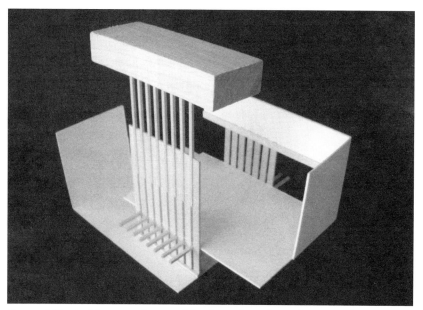

Figure 4.43. In this example, repetition is used as a formal strategy for creating boundaries and crafting joints between perpendicular planes. STUDENT: STEPHEN DOBER—CRITIC: JAMES ECKLER—INSTITUTION: UNIVERSITY OF CINCINNATI

RESIDUE

A remnant or remainder left after something has been removed or destroyed

A memory of a previously existing condition

Generative Possibilities of Memory

The building had been rebuilt time and time again. Its form evolved along with its use and along with the changing cultural norms of the town to which it belongs. At one time it was a theater with a grand spiral stair that brought people to the various tiers of seating. It had been residences, the tiers of seating filled in with apartment units. It has most recently been an architecture studio.

Each iteration left its mark. The stair remains, but it has been transformed: it is no longer as large as it once had been. Giant landings have been converted into small, enclosed spaces with just enough room to pass by them. People continue to live in some of the older residences; others are vacant. Most have been recombined into the larger studio.

The walls bear the signs of having been remade so many times. Patterns of brick differ from one section to another, marking the facade as if it were a timeline recording the history of the building, town, and people. Walking outside one encounters subtle ridges and depressions that mark the existence of the submerged, ancient foundations of a theater that was once much bigger than the current structure.

But despite the degree to which the building has changed from its original form, there remains a residual memory of each stage of its evolution. Those residual instances are reused, repurposed, or transformed. They are characteristics responded to and incorporated into the structure's current design of the structure.

Residue is any portion of something left behind after its removal. Architecture is constantly changing. Buildings are continuously modified over their lifetime. Cities are transformed continuously as new buildings are constructed, old buildings are renovated or torn down, and the street grid is modified. Each of these changes leaves behind some form of residue, even if it is subtle.

How can these remaining fragments be used to inform new ideas? What significance can they have to a design process that is dedicated to making new spaces and new forms? These remnants present many possibilities for the design process. Most architecture is, to some extent, a reinvention or transformation of a preexisting condition. These objects left behind by a building's predecessor carry with them a memory of that past structure. That memory can serve as a subject of analytical study to inform new design through the history of a place. Residual forms can also be retained and translated into components of new design; they can be charged with new program or function.

Space that responds to residual traces of architecture has the potential to emulate program, operation, or composition. This can be a strategy for making space that interacts with certain aspects of a place. Residue might be used to create new space that preserves the cultural traditions for the way people interact with one another. It might also be a way of making space that receives program in a manner typical to its area. Or it could be a design strategy that overlays new architectural objectives on old forms as a record—a reminder of what used to be. The strategy results in spaces in which the evolution of design is made apparent.

Residual objects can also present possibilities for formal composition. Elements left behind might be incorporated into new construction. They might also be used as a template for rebuilding or transforming the past condition. This strategy of formal response can be motivated by the simple desire to preserve elements of the past—a type of material, a method of construction, a general composition. It might be inspired by efficiency and the desire to reuse materials or elements. Or it can become a design objective in and of itself and lead to the creation of a memorial.

These strategies for using architectural residue employ analysis as a form of research toward the generation of new design. That research uses history as a context whose study can lead to the generation of space, form, and idea.

» *See also* Palimpsest.

SHELL

An external protective covering or enclosure

The basic form or gesture of an enclosure

Generative Possibilities of Enclosure

You stand in front of the ruined building. It is small, and a few years ago a fire destroyed it. All that remains is the outer brick shell, a few beams that had once held up the roof, and a wooden catwalk that has miraculously survived unharmed. The catwalk is along one wall at the height of what used to be the second story. The portion of the roof frame that remains intact is over that catwalk. Sunlight streams through the roof frame, casting a shadow pattern on the floor.

The building as it used to be can be understood through using clues left behind in the brick walls. Its orientation, scale, and the composition of its facade provide information regarding its previous use. It is oriented toward the street. Windows and a large opening that must have been the main door characterize the street-front facade. The size and position of the other openings in the shell correlate with the path of the sun in order to control light and temperature within the structure. These attributes are reduced to their most basic form and imprinted upon this ruin. It is as if you are looking at something that has not been completed, a building taken back to a more primitive form early in its design process.

The architectural shell is the primary element that differentiates between interior and exterior. It consists of any assembly that contributes to exterior form or the outermost boundary of a spatial construct. Unlike a skin construction, the shell can be a structural component of architecture.

Other than describing characteristics of exterior surface, facade, or general building form, what roles in the design process might the shell fill? Can it a generative tool? The shell can be an assembly of parts that define relationships and connections between interior and exterior space. It can also be more of a conceptual gesture of built form within a composition. The assembly of the shell determines many aspects of architecture. These

relationships can be developed in many ways, including through the proximity or adjacency of interior and exterior space, and by the way the shell is articulated to permit various types of access, materiality, scale, or thickness. The shell assembly presents the opportunity to design the interface between occupant and architecture as well as the transition between inside and outside. This involves determining the spatial or programmatic

Figure 4.44. The building shell consists of all elements and components that define the outer limits of the structure. It marks the boundary between inside and out. Student: Nathan Simpson—Critic: James Eckler—Institution: University of Cincinnati

relationships and using them as a determinant in the composition of the shell. For instance, a very thick shell can provide a significant ceremony of transition; a thin shell, a close association between spaces on either side of it. The shell's design can also be driven by environmental response and building performance. There are many ways that the assemblies of the building shell define space, but the shell is also the primary tool for negotiating different site forces and the spatial, programmatic, and performative demands of interior space.

Compositionally, the shell presents a profile of form. At the early stages of process, the shell might be little more than a hollow mass that is shaped in response to a possible arrangement of spaces and context.

» *See also* Skin.

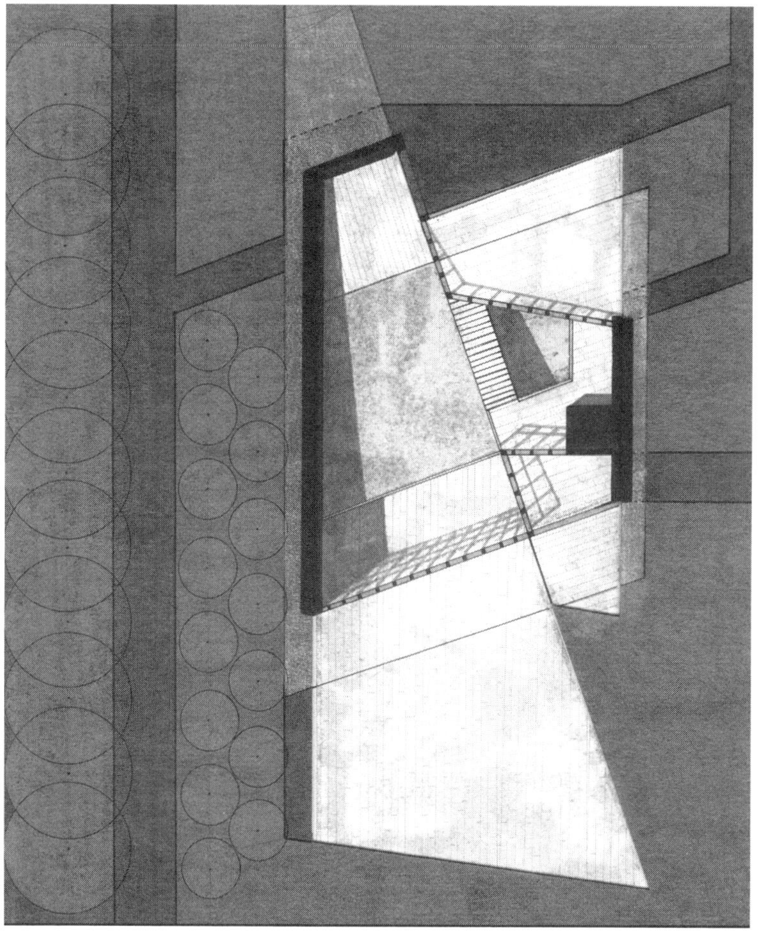

Figure 4.45. *This example shows the role the building shell plays in defining the relationships among interior and exterior spaces. The project is composed of a grouping of interior spaces surrounded by a series of exterior spaces. The shell divides the inside from the outside and determines degree of access.* STUDENT: DEREK JEROME—CRITIC: JAMES ECKLER—INSTITUTION: UNIVERSITY OF CINCINNATI

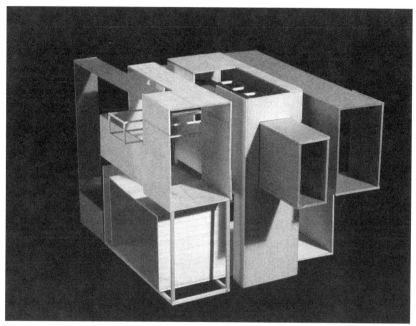

Figure 4.46. *This design is divided into zones, each with a particular spatial character. The shell contributes to that spatial character through its composition, its opacity, and its material.* STUDENT: KENNER CARMODY—CRITIC: JIM SULLIVAN—INSTITUTION: LOUISIANA STATE UNIVERSITY

SKIN

A thin outer layer adhering to a structure

A membranous component in an assembly meant to contain or protect; a component of an envelope

Generative Possibilities in Covering an Armature

A couple decides to build a tree house for their two daughters. They find a group of low-lying branches suitable for supporting the small structure. They create a frame for the platform, the base of the house. From that they build the structural supports for the walls and attach beams that span from one side to the other to support a roof. The basic form of the structure is apparent in the armature they have made. It is long and narrow because of the position of the trees branches that will be supporting it. It is also lower at one end than the other, which determines the pitch of the roof.

Once the structural frame is complete, they go about laying boards across the platform to finish the floor. They leave narrow gaps between them so the children can peer through them to the ground below. They make the roof, and build up the necessary layers to ensure it will keep the rain and snow out of the tree house.

The last step in the process is to make the skin of the outer walls. The skin needn't be structural, as it relies on the framing beneath it. It is therefore made of thin sheets of wood. The sheets are cut to create openings of different sizes. Some will be used to enter, others to look out of. The couple makes sure that the cuts correspond to abutting sheets so that the openings will wrap the corners of the little structure. Once they are all complete, they attach these sheets to the frame. Despite being thin, the skin of the tree house functions to protect the inside from the elements. It also provides a secluded space for the children.

Generally, a building skin refers to the exterior envelope; it contains and bounds interior space. It also differentiates between interior and exterior environments. More specifically, the constructed skin is a nonstructural assembly attached to a structural frame, not unlike a membrane.

How can a skin be used to define space or form? The role of a constructed skin in architectural design is similar to both a membrane and the building shell. There are, however, some distinguishing characteristics that set it apart. The skin is an outer covering, like a building shell. It is not necessarily structural, however, and it defines the entire envelope of space—as opposed to the shell, which refers only to physical construction. This allows skin to be either a descriptor of the physical container or a hypothetical edge. The skin is like a membrane, in that it relies on an interior frame for structure, but it is not necessarily characterized by thinness. It is also an

Figure 4.47. The skin creates an envelope similar to the way a shell functions. However, its formal and structural characteristics are more closely related to a membrane. This example illustrates the form created by a skin that is stretched across an underlying structure and the opportunities for access and light created by its thinness. STUDENT: CHRISTOPHER ANDERSON—CRITIC: TIM HAYES—INSTITUTION: LOUISIANA TECH UNIVERSITY

exterior container of space, whereas the membrane has a greater range of application in design.

An understanding of the specific characteristics of skin relative to other similar terms presents several possible applications to architecture. The skin can be an assembly, or a component of an assembly that defines an exterior condition. It can be thick or thin. And, depending on its formal characteristics, it might be used as a way of expressing the structure of space, or as a way to conceal it.

As a technique, skinning can be applied at a variety of scales toward different design intents. A framed structure can be skinned to form an envelope, whether it is the scale of a building or an object within it. The frame can be used to define the profile and compositional characteristics of form, and the applied skin to define the body of the object. This can be a tool for bounding space, but also for implying mass. A skin stretched across a frame to make a volume without an opening to reveal that it is hollow, can act in the same way as if it were solid. It can behave as an object that blocks your view, or forces you to move around it. It shapes space as if it were a mass. As a crafting technique, this can be applied to the design of a spatial container or to the sculpting of an object.

» *See also* Shell; Membrane.

Figure 4.48. In this example, the roof structure behaves as a skin. It is a thin membrane that defines a portion of the outer envelope. It is also given form by the structure to which it is attached. The folding of the plane has a direct impact on the interior spaces it contains. Student: Jessica Chang—Critic: Valery Augustin—Institution: University of Southern California

SURFACE

A form defined in only two dimensions

An outer boundary of a three-dimensional object or space

Generative Possibilities in Two Dimensions

I walk in and survey the banquet room. My eye moves across the ridges, valleys, and plains of articulated surface. I follow a visible seam between the materials of a wall until my view is interrupted. I am beneath the balcony level of the banquet hall. It wraps around the entire room, creating a compressed space between the entry and the larger volume of the double-height room.

In order to continue my idle observation I move out from under this balcony, and my gaze continues to track the seam upward. I reach the ceiling. It is separated by a piece of molding that connects the relatively smooth wall with the intricate coffers above. Each coffer is perfectly square, and within each there is a set of three smaller beams. They divide each coffer into four rectangular depressions. This pattern is repeated the length of the ceiling. My eye reaches the wall on the other side, which is much like the previous one, and quickly completes its circuit of the space.

The room is composed of tectonic elements. The pieces are of various dimensions and material quality. Textures vary depending on material and crafting technique. Some are smooth, while others are rough. I can see the difference in texture as light rakes across the surfaces, but I reach out and touch them anyway. Smaller components augment larger surfaces. They become ridges or create valleys as they are used to articulate the complex, undulating surface of the coffered ceiling. Each of these surfaces informs the way I perceive and interact with the forms that define space.

A surface can be thought of in two different ways: as the outer limit of any three-dimensional object, or as a conceptual construct existing in only two dimensions. Since every face of every object is a surface, how is it a subject of design? Surface can impact both the spatial and formal understanding of architecture. It can be used as a way of reading and designing boundaries or

Figure 4.49. Surface can be a material attribute. In this image, the surface characteristics of the material are used to control the form's perceived tactility. Roughness is accentuated by shadows and highlights. Additionally, surface is constructed with protrusions used as a means of articulation. STUDENT: ROBERT WHITE—CRITIC: JASON TOWERS—INSTITUTION: VALENCIA COMMUNITY COLLEGE

the limits of space. It can also be considered the one characteristic of form that engages the senses: it is the interface between person and object.

Spatial profile is an articulated surface. It is a result of three-dimensional form, but space can be considered to begin or end at the surface of the forms that define it. Articulating surface can be a way of manipulating the profile of space.

An object's surface is the only way that an individual can perceive or interact with it. It is an interface between the object and the individual. Material characteristics define surface and play a large role in determining the interaction between the object and its environment. The surface might be textured as a way of controlling the perception of space through the sense of touch. The surface of an object might be treated or positioned to receive light in a particular way; this controls the perception of space through the sense of sight.

As a conceptual construct of two dimensions, surface can serve as a compositional aid. Arranging surfaces can determine the scale of space or its position relative to others. The surface may refer to an actual object, or instead become a tool for visualizing the limits of a space at the rudimentary stages of process or analysis.

Figure 4.50. Surface can also be a formal attribute. In this example, the contours that form the surface of ground are extended by the intervening architecture. Student: Hector Garcia—Critic: Allen Watters—Institution: Valencia Community College

TECTONIC

Relating to construction, assembly, or making with parts

A process of making space through the assembly of many smaller pieces

Generative Possibilities in Assembly

A stack of boards waits on a pallet. Several more pieces are arranged on a nearby workbench. Each is long and has been handpicked to ensure it is straight. A craftsman begins joining the pieces together. They are cut to the proper length; the ends are shaped to fit together precisely. More wood is added to either side of the joints to strengthen them, and bolts are strategically placed through the entire assembly to fix the pieces in place.

This component is nearly complete. When it is done it will join other identical components arranged in a series. The pieces rise straight up from the concrete foundations. When they have reached a certain height they reach inward to meet an identical counterpart from the other side. It is as if each had been carefully folded—but in reality the bend occurs at the joint between elements. Already many of these framing elements have been erected in their proper places. They are being prepared for panels of glass that will span between them. This will make them plainly visible, giving the impression of a skeletal structure surrounding the space that is inhabited. They are frames acting to define the perimeter of the space, as well as a structural armature for formal assembly.

The craftsman watches to see if the other workers are ready for the next "rib" to be brought over. There are several groups of craftsmen working. Some, like him, are working on the outer frame of the space. Others are beginning to build the structure's mezzanine. It is to be a relatively thin plane suspended to one side of the interior space. It is a bright white panel, held aloft by a set of columns on one side and a masonry wall on the other. The masonry wall is a plane made with a notch in it; the lighter mezzanine plane will rest within that notch. The columns are another type of framing element, providing structure for the plane above them. The stair that leads to the mezzanine has not yet been begun, but it will consist of thin, overlapping planes as treads. A complex network of linear framing pieces beneath them will support it.

Figure 4.51. *Tectonics refers to the compositional components of formal assembly. It is broken down into three elements: mass (three primary dimensions), plane (two primary dimensions), and frame (one primary dimension). In this example, each of the tectonic elements is utilized in containing and configuring space.* STUDENT: STEPHANIE WILLIAMS—CRITIC: JASON TOWERS—INSTITUTION: VALENCIA COMMUNITY COLLEGE

The foundation was created first, but work still continues. It appears as a solid concrete mass protruding from the earth. This mass has been cut and carved to provide places where other components can be joined to it. Workers continue to add material to it in order to construct solid entry steps. Concrete walls are poured around the outer edge. They are about the height of the workers' knees, and they work with the framing pieces to define the edge of the space.

The frames of the outer walls, the planes of the interior mezzanine, and the massive elements of the foundation are all components of a tectonic assembly. These forms are arranged to define space. They act in service to the space they contain. An act of stereotomic making occurs at the moment the foundation is edited by carving, cutting, scoring, or any other removal of material that occurs instead of an additive, tectonic assembly of parts.

In order for space to be defined, form has to be constructed to contain it. Tectonics is a study of formal composition as it relates to the creation of, and influence on, space. Tectonics can be discussed in two ways: as it pertains to the formal elements and their assembly, and as it pertains to an act of making through assembling pieces into a unified whole.

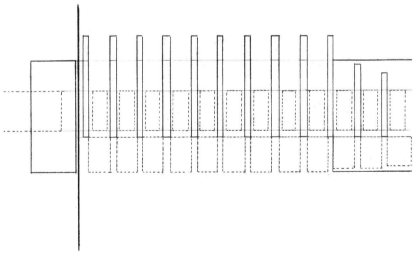

Figure 4.52. This diagram illustrates the composition of tectonic elements in a spatial construct. Student: George Faber—Critic: James Eckler—Institution: University of Cincinnati

In "The Four Elements of Architecture," Gottfried Semper defined a set of fundamental components of buildings. From these, architectural composition and formal assembly can be understood as an arrangement of masses, planes, and frames. These basic components speak to proportional and connective relationships within a composition of elements. In "An Essay on Architecture," Marc-Antoine Laugier describes a primitive hut in which one can identify mass in the base, plane in the thatching of the roof, and frame in its structure. These different elements are brought together and assembled to create architectural space.

Understanding the tectonic elements, as well as the ways in which they can be connected, can drive an understanding of the behavior of space. For instance, how can one create space using a connection between a mass and a plane? A plane and a frame? Where stereotomy seeks opportunities to create space through the carving of masses, tectonics seeks opportunities to create space through the assembly of pieces. Tectonics is the study of the object as it is crafted to receive another; it is the study of connections and physical relationships between forms; and it is a means of reading spatial intent and function through the composition of the forms that contain that space.

The Greek *tektonikós* was used to refer to anything pertaining to building—both the structure or the act. The word's root, *tékton*, meant "a builder" or, more specifically, "a carpenter," who would create things by joining. For the carpenter, tectonics pertains to the act of making rather than the composition.

The act of joining is the primary vehicle for creating space. There is also an implication that the design of space occurs, to some extent, at the scale of the joint. There are many ways to connect one piece to another, of relating one tectonic element to another. Choosing one method for the way elements are joined is a strategy for using the joint as both structure and facilitator of spatial intent.

What possibilities does one type of joint provide that another does not? A joint might be created to hold two pieces away from one another, allowing light to come into a space. Or perhaps they are held away from each other just enough to create a point of reception so another element can be incorporated into that connection. Deciding upon the best way of connecting elements is also designing the space that they are meant to define. The act of assembly can also be an act of decision making, a vehicle for the conception of space. This follows the notion that making and thinking are one and the same.

Mass

A solid body

A tectonic element characterized by having three proportionally similar dimensions

Mass is one of the four tectonic principles defined by Gottfried Semper, and one of the three of those principles that pertains exclusively to formal composition. It is grouped with plane and frame as the basic components of formal assembly.

When considered as simply a compositional element, it is defined as something with a length, width, and height that are proportionally similar to one another. It is also sometimes defined relative to other elements in an assembly. If its smaller dimension is relatively larger than the dimensions of other objects, it can be considered massive.

The mass is the one tectonic element that is correlated with stereotomy. The mass is a tool for making space in two ways: stereotomic cutting and tectonic assembly. The dimensional properties of a mass imply an ability to carve spaces into it. However, joined with other tectonic elements, it has the ability to create space as a component within a larger assembly. What roles might stereotomy and tectonics play in the creation of mass and assembly? Can both principles of making be employed in the creation of space through mass? Perhaps a massive element can be carved to create space at a larger scale, or as a way of creating a joint with other components at a smaller scale. How can this variable act of carving be implemented simultaneously?

As a primary or basic component of formal composition, the mass can play a variety of roles in the composition of space and form. Key to the discussion of tectonic elements is the way in which they are deployed to define or contain space. The mass is a product of the earth; its most direct role is that of base or plinth. However, it can be deployed in other ways, too as well:

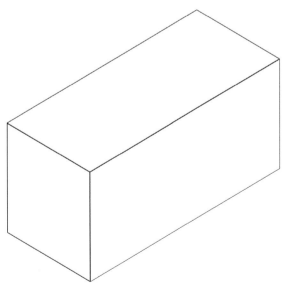

Figure 4.53. *A massive element is characterized by being proportionally similar in all three dimensions.*

Figure 4.54. *This object is considered a massive element because both the main body and the various protrusions are proportionally similar in length, width, and height. These dimensions are not identical, but they are close enough in size that none becomes compositionally prominent over the others.* STUDENT: UNKNOWN—CRITIC: JASON TOWERS—INSTITUTION: VALENCIA COMMUNITY COLLEGE

it can be used to structure or contain space, roles conventionally belonging to the other tectonic elements.

There are several possibilities associated with the conventional role of mass as the foundation of a spatial construct. To explore those possibilities is to ask, How does the base direct the way space is occupied? The surface might be carved to define zones of inhabitation, or it might be carved to receive other elements. One approach uses sterotomy as the process of making, and the other tectonic assembly. How do occupants ascend to the top of the base? How do they enter space through the massive plinth? Perhaps entry is carved into the mass, or perhaps it is attached to it.

Where base as a function of mass presents various possibilities of making relative to spatial intent, the possibilities of mass to be either a structuring device or a container of space are reliant upon both stereotomic and tectonic methods. Whether the mass is being used to hold other elements in place or to define an inhabitable niche, it will have to be carved, articulated, and joined with other components in order to define the way it is to be inhabited. The way the mass is carved or joined with other

elements in a composition determines the way occupants will perceive or interact with their surroundings; it creates an interface between form and occupant.

Plane

A tectonic element characterized by having two similar dimensions proportionally larger than the third

A surface or fieldlike condition; flat

Plane is one of the four tectonic principles defined by Gottfried Semper and one of the three of those principles that exclusively pertains to formal composition. It is grouped with mass and frame as the basic components of formal assembly.

When considered simply as a compositional element, it is defined as something whose length and width are proportionally similar to one another but whose height is proportionally smaller. Which dimension is smaller may change depending on the plane's orientation, but as long as two dimensions are similar and one is smaller, the object can be described as planar. A plane is also sometimes defined relative to other elements in an assembly. If its

Figure 4.55. The enclosure is not composed of massive elements. However, it is resting upon a mass that is notched to receive the enclosure. STUDENT: JAKE SORBER—CRITIC: KATE O'CONNOR—INSTITUTION: MARYWOOD UNIVERSITY

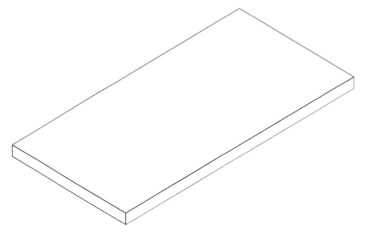

Figure 4.56. A planar element is characterized by being proportionally similar in two primary dimensions.

smaller dimension is relatively larger than the dimensions of other objects, it can also be considered massive.

The plane is a tectonic element that is reliant upon assembly to create space, as opposed to the mass, which can be a part of an assembly or make space through carving. A component of tectonic assembly, the plane is joined to the other components in different ways. A notch in two planes that permits an intersection between them describes space dispersed around that joint. A single plane folded can describe a space and a clear distinction from one side to another. A plane can sit upon a mass and inform the space that is held upon that mass, or it can defy convention and loft the mass upward, holding space beneath it. The frame can pass through the plane, hold it, or be suspended by it. The way in which one element joins another is crucial in determining the spatial condition that will result.

As a primary or basic component of formal composition, the plane can play a variety of roles in the composition of space and form. Key to the

discussion of tectonic elements is the way in which they are deployed to define or contain space. The plane's most direct role is that of barrier, partition, or skin; it is the principle tool for the containment of space. However, it can be deployed in other ways as well. It can be used to structure or base, those roles conventionally belonging to the other tectonic elements.

The conventional role of the plane is as the primary element of spatial containment. Whether it is structural or not, the plane distinguishes one side from another and defines that which is in and that which is out. The plane can be connected to other planes, or it can be deformed to define the limits of a space itself. This use underscores a wide variety of spatial and formal possibilities.

To explore those possibilities is to ask, How does the base direct the way space is occupied? The plane might be thick or thin, a notion that defines the way one might pass through it or the role it may serve in a formal composition. The plane might be opaque or translucent, rough or smooth, dull or reflective. These issues of perception define the interface that exists between occupant and space and between occupant and form. The plane may be a

Figure 4.57. Planes are the primary components that define enclosure in this project. They are assembled out of multiple stacked elements. The elements themselves are not planar, but they are used to make planar components. Student: Tamika Kramer—Critic: Karl Wallick—Institution: University of Cincinnati

Figure 4.58. In this example, planes are the primary elements used in space-containing assemblies. The elements of the assemblies are planes held in place by framing members. Student: J. D. Fajardo—Critic: Reagan King—Institution: Marywood University

membrane stretched across a frame structure, or it may be a dense structure used to hold some other element aloft. The possibilities look toward the way the plane is deployed to contain space.

How does one move through the plane to enter a space? How does one move around a plane to another region of space? Perhaps the plane is cut to allow access through, or maybe it is folded to direct movement around. Perhaps its surface is articulated to create a joint to hold other elements, making it a structure component of a formal arrangement.

Frame

An assembly of linear elements meant to bind, support, or contain

An outline or set of limits

A tectonic element characterized by having one dimension proportionally larger than the other two; linear

Frame can be used in two ways: in reference to a physical bounding or to a tectonic element. As an object or assembly that marks a boundary, the frame is an operative component of a design. As a tectonic element, the frame is a compositional component used to read or generate spatial and formal relationships.

In the most literal sense, a frame is a physical enclosure that holds or structures something within. It defines a spatial limit. Consider a window frame: an assembly of parts that form an enclosed perimeter in order to hold a pane of glass. However, a frame can facilitate spatial operation as well. In the same manner in which the window frame defines and structures a region of glass, a frame might function to define the territory of a site.

What physical element might act as a frame at the scale of site? What site condition is being framed? It might be a field of crops framed by hedgerows or a stand of trees framed by an encircling street. A frame can also be a tool to control the way space and form are perceived. When used in this way, it becomes an operative component of a design. The frame might be used as a way of delineating something of significance within a space or extending view beyond the bounds of that space. For instance, one particular entity might be framed by some element of architecture in order to emphasize its importance and incorporate it into the design of the space.

Additionally, frame is one of the four tectonic principles defined by Gottfried Semper, and one of the three of those principles that pertains exclusively to formal composition. It is grouped with mass and plane as the basic components of formal assembly.

When considered as simply a compositional element, it is defined as something with a length that is proportionally larger than either its width or height, which remain proportionally similar to one another. It is also sometimes defined relative to other elements in an assembly. If its smaller dimension is relatively larger than the dimensions of other objects, it can be considered massive, for instance.

The frame is a tectonic element reliant upon assembly to create space, as opposed to the mass, which can be a part of an assembly or make space through carving. As a component of tectonic assembly the frame is the primary means of joining or linking. It can be connected to other elements in innumerable ways; however, the relatively small section through a frame makes some joints less feasible than others. Absent structural analysis, the frame can still anticipate stability, rigidity, and the direction of force to direct its use as a compositional element in the creation of space.

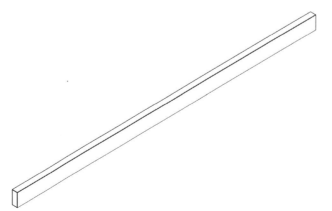

Figure 4.59.   A frame element is characterized by having one primary dimension (a linear element).

How far does it extend before it is supported by another element? How deep is it relative to its length and width? How does it connect to other elements? These issues consider the dimensional properties of the frame from the vantage of creating space. The way in which an element is supported along its space has spatial implications and should be considered in any speculative compositional study. A frame that is connected to a plane at its end will not be as rigid as one that is connected to that plane within some articulation of its surface. That articulation then has the potential to be extended to receive other components or have some other impact on spatial composition. It can be embedded within a mass, as opposed to resting on its surface. The frame can pass through the plane, hold it, or be suspended by it. The way in which one element joins another is crucial in determining the spatial condition that is going to result.

As a primary or basic component of formal composition, the frame can play a variety of roles in the composition of space and form. Key to the discussion of tectonic elements is the way in which they are deployed to define or contain space. The frame's most direct role is that of structure or delineation, or as a unit of assembly of another element.

The frame can physically structure forms as a system of support for other tectonic elements, or it can structure space and physically manifest an organizational system. Space is then defined by the frame's ability to hold elements in place or by a system of arrangement that it establishes. The frame can mark an edge or boundary without being the sole element that establishes it. Spatial arrangement or containment might be implied by the position of frames to denote an edge or boundary. The measure, the proportion, or a module of a space might be implied through the repletion of frames. Multiple frames can be accumulated to emulate the properties of other tectonic elements. The many frames that compose a screen together define space as if the assembly were a plane. Stacked frames might define space similarly to a mass. Of the tectonic elements, the frame has the greatest diversity of roles in a composition, and therefore the greatest number of possibilities for the generation of space.

Figure 4.60. In this example, frames are assembled to define the limits of space. Their direction is determined by organizational structure. They are also used to hold planar pieces inserted into the composition. STUDENT: DAN MOJSA—CRITIC: REAGAN KING—INSTITUTION: MARYWOOD UNIVERSITY

Figure 4.61. Here frames are the primary element used to describe the formal attributes of the project and to delineate between spaces. STUDENT: NICK YOUNG—CRITIC: JASON TOWERS—INSTITUTION: VALENCIA COMMUNITY COLLEGE

Stereotomy

Objects that are massive or carved as opposed to composed of many smaller components

A process of carving or sculpting space from a mass

The first portion of the word, *stereo–*, is from the Greek, meaning "solid." The second portion, *–tomy*, is also from the Greek, *–tomia* meaning "to cut" or "to make an incision." Stereotomy can be thought of as a formal state—maybe even the antithesis of tectonics. In most architectural applications it will refer to something that gives an impression of solidity or of being carved, instead of being a product of actual carving (a brick wall may be a solid mass, but it is not carved, it is assembled of many components).

Figure 4.62.   *Stereotomy refers to the editing of mass through carving. Whereas tectonic assembly refers to crafting with components, stereotomy refers to the subtractive carving away and shaping of material. In this example, both techniques are apparent. The large mass at the center is one that imitates stereotomic mass, but it is not a result of stereotomic processes. (It was digitally fabricated rather than carved). However, it functions compositionally as a stereotomic mass. Around it are tectonic assemblies defining spaces.* Student: Liu Liu—Critic: James Eckler—Institution: University of Cincinnati

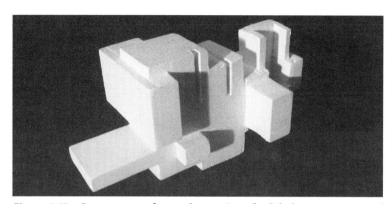

Figure 4.63.   *Stereotomy refers to the carving of solids; however, some other techniques mirror the results. In this example, casting (pouring a liquid into a mold and allowing it to harden) is used to create the mass. After the mass is removed from the mold, sterotomic techniques are applied to it. Tool marks are visible where it has been edited through carving.* Student: Unknown—Critic: Jason Towers—Institution: Valencia Community College

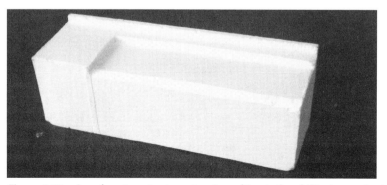

Figure 4.64.   *An advantage to stereotomic making is the ability to manipulate surface characteristics. In this example, the mass has surface textures determined by the material and craft of the mold that produced it.* Student: Laila Ammar—Critic: James Eckler—Institution: University of Cincinnati

The scale of a building would preclude the use of a single giant stone carved to produce space. However, something can be massive and articulated, and therefore sterotomic. Perhaps the use of mass, or the cut solid, could be a strategy for building configuration: building as object, carved to reveal space. Stereotomy could also be employed on a smaller scale, as objects intervening within a larger spatial system, as a way of producing a hierarchy within a space, marking a moment, directing movement, or some other spatial operation resulting from its injection into a space.

Stereotomy can also inform a process for crafting form. This act of making has the potential to frame the way a project is considered. If it is to be considered a solid carved mass, begin building as one. Eventually, the act of making will transition away from this and become an act of assembling pieces. But those initial stages, determined by a conception of space as a result of working and carving a mass, could direct the assembly of those pieces. For instance, working with cast materials like concrete or plaster implies solidity and mass within an assembly. However, casting is not carving. The process could be more about the production of impression than a study of material. What qualities do masses bring to spatial function? How does moving through a heavy mass with a passage through it differ from moving through a lighter assembly of pieces? Stereotomy as a directive of a process of making can help discover new ways of experiencing form.

VOLUME

A space or form considered in three dimensions

A quantity

Generative Possibilities in Three Dimensions

The map shows a pattern of black shapes. It is a figure-ground drawing in which each building is considered a solid volume, an object within the landscape of the city. A woman studies the map in order to find the best route to her destination. Her eyes move across the texture of black shapes until they locate her current position. She rests her finger on the spot. She continues to look across the map to find the place she wants to go. Once found she begins tracing a route from one finger to the other, following the streets that appear as gaps between rows of black rectangles. She memorizes her route and leaves.

On her way through the city, crossing street after street, she recalls an image of the map. She regards her surroundings and correlates the buildings she sees with the black shapes that symbolized them on the map. She mentally tics off buildings as she passes them to ensure she continues to walk in the right direction. The black shapes were very accurate in their depiction of the outer profile of these buildings. From those shapes, representing the proportions and scale of each structure relative to the others in the immediate vicinity, she could discern many volumetric qualities of the buildings. It seemed as if the black shapes had been extruded to create solid masses of material.

As she arrives at her destination, she walks into the building and sees the inverse of what her map would have her believe. Once inside one of those black shapes, volume takes on a different set of characteristics. Here volume is space; it is void; it is inhabitable.

Volume is the measure of three dimensions: length, width, and height. It describes properties of dimension and proportion of both space and form. There is an obvious application of volume to the measurement of architecture. Aside from that application, are there ways that an understanding of volume can inform the study of architecture or the creation of space? In as much as volume describes the physical characteristics of form, it can be a

Figure 4.65.   Volume can describe either space or form. It is a measure of three dimensions. This example is a composition of both spatial and formal volumes. Form surrounds and defines spaces. Spaces occur between forms.   Student: Ryan Simmons—Critic: Allen Watters—Institution: Valencia Community College

tool for research and inquiry. Through documenting the volumetric characteristics of a design, one might be able to make certain associations between the measure of space and its function, or between the dimensions of an object and its formal relationships with other elements of a composition. The use of volume in design is not limited to documentation, however. It has the potential to impact analysis, composition, and the creation of space.

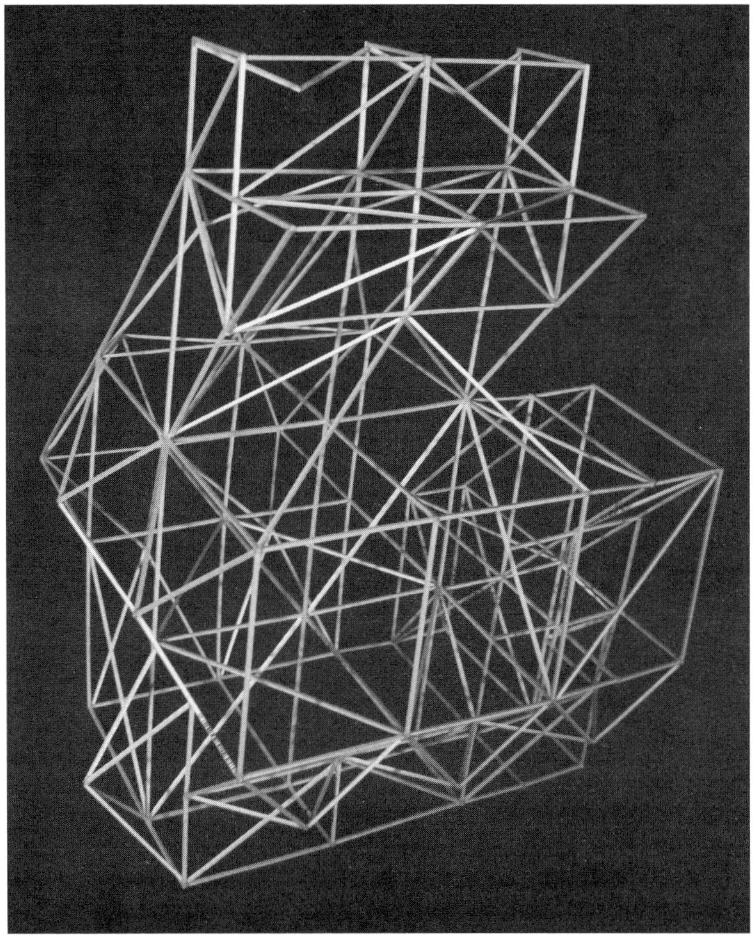

Volume must be understood in two ways: as a measure of mass, and as a measure of void. Relationships between mass and void are the primary ways of making and reading architectural space. In order to make space, there must be form to contain it. That space can be described in terms of its volumetric characteristics, but so can the formal components of the assembly used to define it.

This understanding of volume as either mass or void is manifest through different techniques for representation. The figure-ground drawing is principle among them. It is simply a mapping of filled space and open space. It marks where objects exist and the interstices that occur between them. This type of document can be used as an analytical tool. Existing conditions can then be documented to determine the compositional principles that govern their creation.

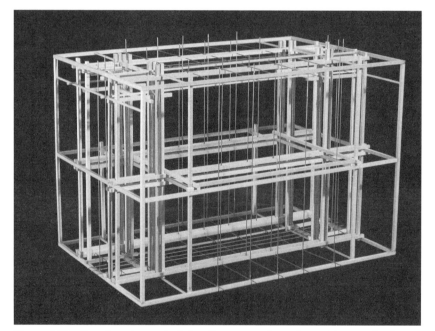

Figure 4.67. Framing elements define the parameters of an orthogonal volume. As in Figure 4.66, the volume is defined as neither spatial nor formal, but is considered absent of character or configuration. However, in addition to proportional information, this model also studies zones and hierarchies through the inclusion of elements of different size. STUDENT: TYLER FROST—CRITIC: JIM SULLIVAN— INSTITUTION: LOUISIANA STATE UNIVERSITY

Figure 4.66.   In this example, an angular volume is delineated by an outline of framing elements. Proportions are isolated to be studied absent of spatial or formal character. STUDENT: COREY KOCZARSKI—CRITIC: VALERY AUGUSTIN—INSTITUTION: UNIVERSITY OF SOUTHERN CALIFORNIA

The figure-ground drawing is also a way of determining typology based upon volumetric characteristics, such as the difference between the long narrow space and the relatively larger open space. Those typologies might then be associated with function or spatial operation. The types and roles of form can be determined based on the way they were used to create that space. The figure-ground can also be used to create space. The sculpting of objects results in the manipulation of the profile of space that exists between them. The figure-ground is a medium for these types of studies.

The crafting of space can be performed in two ways relative to volume: through the accumulation and assembly of objects to contain space, or through the subtraction of mass. The figure-ground description above refers to the manipulation of the profile as a way of constructing space.

That profile can be a construct of either tectonic assembly or of stereo-tomic carving. These two attitudes toward the construction of archi-tecture reflect a position taken by the design regarding habitation. The tectonic assembly of space makes it possible to construct volumes with a profile composed of minute variations and with a complexity necessitated by multiple connections amongpieces. The stereotomic carving presents mass as the primary medium for the making of space. Space is defined through thickness. Methods of construction can be hidden within simpler or more homogenous profiles. This idea of carving space from the mass, making large areas filled with material, is sometimes called poche space, which is the representation of mass and void through blackened volumes that more clearly illustrate the pockets of space they define.

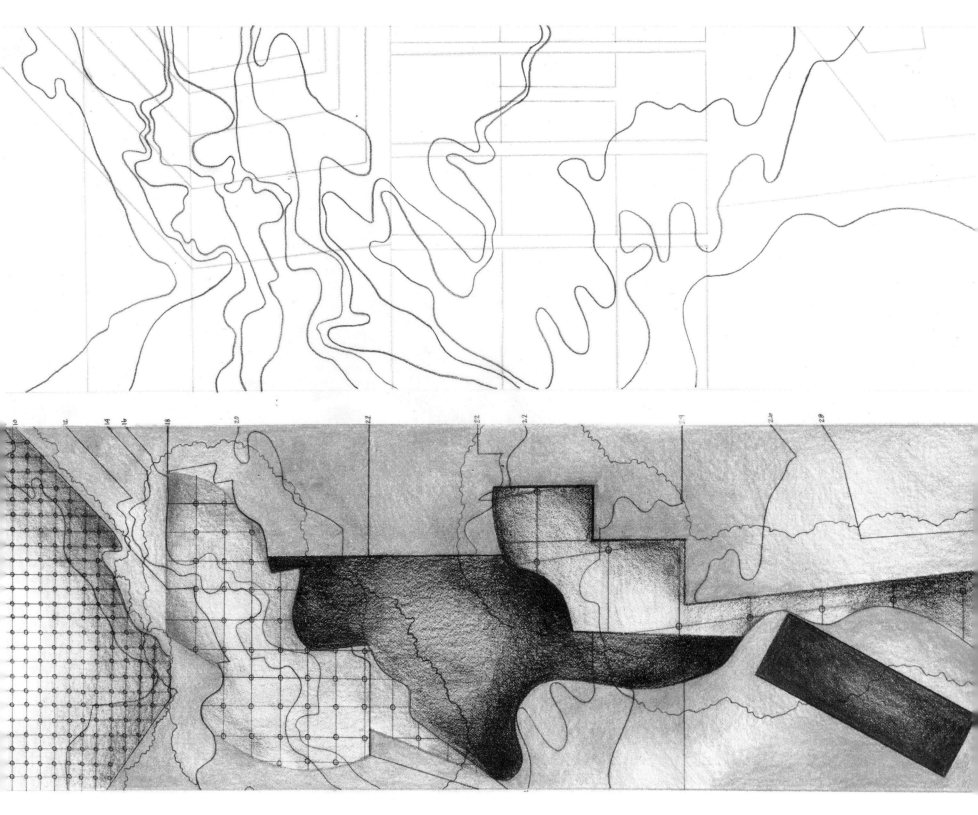

5. TERMS OF REPRESENTATION AND COMMUNICATION

AESTHETIC

Pertaining to beauty

A set of standards that governs visual communication

An established language of form, space, material, and assembly that conveys information through a consistency of application

Generative Possibilities in Appearance

I looked around as I stood in the space. There were no signs or symbols that told me this space was meant to be public. Nor were there any markings that told me that there were private spaces upstairs. But this was obviously a public space— because of its size, its height, the amount of light streaming through the glass walls, and its placement in relation to other parts of the building.

The stairs were narrow and set to the side of the space. Although they weren't physically separated from the public area, they were somewhat removed from it; they could also accommodate only one or two people at a time. These elements of the architecture made apparent my role in this place—where I was welcome, where I was not, what I was and was not to do, and so on—through the composition of space, form, material, and scale of my surroundings. Those aesthetic principles controlled my perception of the space by controlling what, and how much, I could see, hear, and touch. The designer of this space used an aesthetic to guide his or her decisions in making this space so that people could understand its purpose through intuition rather than signs or labels.

Aesthetics is commonly used to refer to elements of a subject that cause it to be beautiful or pertain to its beauty in some way. However, understanding aesthetics in a way that is less subjective can be more beneficial to a designer. The origin of the term is the Greek *aisthit,* which referred to anything pertaining to the senses. Similarly, aesthetics in an artistic discipline are principles that govern the visual communication of ideas. These principles establish some measurable criteria for success in design.

Often, the phrase *aesthetically pleasing* is used as justification for making decisions. This use of aesthetics, while technically correct, is not beneficial, in that it can not be critiqued—nor can it generate other possibilities for better solutions. It is removed from the process of thinking and making that governs design. Instead, when aesthetics is thought of as an established language for making space and form, new possibilities for a project can be discovered. In this instance an aesthetic can be used as a strategy for conception, composition, or assembly of architectural elements. As a strategy rather than a prescription, it becomes possible to test variations and make discoveries through iteration. Those discoveries can then be justified based upon a set of goals for the project rather than taste or preference.

The use of an aesthetic in architecture is unavoidable. We all have different ways of thinking about form and space, and those invariably show up in our own styles of representation. The challenge is to use that aesthetic as an advantage in design. Typically, that advantage will come through consistency in application. Subtle shifts in the application of an aesthetic strategy to different instances of making space and assembling objects can be more informative than a reinvention of the language for each component of a design. A consistent application of aesthetic language to the design process can be used to reinforce and define relationships among components. An inconsistent application of an aesthetic language can cause turn those components into isolated events that do not contribute to a larger whole.

ARCHETYPE

The first or quintessential example of something

A model to which other examples of a kind or type are compared

Generative Possibilities in Research and Precedent

The site was very large. The terrain was sloping and mostly grassy, and there were other buildings scattered around. The charge was to design a new building in this place. The first decision that the architect made was to investigate the existing buildings on the site. Most of them were completely abandoned and were going to be torn down. They had stood on that site for a long time and had been used for a variety of purposes. While investigating those buildings, the architect noted their orientation, the way they were positioned partly submerged in the ground, the materials, and construction techniques. Although the new design would be radically different in scale and program, there was a lot that could be learned from these buildings.

These structures became the archetype for the new design. They defined a pattern on which the new design could be based. The architect was able to present and justify many of the decisions that she made based on the successes of those previous structures. She was better equipped to present her ideas for making space, and placing that architecture in the site, by referencing those original structures. They gave her clients examples that they could identify with and aided in their decision-making process.

Archetypes can be useful in several ways. One way is as a kind of precedent. As in the narrative, the archetype can be used as an example that directs design decisions based upon the successes and failures of a previous design. In effect, the new design becomes a member of a type that is defined or represented by the archetype. It can be compared with that archetype as a way of measuring success. The comparison between the archetype and subsequent examples within a type does not necessarily imply architectural replication. Instead, the similarity may lie in an architectural strategy for a specific design issue (foundation type, spatial sequencing, or even something as fundamental as a spatial proportion).

How then, does this aid in the representation or communication of the ideas in a project? An archetype can be used as a design generator; at that point, it is more of a precedent than an archetype. The archetype becomes representative of a group based on some similarity. And it is that similarity that gives the archetype an ability to present information. By using an archetype as a representative of a proposed project, one can observe and test the performance of the similar aspects of the design.

Additionally, the archetype can be more generative: it may be a designed portion of a project. It could be a piece of a design that sets a standard for subsequent decisions. Perhaps it is a primary structure in a compound of smaller buildings, or a small part of a larger design that is referenced as an example used or repeated elsewhere. In this scenario it establishes a language for making, or an application of some other design strategy that can be used to build consistency within a project. The successful use of an archetype in the generation or presentation of a design will be based upon asking, What aspects of the example should be incorporated into the new design, and which should be abandoned?

» *See also* Precedent.

ARTICULATE

In common usage, refers to clear, intelligible speech or expression

Pieces or parts fitting together to create a distinct or complete element

The assembly of pieces to present a clear understanding of formal and spatial composition

To detail; an act of detailing form

Generative Possibilities of the Joint

In a museum there are three interior walls. Two are used to house display pieces, and one is left blank. The first wall is opaque and filled with many different holes, niches, and depressions. Each of these creates a small space for an object to be held in, and each object has a place—a specific hole, niche, or depression it is meant to occupy. This wall is specifically articulated to receive each object that is put on display. This is a permanent collection, so the pieces will remain in their spaces for the foreseeable future.

Parallel to that wall is the other, devoted to the display of artifacts. This wall is predominantly clear and constructed along a regular grid. The grid is apparent in the brackets that hold the glass together, the structural supports that suspend the panes above one another, and the positioning of the pieces on display. This houses various traveling collections and is articulated in a way that presents a strategic ordering system for the placement of objects. The grid is an articulated pattern meant to be a tool for the arrangement of pieces.

The third blank wall also runs parallel to the others but is closer to the entrance of the gallery space. Here people are encouraged to sit and look at the displays or wait for a rendezvous with family members. Benches to support that loitering emerge from grooves carved in its surface. Small depressions just large enough to give an individual some level of containment push into the wall surrounding those benches.

Each of these instances—the permanent display, the traveling display, and the gathering place—are articulated to communicate a purpose and to function in a particular way.

The earlier versions of the word *articulate* referred to the division of meat at the joint. Eventually it evolved into a word that speaks to the connection

Figure 5.1. Articulation is the expression of the function or characteristic of joints. Here the method for joining two materials is expressed through the groove pattern that extends beyond the linear pieces that fit within it. STUDENT: MICHELLE MAHONEY—CRITIC: JAMES ECKLER—INSTITUTION: UNIVERSITY OF CINCINNATI

of parts through joints; this is the meaning that has the most impact on design thinking.

There is an obvious duality to the term *articulate*. It is a word that describes speech and communication, while simultaneously opening up possibilities for the creation of form and space. What possibilities does the act of articulation have to guide the design form or space? How might it be a conceptual tool to frame the way one makes? There are several possibilities for the use of articulation as a design tool. It can be a vehicle for establishing relationships between forms by marking them as similar or dissimilar. It can also influence relationships between forms through physical connection or joinery.

The articulated form can be used in three different ways to impact both design of space and its inhabitation. First, articulation can be used to define a relationship between different forms. The physical qualities of one element are reflected in the designed response of the other. Second, articulation can be a formal ordering device, a system for the arrangement of objects. In this way, articulation becomes the physical manifestation of a design strategy or design intent—possibly an idea carried through from the very preliminary stages of process. Third, articulation can be a way of designing the

connection between two objects. It is manifest in the details and joints in an assembly.

In design and design process, the question is not *whether* to articulate forms and spaces but rather *how* to articulate them. Every act of making is accompanied by some means of articulation: the use of one material or another, the crafting of connections, or any other manipulation of form. However, consciously using articulation as a design tool can be both a powerful communicative device and a generative tool for exploring possibility and variation.

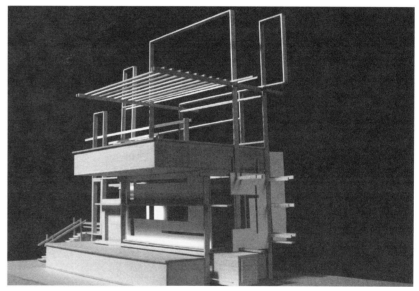

Figure 5.3. *Articulation is seen at a larger scale as it contributes to the overall construction. Consider the slots in the planar elements of the skin and the way linear elements pass through those slots. These joints provide an opportunity to build vertically. In this instance, the smallest articulations facilitate larger compositional design goals.* STUDENT: RACHEL MOMENEE—CRITIC: JOHN HUMPHRIES—INSTITUTION: MIAMI UNIVERSITY

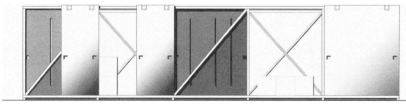

Figure 5.2. *Articulation can be points where a surface is marked or expresses details of its construction. Here those surface articulations are exaggerated by allowing light to be cast across them. This leaves shadows within the depressed articulations of the surface.* STUDENT: TROY VARNER—CRITIC: MATTHEW MINDRUP—INSTITUTION: MARYWOOD UNIVERSITY

CODE

To implement a system of symbols to communicate information regarding group, type, or characteristic

Generative Possibilities in Typology

Before drawing the space she observed the way it was used and generated a list of spatial characteristics that it exhibited. She then drew each characteristic of the space using different techniques, conventions, or media. The different techniques she employed acted as symbols representing the various characteristics of the space. Her drawing became a coded diagram.

Code is relevant both as a communicative system and as a process of representation. Both understandings are associated with a set of symbolic conventions for the representation of space, form, or idea. The communicative system refers to the convention itself and the way it is read. The process of representation refers to an act of developing a set of conventions that can be universally applied to design documents or models.

A code is a way of simplifying otherwise complex conditions. It does this by relying on an assumed understanding of the content on the part of the viewer. A color code might be applied to distinguish between programs, zones, or types. In order for the color code to communicate effectively, the audience must have a preconception of what each group is or how it works. The code will do little in communicating function or characteristic, as it is in many ways a system of naming or labeling.

A code provides a key to preconception. It marks placement, organization, or relation. It can be used to differentiate between subjects based upon type or characteristics. It can be a vehicle for embedding information of multiple scales within a document. For instance, the symbol used to mark a bridge on a map allows the scale of the region and the scale of the element to be presented simultaneously. However, it relies on your understanding of what a bridge is. It also carries no specific information about that particular bridge.

What generative design potential does coding have? At what point in the design process is it most relevant? Often coding is a useful tool in the development of the diagram or an organizational scheme. It can be used at the

beginning of a process to generate a preliminary understanding of situations that are not yet fully developed. It is also commonly used as a method of simplifying elements or ideas that have reached a highly developed state in order to make those notions more accessible to others.

There is, however, also a potential for coding to compromise a design process. Because coding relies on preconception to effectively communicate an idea, it may undermine invention. The coded diagram becomes a map of the previously developed components reconfigured. That process skips

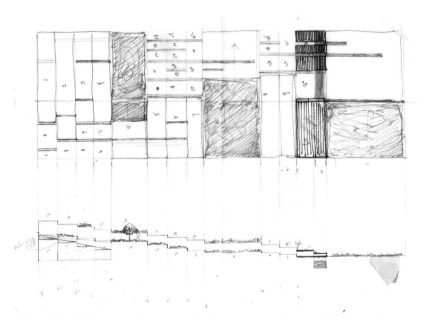

Figure 5.4. This image shows a code of measures and types of zones as they are used to compose and configure a field. STUDENT: ELIZABETH SYDNOR—CRITIC: MILAGROS ZINGONI—INSTITUTION: ARIZONA STATE UNIVERSITY

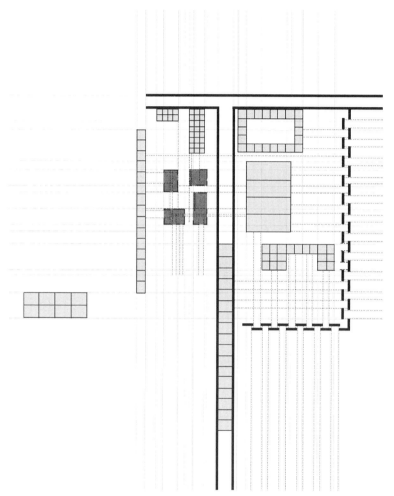

stages of thinking that permit specific design response to unique conditions or situations.

How does one prevent the code from undermining precise design intent? A simple rule of thumb is that the code should not be used to present design information, but to supplement information that is already there. If the code and legend were removed, would the design still be legible? When used as a schematic tool it should eventually be abandoned in favor of more specific design choices, and as a communicative tool it is most useful as a means of clarifying information that is already present.

Figure 5.5. In this example, symbolic convention becomes a code to illustrate the placement and function of elements within a field. Tones prevent movement, lines indicate direction and alignment, and gaps indicate thresholds. STUDENT: BRITTANY DENNING—CRITIC: JAMES ECKLER—INSTITUTION: UNIVERSITY OF CINCINNATI

COMMUNICATE

To convey information

To present or express an idea through any representational language, spoken or graphic

Generative Possibilities in Presentation

She had to present her project. She had many ideas that shaped her concept of space, form, and composition for this building. She tested and developed those ideas through models and drawings. Each of her sketches, diagrams, studies, and renderings provided information for her to draw upon. Each was a communicative device. The way she spoke was also designed. Her terms and phrasing were specifically choreographed to clearly and succinctly present her ideas. She used the models and drawings to demonstrate and reinforce the ideas about which she spoke.

To do this effectively, she arranged her work in a way that followed the sequence of her presentation. That was not the order in which she had made each piece, but was instead was based on the ways ideas related to one another from one product to the next. Design is dependent on the ability to communicate the ideas that generate it.

Much of what we do as designers is based in communication. Sometimes that communication is for the benefit of others trying to understand our projects. And sometimes that communication is for ourselves, a way of documenting ideas so that we can see if they will work. Communication's intent is to illustrate an idea, and to do that it is reliant upon a language that is either commonly understood or able to be interpreted. Architectural language has elements of both conventional and interpretive aspects. However, whether relying on commonly understood conventions or an interpreted meaning, architecture communicates in three ways: spatially, formally, and graphically.

Spatial communication can either be the portrayal of information about spatial attributes or the use of spatial attributes as a means of communicating. Space, as the primary condition of architecture, is the subject of most architectural representation. That representation seeks to illustrate spatial composition, characteristics, functions, or means of habitation. However, space can also be the medium through which information is communicated. How can space be used as a communicative medium?

The attributes of space that impact experience can also be used in a way that makes ideas regarding design intent explicit. The composition of spaces can be used to establish a hierarchy of spaces. Or the physical characteristics of space might communicate the events that are to occur within it. There are many ways that space communicates information, ranging from an illustration of the generative principles used in the conception of the architecture to the location of certain programs in a composition.

As with spatial communication, form can either be the subject of representation or its medium. As space cannot be defined without a formal device for its containment, the representation of form indicates properties of the architecture. Those properties might be issues of performance, composition, or craft. However, formal communication can also become dedicated to novelty, or making architecture that prioritizes sculptural characteristics over the spaces it contains. How can form be used as a communicative medium? Insomuch as form is a measure of spatial attributes, it communicates in the manner described above. Form can be the primary condition of architecture, depending upon the needs of the design. Architecture considered as object gives precedence to building form rather than space, and image rather than habitation. It can use form as an icon or symbol. It can use form as a physical manifestation of a generating idea, such as a metaphor. The form may also be a descendent of an initial gesture; the formal properties become a frame for design thinking through the iterations of process, from gesture to building.

Graphic communication is the documentation of volumetric properties in a flat medium. A graphic communication is one delivered through the treatment of surface. That may be a drawing or the treatment of a surface in a three-dimensional format.

» *See also* Language.

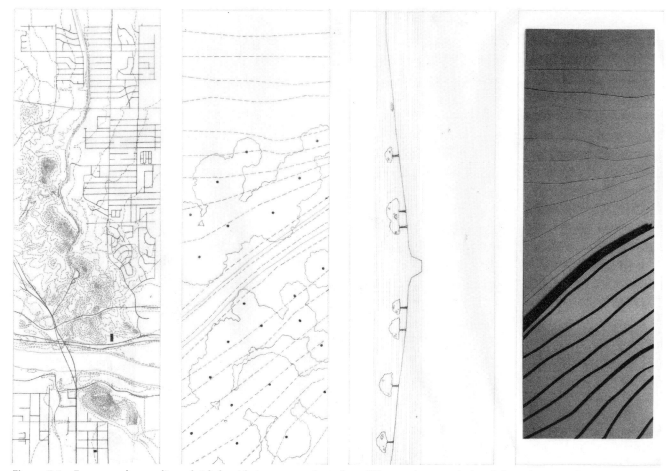

Figure 5.6. Four panels are aligned side by side to communicate four different characteristics of site: a large-scale mapping of the site, the distribution of trees across the site, the topography of the site in section, and the topography constructed in model form. Each relies on different media or means of representation to communicate information pertinent to that aspect of the study. STUDENT: ELIZABETH SYDNOR—CRITIC: MILAGROS ZINGONI—INSTITUTION: ARIZONA STATE UNIVERSITY

CONTEXT

A setting or circumstance surrounding a thing or event

The region of space that surrounds a site; the composition of the surrounds

Generative Possibilities in Reading Place

Looking at the building in its context caused several of its designers to change their minds about some of the decisions that went into making it. The model functioned perfectly well when set apart and understood on its own. However, in placing it in a context that was analogous to the project site, the team could see that it was out of place. It didn't function properly with the buildings around it. It was out of scale, towering above the other buildings in the area. It interrupted the public promenade that connected it to its surroundings. If built, this would disrupt the public space and limit commerce in the area. That would, in turn, limit the effectiveness of this project, which depended on the commerce promoted by the large social space.

They studied the context more, and the way other buildings were designed in response to the promenade. They gained information from detailed mapping studies, photographs, and physically experiencing the site. They edited their design in response and created a building more integrated with the conditions that surrounded it.

The term *context* derives is from the Latin *contextus*, meaning "to weave together"; it has become a reference to surrounding elements of a text. Architecturally, context can be understood simply as surrounding elements. Context, as a design principle, defies codification through the conventions established by this text. The architectural context is at once an organizational structure for the association of objects, a field constructed of objects, a spatial construct that is determined by program and experience, a framework for a process of response, and a testing ground for iterative study. It is a constructed form from which architectural needs and ideas can be gleaned through study and observation. The architectural intervention, assumed to be a proposed addition to this structure, can be responsive to any, or all, of these conditions.

The communicative potential of a context lies not so much in the presentation of an architectural idea but in the way it can convey conditions to which an architectural intervention might respond. In what ways might a

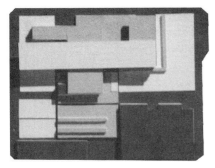 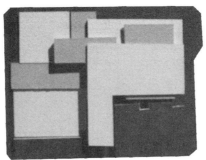 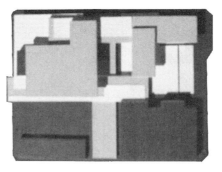 

Figure 5.7. Context is a set of surrounding conditions. It can be used as a means of gathering information in order to design an intervention that is responsive to its surroundings. In this process set, the student experiments with various configurations derived from contextual information. Aspects of the context can be used as communicative tools to obtain and relay information about a project. STUDENT: LARISSA BURLIJ—CRITIC: JAMES ECKLER—INSTITUTION: UNIVERSITY OF CINCINNATI

context communicate issues that could direct the development of a design? In what ways might it be used to relate issues of the design itself? Observing, analyzing, and documenting the context of a project can generate a large amount of information. The density of structures and their proximity to one another might give the designer information about an appropriate relationship that the new design should develop with neighboring buildings. The scale and program of surrounding structures might present information regarding the types of events the new design should hold or the way it should meet the street. Understanding the way people engage surrounding structures can provide knowledge of the relationship between public and private spaces or the way someone might move through a place in order to arrive at the new design. Understanding where and how people gather, or the type of transportation used, or the activities that take place in the civic realm, can provide information that pertains to a local culture and the ways that architecture might respond to it. There are many ways that information gleaned from a contextual condition can impact directly on the establishment of architectural intent and the generation of space and form. That information, when used as a kind of research, can then be used later as a way of justifying positions taken and decisions made with respect to space and form. It establishes a measure of success in the way a design relates to its surroundings.

Context engages the design process as a testing ground for decisions made and the spaces and forms that result from those decisions. The architectural context is a part of the design process in that it establishes a measure for the success of a design in relation to the role it plays in a larger construction. If a surrounding set of conditions is understood to be both influenced by the new design and an influence on the new design, addressing context becomes a consideration of process.

How does one address a context? Responding to the needs and characteristics of context requires analysis and testing. A process of contextual response may follow a method, such as reading and analyzing the surroundings, strategizing ways that a new design should relate to those surroundings, generating a spatial construction within the limits defined by the strategy, reanalyzing the context to account for the new addition, or reconfiguring the design in response. This process acknowledges that whatever is inserted into an existing condition can be generated by it, but it will also,

inevitably, alter its defining characteristics. That alteration should be anticipated and incorporated into the process of response in order to ensure successful relationships between context and intervention.

Context is an organizational tool in that it provides an existing structure or pattern that the design can respond to. Contextual organization occurs at a variety of scales. An urban context may be a regular grid of streets or a radial pattern around a monument. Within that larger structure there may also be smaller neighborhood organizational patterns, or even differences in the way structures within a block are organized. In what ways can an intervention respond to the existing organization of context? Relative to design intent there are three positions to take regarding organization and context: the design can perpetuate the existing organizational pattern, it can disregard that pattern and facilitate change, or it can anticipate that the pattern will change and respond to that projection.

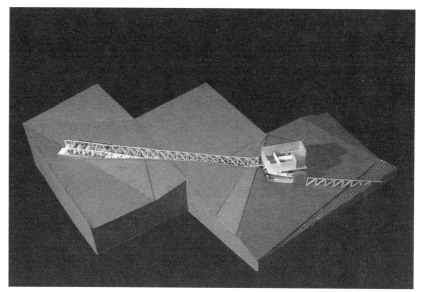

Figure 5.8. In this example, the information discovered in context pertains to the topography of a site. This information generates strategies for the ways that an intervention is to respond to the site. In this instance, extensions are embedded within the slopes of the terrain. STUDENT: HOUSTON BURNETTE—CRITIC: PETER WONG—INSTITUTION: UNIVERSITY OF NORTH CAROLINA, CHARLOTTE

Context is a principle of object and assembly in that it implies a texture at a very large scale and other physical attributes when understood at the scale of a block, street, or individual building. The physical context can be understood as a construct of masses and voids—the figure ground. When viewed at a large scale, these figure-ground relationships will define a texture that will correspond to the organizational pattern of the context. That texture is a composition that engages many other formal principles, such as hierarchy, proportion, and density. When viewed at a smaller scale—that of the block, street, or building—other physical attributes can be determined. These attributes represent a more precise understanding of the way architectural elements relate through varying types of mass and void, orientation, physical connection, proximity, material, surface types, and so on. In what ways can an intervening design respond to the physical properties of context? These issues of contextual physicality can generate design through material composition, physical connections, and formal typology. As with the organization of context, the designer can take one of three positions with regard to physical context: to perpetuate existing formal characteristics of a place, to disregard those characteristics, or to anticipate that they will change and to respond accordingly.

In what ways can context be read as an operative or experiential construction? Context can be understood as a composition of spaces and events, just as a building can. There are, for instance, both public and private spaces. There are streets dedicated to shopping and streets dedicated to manufacturing. There are movement patterns and places for rest. There are narrow passages with little light and wide passages flooded with light; contained spaces and open spaces. The operation and experience of a context can contribute to the way an intervention relates to its surroundings by controlling path, approach, points of access, or the programmatic relation between intervention and context. Entry might align with one street and not another, or an open space might join a park and give a fragment of program over to the public realm. Experience of context inevitably determines the nature of the transition between spaces exterior to the project and the spaces contained within it.

» *See also* Site; Intervene.

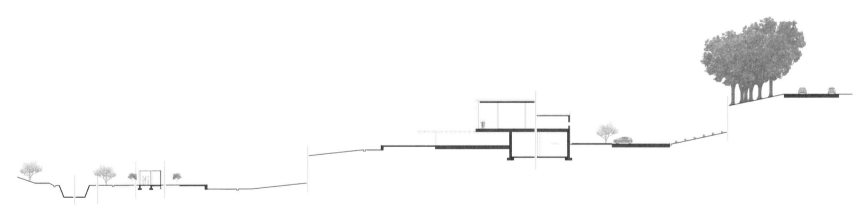

Figure 5.9. *The contextual information important to this document is topography and programs of the field. It is used to define relationships between site conditions and built form.* STUDENT: JENNIFER COLLEY—CRITIC: JAMES ECKLER—INSTITUTION: UNIVERSITY OF CINCINNATI

DEFINE

To describe the qualities or characteristics of something

To clear away an ambiguous understanding of something

To precisely delineate the formal or spatial quality of a volume

Generative Possibilities in Clarity

The project developed according to a series of studies. The first was a model that included a piece of clear material to indicate transparency. It was crudely attached to opaque pieces that enclosed a space to one side of it. The next study involved scoring lines into the surface of the transparent material to indicate structure and modulation, a way that transparency would be achieved through tectonic assembly. The third study was a model that replaced the transparent material with elaborately constructed wooden frames that indicated ways in which a transparent material would be held in place. In this last iteration, the joint between the transparent plane and the enclosing elements was considered in greater detail.

This process progressed into more modeling and drawing that indicated technical construction methods and technologies for building and structuring the housing for a piece of glass. With each iterative step, the detail became more defined. Each step also brought more conceptual definition to the role that the transparency played in the compositional strategy for the project.

In design, definition refers to a level of representational resolution that permits the identification of use or characteristics. This is communicative in that it pertains to informing, and it is related to process in that it implies development, wherein an element becomes gradually more specific in its composition and function.

Spatial definition refers to the ability to identify attributes of habitation and composition in relation to other spaces. Spatial definition might include attributes such as program, experience, or the relationship between, or link to, other spaces. How is space defined? Spatial definition is achieved when its characteristics are developed and represented to a degree that permits an intuitive understanding by an audience. However, a spatial study may also

be focused on one particular characteristic, in isolation from the others, that would typically contribute to function or the composition of the architecture. In that instance, spatial definition may be dependent only on the resolution of the characteristic in question.

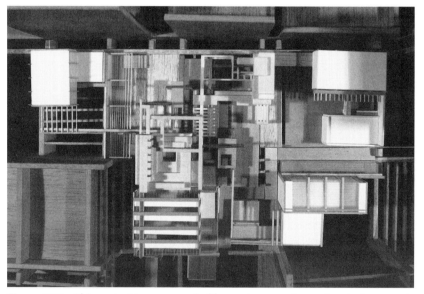

Figure 5.10. *This project is composed of four primary volumes located, approximately, in the four quadrants of this image. A specific spatial character defines each. They are distinguished by employing a slightly different graphic language for each. Although they are connected by a set of smaller interlocking spaces distributed across the field between them, their boundaries are clearly delineated by the assemblies that join the smaller constructions with the primary volumes.*
STUDENT: MICHAEL ROGOVIN—CRITIC: JAMES ECKLER—INSTITUTION: UNIVERSITY OF CINCINNATI

Formal definition refers to the composition of objects or assemblies that can be identified for the role they play in the architectural construct. Issues of formal definition may include decisions regarding material, materiality, the assembly of parts, or systems of structure or enclosure. How is form defined? Formal definition refers to a coherent articulation of elements as they contribute to the function, experience, and perception of space. Elements, when assembled, take on roles that surpass the needs of composition. Formal elements are given specific purpose for the operation of space. They are reconfigured in order to fulfill that purpose.

In either scenario, definition of space reflects a process in which space is developed beyond the limits of the gesture, the intent, or its initial conception. The ability to identify spatial characteristics is a result of specificity of form and function. There are degrees of definition: elements can be more or less defined. Definition is one aspiration of process, and with each stage the design process should bring greater definition to the characteristics of the architecture. Definition is the direct product of an evolution of the architectural idea.

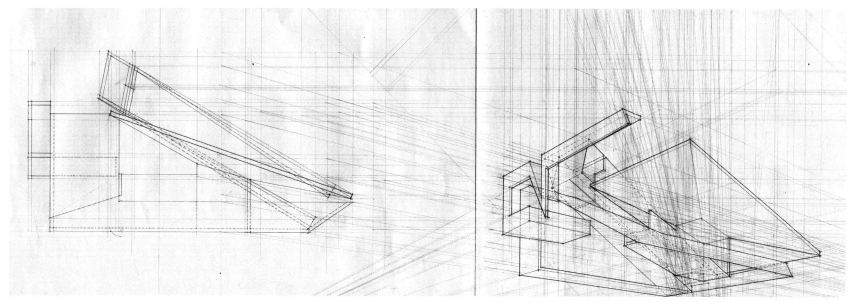

Figure 5.11. *This example shows development through craft. The drawing brings resolution to the project as it is crafted and as it is used to generate a corresponding axonometric. The gesture is made more specific by the inclusion of dimension—by thickening walls and illustrating the location of hidden elements. Spaces and assemblies become further defined as they are translated into a three-dimensional view.* STUDENT: TAN VU—CRITIC: JIM SULLIVAN—INSTITUTION: LOUISIANA STATE UNIVERSITY

DIALOGUE

In common usage, conversation between multiple people

An exchange of ideas

A system of formal or spatial response, matching, or registration; a responsive relationship between spaces or forms

Generative Possibilities in Response and Exchange

He configured the facade in response to the composition of the building across the street. The articulations of the surface he was creating aligned with those of the opposing facade. Where the existing surface jutted out, so did his design. Where windows defined a module in the previous, he continued the module in the new. He indicated levels that were roughly the same height as those in the other building. The result was continuity in scale in the way the street was framed. He presented his process as if the two opposing facades were in dialogue with each other, a relationship of interaction and response.

In common usage, a dialogue refers to the exchange of ideas, most often through conversation. However, understanding a process of spatial, formal, and organizational response as a dialogue is helpful for both the generation and communication of architectural intent. When a design is placed in relation to something existing, or if two design elements are being developed in association with each other, a dialogue exists between those elements. That dialogue is a series of responses, actions, and reactions through the process of design. It can be manifest through formal or organizational registration, joining, spatial sequencing or a myriad of other possible devices for relating components. In the process of generating a dialogue between architectural elements, design intent is developed or resolved. Similarly, explicit responsiveness between spaces or forms is often an effective tool for communicating design intent.

Space responds to other spaces in many ways. The dialogue is a method for scripting or focusing that interaction. If a new construct is created in relation to existing spaces, it can become a part of a sequence that incorporates both old and new. Its placement could redefine the relationships between existing spaces. Two spatial components developed in association

with each other may be related through interlocking, overlapping, separating, or linking. However, the dialogue between these spatial elements is dependent upon a series of responses in process. As one space develops in one way, the other is altered in turn. This system of action and response is

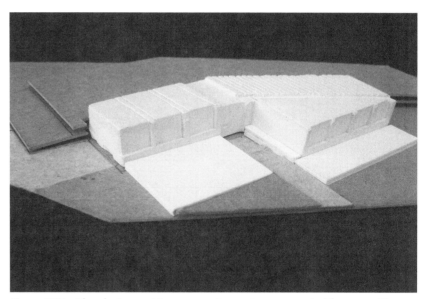

Figure 5.12. The plaster cast is a responsive gesture generated from specific characteristics of site orientation, topography, and organization. It is in dialogue with its immediate surroundings because of the mutual response that occurred throughout the process of its generation. Every time a decision that affected the configuration of the plaster cast was made, corresponding transformations of site followed, and vice versa. This continued until the site and intervention were conceived as interdependent. STUDENT: BRITTANY DENNING—CRITIC: JAMES ECKLER—INSTITUTION: UNIVERSITY OF CINCINNATI

the catalyst that will generate any of the relationships listed above, as well as any number of others. Given the characteristics of a space, or the events it is to hold, how will it be connected to those spaces around it? Once that decision is made, this process of response can drive the design of that relationship.

In addition to spatial interaction, formal and organizational dialogue can inform the relationships between elements, or facilitate the relationships between spaces. The assemblies that contain space might be the vehicles for defining one of the interactions above. Surface may be manipulated to match or correlate with a surface opposite. Components may extend and interlock with the assemblies of an associated element. An organizational strategy may be applied to architectural elements in order to facilitate a relationship or interaction through alignment, registration, proximity, or arrangement. How are spaces to relate? How might form or organization impact the generation of that interaction? The dialogue between elements is usually carried out in a multitude of ways. Forms are created, and other forms are altered to receive them. Elements are positioned, and others are repositioned in order to correlate the components. This generative exercise scripts the interaction between spaces. The clarity of dialogue in space, form, or organization can communicate strategy.

Figure 5.13. *These two projects were designed simultaneously. Although they were independent of each other, they were developed on a single site. As a result, each was produced in response to developments made in the other. This created a kind of formal and spatial dialogue that correlated the projects.* Students: Jessica Helmer and Chad Gleason—Critic: James Eckler—Institution: University of Cincinnati

GRAPHIC

Unmistakable or unedited imagery

Pertaining to the use of writing, drawing, or other two-dimensional forms of communication

Generative Possibilities in Drawing

In developing her project, she needed to make a series of diagrams. Each was drawn and therefore required her to create a set of drawing conventions so they could be read and interpreted. She used lines of varying thickness, patches of color, and symbols. The conventions she developed determined the meaning that would be attached to the different parts of her diagrams. Colors that overlapped would indicate one piece of information, while a separation would indicate another. Hierarchy was established through the thickness of lines and area of tones. Each symbol she used referred to a specific element of study. The whole of these conventions comprised a graphic language used to read and understand her drawings. The language was consistent from one diagram to the next.

The term *graphic* originally referred to writing or drawing using either pencil or pen. It has since come to refer to any two-dimensional medium of representation. For the architect, that includes any drawings, diagrams, or sketches and can be created either digitally or by hand. However, graphic communication can reflect different intentions on the part of the designer in relation to both presentation and design process. Graphic communication is dependent upon language in order to portray information regarding three-dimensional space or form. That graphic language can be conventional or interpretive.

A language of conventions relies on commonly accepted symbols that indicate information. This works because there is a standard system that governs symbolic meaning. That system may exist as a key that is used to interpret that specific document, or a system of representation determined by the discipline that maintains consistency in documenting and interpreting information. How does a conventional graphic language impact the design process? Because it is universally accessible, this type of graphic representation is often used as a presentation device. However, there are systems of

drawing conventions that are valuable to the invention of space as well. For instance, line weight, as a designator of hierarchy is often necessary even at the beginning stages of the design process.

An interpretive graphic language is one that is driven by composition rather than standardized drawing conventions. Information is received through the interpretation of meaning. Elements are composed in a particular way that causes an audience to assume the content of the image. If an

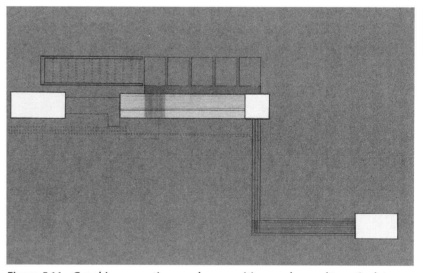

Figure 5.14.   Graphic conventions and composition can be used to articulate the characteristics of three-dimensional space and form. Line weight, contrast, line type, and consistency in representation communicate relationships and qualities of space. Combined, these graphic techniques comprise a graphic language, one that relies on the consistency of conventions to communicate ideas.   STUDENT: LAUREN WHITEHURST—CRITIC: JAMES ECKLER—INSTITUTION: UNIVERSITY OF CINCINNATI

interpretive graphic language is subjective then how can it be used to accurately represent architectural intent? The interpretive graphic language is often one of abstraction. Both abstraction and interpretation can be used as tools for discovery in addition to communication. Choosing to represent an architectural idea in a way that is more implicit than explicit presents greater opportunities for discovery and transformation.

Although graphic representation is two-dimensional, it can play a role in the development of three-dimensional volumes. A graphic language can be a means of the treating surfaces that delineate volume, or a way of articulating surface in order to inform the way space is used or perceived. However, a space or form that has a "graphic quality" may be an indication that certain aspects of the design are unresolved. In this instance referring to a design as being 'graphic' can imply that volumetric elements are not contributing to the definition of space. This may be the case if elements are assembled in a way that denotes pattern more than a function. For instance, one might assemble frames to define a surface. One approach might be to create a surface of bands (graphic pattern); another might be to make louvers (light filter).

» *See also* Language.

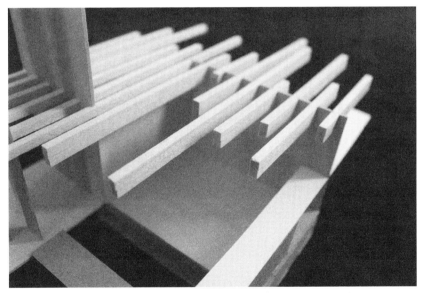

Figure 5.15. *The same principles that govern graphic communication can sometimes be applied to formal assembly. Repetition, rhythm, orientation, and hierarchy can determine the role a particular piece plays in the composition and operation of an assembly.* STUDENT: JAKE SORBER—CRITIC: KATE O'CONNOR—INSTITUTION: MARYWOOD UNIVERSITY

Figure 5.16. *Because of the conventions that permit them to be interpreted as three-dimensional space and form, graphic principles can also be valuable tools in a design process. They can be interpreted and translated into a physical object, component, or assembly. In this example, an analytical diagram composed graphically is transformed into a physical construct. Remnants of the graphic generator are left as markings or articulations of surface.* STUDENT: NIKA BANAPOUR—CRITIC: JOHN MAZE—INSTITUTION: UNIVERSITY OF FLORIDA

ICON

A representation based on characteristic similarity

A type of semiotic element; a type of sign that embodies certain characteristics of the subject it represents

One member of a larger group that is a quintessential example of the elements of that group

Generative Possibilities in Semiotics

She was making a model that detailed a wall assembly. She was building the model at a small scale, so she could not include every piece that would be required of a full-scale assembly. She was using glue and small wooden members, as opposed to the bolts, screws, and steel structure that would be used in the full-scale construction. In order to effectively represent the assembly and the types of joints involved, she chose to include only the most prominent members. They were scaled down to the appropriate size for the model and joined using glue. It represented the would-be full-scale construction as an icon. The representation was based upon organizational and formal similarity rather than assigned meaning.

The origins of the term *icon* lie in the Latin *¥cÿn* and the Greek *eikÿn*, which referenced a likeness or image. Currently, the word refers to an element that represents another through similar characteristics. However, the latest incarnation of the word in the English language establishes it as a facet of linguistic theory called semiotics. In *Peirce on Signs: Writings on Semiotic*, Charles Sanders Peirce refers to the icon, along with symbol and index, as a type of sign. An icon is distinguished from a symbol or an index because it relies on an interpretive similarity to the subject it represents: a curved arrow on a road sign signifying a U-turn, or a drawn line signifying an edge, for example. Without the similarity between the arcing arrow and the turning vehicle or the proportions of the line and the edge of a form, these icons would merely be marks or patterns without communicative value.

The role of an icon within a system of representation lies in its ability to exemplify the characteristics of a group or information set. Iconic representation may be an explicit figural documentation of some spatial or formal condition that acts as a pattern, template, or strategy for the way other instances

are interpreted. The designed detail of a connection between parts may be iconic in that it establishes a language of assembly that is applied to other instances in a design. The gestural form that does not yet contain space but

Figure 5.17. This construct is an exploration of several compositional and operative conditions. Organization is studied through the distribution of pieces. Filtering is explored by passing light through the gaps between uprights. It does not define a space, nor is there a formal logic to which it adheres. Instead it seeks to create those characteristics without applying them to a spatial or formal intent. It is an icon representing the characteristics described. It is not a symbol because it shares characteristics with what it represents. STUDENT: VICTORIA TRAINO—CRITIC: KATE O'CONNOR—INSTITUTION: MARYWOOD UNIVERSITY

alludes to it can be an icon of a spatial or formal compositional pattern. A primary space or form might be iconic in that it indicates a function or orientation of a project.

Additionally, projects themselves are often referred to as iconic because they represent a quintessential example of some architectural type, use, conception, or history. Here the icon is understood as a precedent pattern to emulate or a contextual condition to which a design should respond. How does one use an iconic architecture as a precedent? How might a designer respond to an existing architectural icon? Studying examples of successful design is important to the advancement of new design. Icons are most often established as the most successful examples of one design or another. Using them as a subject of study to influence the way a new project is being developed can be a valuable exercise. That exercise can also aid in a process of contextual response. Understanding the way that an iconic structure informs the regions around it will better enable the designer to intervene within those regions—to define a particular relationship with whatever iconic structure represents a context.

» *See also* Symbol.

LANGUAGE

A medium for the communication of thoughts

A standard set of rules established for the communication of thoughts or ideas; a system for communication

Consistency of representation; guides for making or drawing that facilitate a communicative quality

Generative Possibilities in Representing and Communicating Ideas

In front of her were two drawings she had created. One was made at the beginning of the design process; the other was the most recent documentation of her project. The first was a diagram; the second, a section.

The diagram combined blocks of tone with lines of varying thickness. In it, composition was used to imply certain relationships among elements. The

graphic language in this drawing reduced elements to generic compositional components to test these relationships.

In contrast, the section relies upon the conventions for drafting in order to communicate the design. The elements that were general in the diagram are now made specific. Although the section drawing is still representational, it

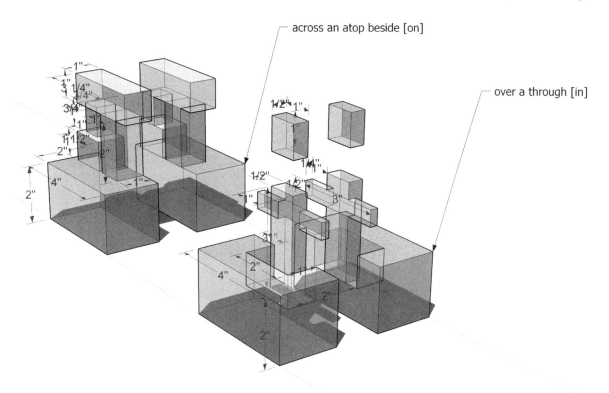

across an atop beside [on]

over a through [in]

Figure 5.18. *Like this text itself, this example illustrates the potential of language to generate design. In it, the student uses prepositional statements as compositional generators. The prepositions define a set of criteria that determine one object's relationship to another. When combined, the resultant assembly speaks to formal logic.* STUDENT: CONOR BRADY—CRITIC: JOHN HUMPHRIES—INSTITUTION: UNIVERSITY OF CINCINNATI

explicitly indicates unequivocal information about the project. There is no need for interpretation of such a drawing. Whereas the diagrammatic language seeks to discover qualities of architecture that could be used in the design, the conventional graphic language seeks to communicate qualities of architecture already decided upon.

Language is the medium of communication. Language is commonly understood as primarily written or spoken. However, with communication as the singular objective of language, our understanding of what defines language can be broadened. Different languages are governed by different rules in the communication of an idea. There are many inherently linguistic aspects of architecture; it is reliant upon communication to direct function and inhabitation. Architecture is an inhabited construct; the implication of inhabitation is experience. The narrative of space—a scripted experience—is one written in spatial characteristics and the forms that generate them. The language of architecture is manifested graphically, formally, and tectonically in the way space is perceived and generated.

The language of architecture directs use and interaction. It determines the way space is read. Architectural language is comprised of those elements that allow an occupant to understand use or type intuitively. How does one know that a space is public or private, that an entrance is primary or not, that a space is used for staying or moving through? All of the elements that generate that impression of space are components of an architectural language. Identifying and responding to those elements is an act of reading space and form.

Language is also useful as a guide toward invention. As a communicative device, language can also play a role in making and representing throughout a process. In this regard architectural language can be divided into three categories: graphic, formal, and tectonic. Each refers to convention, a consistency that controls the way design is read and documented. Drawings will employ graphic conventions to consistently communicate spatial ideas. The way hierarchy is established, types of lines are used, or what patterns or tones indicate will be consistent from one drawing to another.

What spatial information is being presented at different stages in the process and how does that impact the graphics used to convey that

information? Similarly, formal conventions will work toward communicating gestures and schemes for the arrangement of, and relation between, spaces. In what ways does form contribute to the understanding of space? How is it represented at different stages of the design process? Tectonic language defines a convention for the way elements are joined or made. What kinds of joint will best contribute to the formation of space in a project? How might that type of joint be adapted to different situations within a project? Language, as a process-related device, can work toward establishing a strategy for thinking, making, and representing spatial ideas.

Explicit Language

That which is clearly expressed without possibility of interpretation

That which is directly communicated without ambiguity or implication

A clearly defined and resolved formal or spatial design

Something that is explicit communicates an idea, function, or characteristic clearly and without room for interpretation. It is generally a point of resolution that results from many iterative stages of development. It is also usually a literal representation rather than a gesture or some other abstraction.

A design that explicitly represents space and intent leaves little room for further development. Explicit representation is a reflection of a stopping point. It can communicate precise information, but if that information doesn't lead to advancement, how can explicit representation be generative? When thought of as a "complete" design, explicit representation has little to no impact upon process or development. However, it can be a tool for testing variations in a precise and measurable way. If ideas are becoming resolved and are manifest literally, there can be an accurate measure of how that designed space or form will operate within a design. That measure can then impact decision making. Depending upon the outcomes of testing, the explicit design can drive one to redevelop a previous iteration, thereby changing the outcome. It can redirect process in a cyclical way as long as it is used as tool for inquiry rather than one that is exclusively communicative.

Explicit representation can also reflect varying degrees of resolution across the scope of a design. Fragments of an element may be well resolved and explicitly represented, whereas other components of that element may still be gestural, speculative, or implicit. This variance is helpful: the explicit components can lend more information to the implicit ones. This is one process-driven method for testing precise variables. The resolved components provide a standard, immutable armature against which the speculative can develop. The resolved pieces become a driver for the development of the unresolved pieces.

There is a cyclical implication in this type of process as well. As the speculative becomes more developed, it has more capacity to challenge what was once thought of as resolved. The definition of the different parts will gradually converge as they are reconfigured relative to one another.

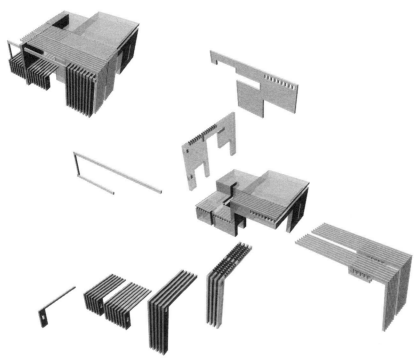

Figure 5.19. *This exploded axonometric details components and the way they are joined together in the final assembly. Because the information in the drawing requires explicit communication, critical points of the various components of the assembly are aligned. Through that alignment, one can see points of connection and the type of joint being used.* STUDENT: STEPHEN DOBER—CRITIC: JAMES ECKLER—INSTITUTION: UNIVERSITY OF CINCINNATI

Implicit Language

Expression that relies upon interpretation

That which is indirectly communicated through implied meanings

Information held in the nature of something rather than specifically expressed

An unresolved form or space that is understood for the possibilities it presents rather than its existing qualities

Implicit information is the basis of generative representation. Implicit information is contained within the drawings and models that, through rudimentary or unresolved language, speculate toward the possibilities of design. Implied information is important to the discovery and inquiry of spatial intent. The diagram, the study, the gesture: each are tools for representing implicit information. Discovery is an unexpected product of process.

Implicit elements have the ability to foster discovery through interpretation of spatial condition, composition, or arrangement. This discovery is a testing ground and a facilitator for the advancement of design. As a testing ground

Figure 5.20. *Implicit information is often used in generative documents like this one. Broad, nonspecific compositional relationships are created. The hybridization of various media presents opportunities for interpretation that can be starting points for future design iterations.* STUDENT: RENÉE MARTIN—CRITIC: JOHN HUMPHRIES—INSTITUTION: MIAMI UNIVERSITY

where interpreted information can become recast or reconfigured through iteration, implicit representation becomes a tool for inquiry. The implicit representation of architectural intent enables the designer to generate questions that guide exploration. Questions drive the creation of variants that satisfy design intent, and those variants can be tested relative to other issues being explored.

What formats of representation are implicit? At what stage in the process do they most impact design thinking? Implicit representation is typically based more on content than format, in that the subject being represented is more generic than specific, more of a generator than a documentation. Any component that implies spatial properties without specifying them is an implicit representation of design intent.

Implicit information is primarily produced in the initial stages of a process. It is a frame for developing or exploring a spatial concept. As a foundation for design development through the course of multiple iterations, the generic becomes more resolved; the implicit approaches the explicit. However, remnants of the initial implicit spaces, patterns, or forms can linger. The implicit representation might be used to generate an architectural language that translates through each iterative stage. That language may be one of formal composition, a strategy for joint-making, or a pattern of spatial composition. Can these residual instances be used to further design intent? What impact might they have on spatial conditions?

Implicit information can also be an integral component to a resolved architecture. It may be comprised of elements that recall the generative concepts or strategies for the architecture. It might be a spatial configuration references some other analogous condition. Or it could be embodied in the details that define space and direct the ways in which an occupant is supposed to interact with it.

» *See also* Aesthetic.

MANIFEST

To show or make plainly visible

To articulate in a specific way

Generative Possibilities in the Physical Embodiment of Concept

He did the drawings over and over again. Each was well crafted, but none was effective in communicating his ideas about his project. He continued to employ different techniques and variations of media application. As he progressed through each drawing, his ideas became clearer, and his project more sophisticated because of it, but none of the drawings adequately reflected the underlying concept.

He continued to draw. Finally, the last set embodied all of the relevant ideas used to generate his project. Each detail communicated strategies for assembly. The media and composition reflected principles of spatial organization. Every idea that he had for this project was manifested in this last set of drawings. The set was a valuable communicative tool for the presentation of his project.

A manifestation is something that is evident in or about space. When architectural intent is manifest in space, the spatial construct becomes a clearly understood embodiment of that concept. The manifestation of an idea in architectural form is inherently communicative in that it causes the idea to be accessible to an occupant. It can also be understood as a communicative tool in representational media. Certain media or formats lend themselves to the communication of certain types of information, which may cause an idea to be manifest in one type of presentation and not in another. Choosing the correct media and format is important to the clarity of communication.

In what ways can an idea be made apparent in architecture? Compositional devices are the tools that designers have at their disposal in order to make concept or intent manifest in space. Articulating a containing form, arranging spaces, or defining proportions can impart an intuitive understanding of how a space is used, how it is to be experienced, or the generative principles that spurred its conception. Compositional principles can configure space and form in order to illustrate design intent.

The notion that an idea can be physically embodied in some aspect of architecture implies a level of translation or transformation. Translation occurs as an idea discovered while working in a graphic format is applied to the physical construction of a space. The idea, as information, is translated from a process document into a constructed format. Transformation is a result of spatial or formal manipulation toward the manifestation of concept. These issues impact design process as they result from and encourage iteration.

METAPHOR

Speech normally used in reference to one subject instead being used to reference another

An invented correlation between two seemingly unlike subjects

The presentation of one subject to symbolically represent another in spoken, graphic, or formal modes of communication

Generative Possibilities of Symbolism

The project concept was difficult to explain. Perhaps it was difficult to understand the way architecture could function according to the concept presented. The catalyst for her thought process in developing the project was the structure of a leaf. She was fascinated with the way the veins of the leaf were intertwined and became smaller as they extended away from the stem. She also considered the thin membrane stretched between the veins. Her ideas for organizing her project were based on the leaf's structure.

She decided to use that same simple idea to present her building design. The complex and sometimes convoluted organizational scheme of her building was more easily understood when she compared it to the leaf. The leaf is commonly understood, a simplified version of her architectural creation. The building worked like a leaf; this was the metaphor she had used from the beginning. And now, she used it as a key so that the panel offering critique could better understand her project.

Coming from the Latin *metaphora,* meaning "a transfer of meaning from one word to another," a metaphor is a communicative device whereby the characteristics of a subject are presented through the description of something different. It is a way of generating complex spatial, formal, and experiential conditions in architecture at the beginning phases of the design process. It is also an effective method for the communication of those complexities by giving an audience a comparable condition that it already understands. Metaphor can be a generative tool as well as a communicative tool for uncommon architectural notions. It can also be an aid in understanding a unique condition by using a commonly understood condition as an analogue.

As a conceptual catalyst, the metaphor is an examination of an unrelated subject in order to communicate ideas of space, form, or organization. What subjects of study translate to architecture? How does one look for a subject from which architectural information or inspiration can be derived? The metaphor comes with a versatility of application. Any association between the architectural outcome and the generating metaphor is contrived. Therefore, there are no inappropriate subjects to study and translate into architectural information.

Because the metaphor is based on a subject the designer knows well, it is often an effective tool, eliciting characteristic similarities between its properties and a goal of the design. A space may be a "sponge" in the way it permits continuous access from all sides, thereby mimicking absorption. An assembly may be a "sponge" in that it is porous. A pattern of movement may replicate certain characteristics of a biological circulatory system, or it may be a river flowing in some direction. The metaphor becomes a key for generating the architectural idea. It simplifies complex notions so that they may be more easily developed through process.

As a generator or communicative device, the metaphor can be a valuable asset to a design. However, it is not an outcome or intent of design. There comes a time in the process of developing architectural conditions when the metaphor will lose relevance. Translating information from one subject of study to another results in transformation, which will cause the inevitable deviation of the architectural outcome from its metaphoric generator. This is a result of the design process guiding decisions relative to space, form, and organization independent of the characteristics of the metaphor. As the design intent becomes more resolved, the subject of the metaphor will once again be unrelated. If the priority of the design lies in the preservation of metaphoric characteristics, the intent becomes semantic rather than architectural.

NARRATIVE

A story, or related to storytelling

A description of an event or environment as if perceived or experienced as a story

A perceptual or experiential function of space

Generative Possibilities in Storytelling

Instead of presenting his projects in technical detail, he found that explaining them as if telling a story was more effective. It enabled his clients to better understand his ideas. He explained their projects as if he were guiding them through their new house. He told them what they would encounter and the experiences they would have. He described the feel of the door handle, the light washing into the space from skylights overhead. He talked about the size and what they could do inside. He spoke to them about the way the materials looked and felt. To him, his projects are a type of story in which every occupant becomes a character within the environment he creates.

A narrative is the communication of experience. When a story is told or read, a character's experience is understood through a description of events. Experience is described through the objects with which the character interacts, through the way they look and feel. It is described through event—through what a character does. The place of the event is described as well as the reason it takes place. Experience is relayed through descriptions of an environment with which an audience can identify. These notions of experience and event can be used to generate architectural intent and the composition of space. And just as in a story, intent can be communicated through the characteristics of space and form.

Although desired experience or event can be conceptual generators for spatial composition, the concept itself can be communicated through narrative. If narrative is understood as a sequence of experiences and events, then the architectural narrative is one in which inhabitation is defined through order, perception, interface, and function. How can the architectural narrative be a communicative tool? In what ways can it generate ideas for space? The narrative can illustrate spatial intent through the description of habitation: what occupants do when they enter a space, how they move through space, what they see, hear, or touch. The architectural narrative gives an audience insight into the way spaces are conceived relative to one another from a vantage of habitation. It enables an audience to understand the architecture as if it were to occupy it.

In what format is an architectural narrative communicated? The difference between a literary narrative and an architectural narrative lies in their subject. Both pertain to the experiences of individuals and the actions they take. However, the architectural narrative places priority on the ability of space and form to facilitate those experiences and actions. It can be communicated through a wide array of formats and media, rather than relying strictly on writing or speaking. A drawing that denotes space as a composite of material and light as a means of providing a place for an event describes a portion of the architectural narrative. The arrangement of spaces within a structure speaks to ordering a sequence of experiences and events. The architectural narrative can be communicated in any way that imparts information on the relationship between space and form.

Narrative can be a driver for choreographing the occupation of space. Space can be conceived using a desire to structure particular experiences and the events they facilitate. Understanding the order in which one should encounter certain spaces or perform certain tasks can outline a set of decisions regarding experience and the way that the architecture can create that experience. As a process tool, narrative can be employed as a way of using spatial and formal composition to control the various experiences within a set of spaces.

» *See also* Experience; Event.

PROPORTION

A comparative relationship between parts

The relative dimensions of an object

Generative Possibilities in Relative Size

Placing a scale figure into the drawing was one of the tools she used in order to communicate the proportion of the space she was designing relative to a typically sized person. There were other cues that helped establish a scale that could be read in the drawing without referring to the small legend at the corner of the page. She included small elements, immediately recognizable and with understood dimensions: a set of steps, a handrail, and an articulated surface. These smaller details offered a greater understanding of the proportion of the larger space. The range in size from small detail to large space provided a visual understanding of proportion—a way of comparing. The scale figure only served to reinforce the proportional information already inherent in the section drawing.

Proportion refers to a comparison of relative size or quantity. This comparative measure can be a communicative vehicle for understanding either spatial or formal relationships. It can also be a way of defining or classifying volume.

The communicative aspect of this principle is that dimensional proportion between spaces or forms is an indicator of the relationships between them. Hierarchy may be communicated by one element being proportionally larger or more prominent than another. Program may be communicated using the same tool. The way proportionally different spaces or forms intersect provides evidence for the way they function. Is one a primary space or a support space? Is the proportional difference marking a location of some spatial function? A transition between spaces? An extension of the larger volume? Proportion is one communicative layer of information that aids in presenting information regarding spatial relationship, function, and hierarchy.

Proportion is also a useful tool for defining volume, either formal or spatial. In reference to tectonic classification, proportion is used to determine the difference between masses, planes, and frames. The dimensional proportion

between length, width, and height will determine the type of object it is. Similarly, spaces can be classified as horizontal or vertical depending upon dimensional proportion. Spatial proportion might also determine, or be

Figure 5.21. Proportion measures the relative dimensions of elements. This drawing is a study of the proportion of each component of an arch relative to the others. STUDENT: MELODY PRESCOTT—CRITIC: JIM SULLIVAN—INSTITUTION: LOUISIANA STATE UNIVERSITY

determined by, the event that is to occur within. Interaction between an occupant and the built form that defines a space is also largely dependent upon proportion. Is a space compressed, extended, tall, or short? What can be touched, and what is out of reach?

Proportion can also refer to the density of a group of objects. This kind of proportion does not reference dimension as much as quantity. One group can have proportionally more of something than another. This has implications on design, as it differentiates strategies of formal and spatial operation. How many spaces are present in order to facilitate certain events? Can many different activities occur within one larger, more generic space? These questions address the density and configuration of spaces within a design.

» *See also* Scale.

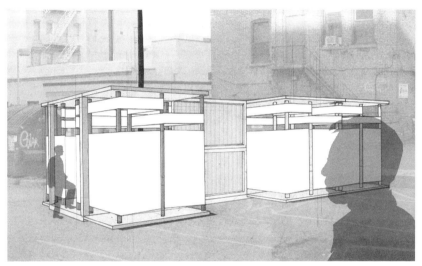

Figure 5.22.   *In this drawing, proportion is communicated in several ways. The proportion of the project is understood relative to its surroundings. Proportion is used to define certain contextual relationships. Proportion is also indicated in a way that relates the human body to the form of the design. The level of interaction between architecture and occupant becomes clearer from the proportions presented.*   Student: Bart Bajda—Critic: Matthew Mindrup—Institution: Marywood University

Figure 5.23.   *The proportion of the human body is compared to the interior space of the design by placing scale figures within the drawing. Additionally, the proportional relationship between space and occupant is understood through the inclusion of known elements—a staircase, a handrail—in contrast to the size of the spaces that hold them.*   Student: Derek Jerome—Critic: James Eckler—Institution: University of Cincinnati

REPRESENT

Communication that involves the creation of an analogue or symbol to stand for an actual condition

Generative Possibilities for Creating Communicative Products

He glued small wooden members to one another, making a frame. Additional pieces were added to attach the frame to a larger plank of wood. The larger wooden plank was just one piece of a larger enclosure that bound the frame. In all, the entire model could fit in the palm of his hand.

The frame held no glass or transparent material. It was not built as it would have been in an actual full-scale construction. However, the members of the frame defined a limit to the space within the model. They left that surface open, and represented transparency through the absence of material. The entire construct represented actual assembly by defining points of connection and general strategies for joinery.

Representation refers to the manner and media in which architectural ideas are communicated. There are different types of representation, used at varying stages of the design process and with varying goals. Symbolic representation is any communicative strategy that relies on symbols to stand for architectural elements. Generalized representation is any communicative strategy that implies general information regarding spatial condition and formal characteristics. Analogous representation is any communicative strategy through which the actuality of the architecture is replicated—the creation of an architectural analogue.

Symbolic representation is reliant upon convention. In order for symbolic representation to effectively communicate an idea, symbols that have an understood value or meaning are deployed. The architectural qualities being communicated are not inherent to the symbols themselves but rather to the element that the symbols reference. Patterns that denote material, line weight conventions, or colors of a color-code system are all examples of symbolic representation.

Generalized representation communicates through implicit information. Spatial and formal content are interpreted from the media rather then documented. Products of abstract representation communicate general characteristics of architecture. They are the products of preliminary ideas

and unresolved design intent. General representations tend to be deployed at the beginning stages of a process and used as generative products rather than documentation products. A massing model, a tonal diagram, and a figure-ground pattern are all examples of generalized representation.

Alternatively, an analogue can be used to communicate spatial and formal information. Analogous representation seeks to replicate the realities of a complete architecture as closely as possible. The analogue is a product of resolved ideas and meticulous craft. The analogous representation is communicative in that it precisely demonstrates the behavior and characteristics

Figure 5.24. Representation is a means of communication through the use of conventions, symbols, or analogues. This image illustrates the relationship between two different modes of representation. The drawing and model communicate similar spatial information using very different materials, formats, and conventions. Student: Brittany Spruill—Critic: Jim Sullivan—Institution: Louisiana State University

of the architectural form at a minute scale. The delivery of information is explicit—it precisely indicates attributes of the architecture in order to eliminate interpretation. Because of the commitment to the resolved architectural idea, this "finished model" is typically divorced from the design process; it is a result of decisions made through figural representation techniques rather than a tool for exploring ideas. Any model or drawing that seeks to replicate architectural details or building form is an analogous representation.

For each of these representation types there are three different formats: graphic representation, formal representation, and spatial representation. Each of these formats has myriad media options and communicative outcomes. However, each has certain characteristics that make it more or less applicable to different types of study or presentation. Graphic information refers to any mode of representation that is two-dimensional. It is an ever-present format for conveying information throughout the design process, from diagrams and sketches to detailed schematics and pictorial renderings. Model building, whether digital or manual, is an exercise in both spatial and formal representation. The intent of the three-dimensional representation

determines its format. A model of a detail or assembly will make it a predominantly formal representation, whereas a model that studies spatial or experiential conditions will be a spatial representation. As in other facets of architecture, these two modes of understanding a design are intertwined.

How does one determine which type of representation is appropriate, or which format to use? Representation should have a direct correlation to an outcome. Is the exercise to be a study or documentation? What aspects of architecture should it communicate: spatial, formal, or systemic? A diagram may be used to create relationships among elements. If proportions of length, width, and height are important to those relationships, perhaps it is a massing model, a figural representation of generic pieces joined. Or if it is only to establish a network of pieces, a graphic mapping of elements may be a more appropriate format. Each act of representation should be tailored to the specific study being performed and the content being presented. Representation as an act of making is also a device for discovery. When it is only communicative, it has no engagement with process.

» *See also* Symbol; Implicit; Explicit; Graphic; Space; Form.

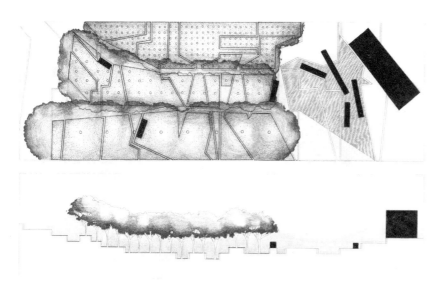

Figure 5.25. Symbolic representation is the creation of something to represent a more complex condition. In this drawing, symbolic representation is used to signify the location and relative scale of trees. Each tree is depicted by a consistent shape that varies in size according to the proposed size of the tree. STUDENT: ELIZABETH SYDNOR—CRITIC: MILAGROS ZINGONI—INSTITUTION: ARIZONA STATE UNIVERSITY

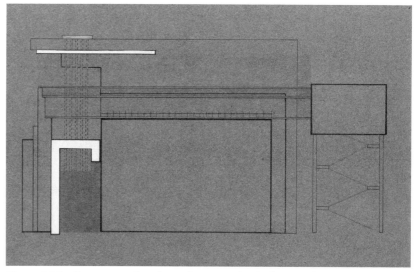

Figure 5.26. Representation through convention is the use of commonly understood symbols or application techniques for the communication of information. It is a common standard that hierarchy is determined by line weight and that a dashed line depicts hidden elements. These conventions allow the drawing to be read and spatial information interpreted from it. STUDENT: LAUREN WHITEHURST—CRITIC: JAMES ECKLER—INSTITUTION: UNIVERSITY OF CINCINNATI

SCALE

A proportion used to determine the dimensional relationship between a representation and the subject that is being represented

A standard of measure for proportion

To make uniformly larger or smaller

Generative Possibilities of Proportion

She made the model so that $^1/_8$ inch was equal to 1 foot. As she was making it, she knew that a person would be a little less than $^3/_4$ inches high. She knew how it would fit on the site for which she was designing. She also knew when she was creating spaces that were too big or small for their functions and when forms were unrealistically large or small.

The scale provided a system of measure that governed her compositional exercises. It defined the proportions she was to use. It provided a clear understanding of how her design would work if it were constructed at its intended size.

In the most conventional sense, scale is a measure of proportion between a representation and the subject being represented. It is commonly indicated by a mathematical relationship: $^1/_4$ " = 1'-0", for example. This means that every $^1/_4$ inch of a model or drawing equates to 1 foot at full size. However, there are also generative implications of scale. As a proportional system, it can be used to understand the size of a person relative to a space, or the size of a building relative to its context. Scale can also be a generative principle, in that proportion between elements impacts spatial and formal relationships.

Understanding scale as a relative proportion is sometimes a necessary part of a design process. At the beginning stages, absolute dimensions are not yet realized and are in a flexible state. However, understanding a relative proportion can be beneficial for determining spatial relationships, habitation, narrative, and other aspects of a conceptual scheme. For instance, deciding on the dimensions of a space too early can often lead to overlooking many viable possible arrangements for a space. Conversely, creating relationships among volumes using the relative proportion of habitation or event leaves the design open to more consideration and design possibilities. How many

Figure 5.27. Scale is communicated in several ways in this image. As a measure of proportion, the dimension of a known value relative to its surroundings determines scale. In this case, the scale figure has a known, approximate dimension. The dimensions of the other elements that comprise this project can also be understood by comparing them to the scale figure. Additionally, a diversity of size establishes scale: smaller elements will have a different relationship to the human body (a known value) than larger elements. The steps, screens, and small linear framing pieces all provide an approximate understanding of the size of the larger components because experience will inform an observer that these elements can be stepped on or grasped. Student: Hector Garcia—Critic: Allen Watters—Institution: Valencia Community College

people must the space hold? What will they be doing? These questions of scale, rather than preset dimensions, will provide a set of limits that respond to the demands of a project without compromising the ability to iterate or test variation.

Establishing that scale of proportion in the various media in which a project is represented is an issue of communication. Just as scale measures the proportion between elements, communicating scale requires the presence of a known quantity. The ability to intuitively measure a space in a model or drawing is often established through the inclusion of elements of human interaction. The stair is a common dimension; it is intuitively understood. Likewise, any element that is to be grasped provides scale, in that whoever is viewing the drawing has an innate understanding of the hand and what it is able to hold. Those visual keys exist in a representation's density of detail. The more easily understood proportional information in a representation, the more legible that representation will be.

» *See also* Proportion.

SYMBOL

A representation based on a standard convention

A type of semiotic element; a type of sign that relies on previously understood meaning

A simple gesture used to articulate the characteristics of a more complex condition

A simple gesture that references a more complex condition

Generative Possibilities in Semiotics

She was making a drawing that detailed a wall assembly. In it, each piece had to be indicated. The drawing was to precisely depict the way each component would come together to create the wall. Because of the scale of the drawing, however, if each component were precisely drawn, the entire document would become a confusing mass of lines and shades. Instead, she drew some components as simplified versions, or representational symbols. Each symbol was identified in a key set off to the side of the page. In this way each component was accounted for, but documented using a convention through which different types of marks were assigned various meanings.

The origins of the term *symbol* lie in *simbal*, from the Latin *symbolum*, meaning "a creed, token or mark." Currently, it refers to any element that stands for another. However, the latest incarnation of the word in the English language establishes it as a facet of linguistic theory called semiotics. Charles Sanders Pierce refers to the symbol as a type of sign, along with icon and index. What distinguishes a symbol from either an icon or index is that the reader must already know what the symbol represents. Without prior understanding of its meaning, a word or a letter would merely be an unintelligible sound or a curled line. A dot on a map symbolizes a town only because the reader knows that is how this particular map indicates the position of a town.

Its role within a system of representation lies within commonly accepted conventions. Drawing conventions and communication through coding are symbolic means of communication. They utilize an understood correlation between meaning and the symbol used to represent it in order to present information. For instance, certain hatch patterns are symbols

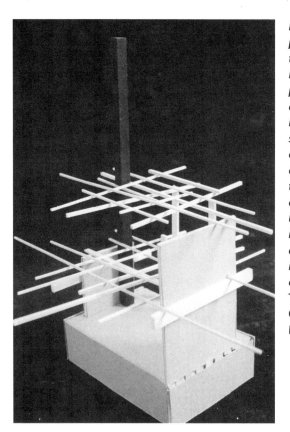

Figure 5.28. The black post toward one side of this model is a marker. It is used to indicate the presence or location of a substantial element. Its height and width signifies a hierarchy over other components. Its color signifies its distinctiveness from other components. It is a symbol because it has been invented to represent a condition with which it shares no common characteristics. STUDENT: TARA WYATT—CRITIC: KATE O'CONNOR—INSTITUTION: MARYWOOD UNIVERSITY

used to denote material in a drafted document. Colors become symbols of content in a color code.

Other designed uses of the symbol function as conceptual generators. Some spatial condition or formal assembly might be symbolic of another idea or cultural significance. The architectural gesture might come to represent a meaning divorced from the issues of space or form that define architectural thinking. In this way the symbol becomes a link between architectural thinking and the understanding of some other discipline, philosophy, or cultural condition.

What can a space symbolize? I low does that representation influence design thinking and the process of invention? In order for the architectural space or form to be symbolic of something else, that other condition must be understood by the audience intended to receive that information. Moreover, that information must be directly correlated with the spatial or formal composition used to represent it.

The memorial is an example of symbolic space or form; it requires some preexisting understanding for the underlying cultural message to be delivered. Understanding is the tool for interpreting symbolic information. As for the process of developing symbolic spaces and forms, a spatial or formal language must be established and carried through the iterative stages of a process. That language will be the way that cultural information is delivered through architectural composition.

» *See also* Icon.

TRANSLATE

To communicate an idea in another language

To alter the mode of communication (linguistic to graphic, or diagrammatic to precise)

To shift from one place to another

Generative Possibilities in Shifting Between Media or Format

Another person on the design team handed him a sketch. It detailed an idea for the building's entry sequence. He liked it and decided to continue working on that idea. He determined the best course of action was to build a model, and he began constructing elements that were only implied in the sketch.

He manipulated some parts so they would interlock more securely. He interpreted information that was undefined in the sketch in order to make constructing the model possible. Translating information from the graphic medium of the sketch to the spatial/formal medium of the model advanced the design by working out details that weren't considered in the drawn version.

Translation can be either a communicative act or a physical process. In the communicative act, information is moved from one mode of representation to another. The physical process refers to movement itself.

There are many spoken languages. Information that is communicated in one can also be communicated in another through a process of translation. Since design representation is a communicative act, there are also many ways that spoken language can be compared to the various languages of artistic representation. One point of comparison is in the possibility for information communicated in one medium to be translated to another. In reference to architecture, there are two ways that translation might impact process and communication. One is through transferring spatial information from one architectural medium to another; the other is transforming or interpreting information from a separate discipline into architectural media (ink, wood, pixels, vectors, etc.) and formats (section, model, diagram, digital model, etc.).

Translating information from one architectural medium or format to another is performed with an understanding that the same information can be portrayed in either. What advantage is then gained through translation? How does it impact the process of generating new architectural information? In this instance, that translation of information is valued for its potential to facilitate iteration and the opportunity to evaluate a design using different kinds of information. Iterative process is often spurred through translation.

Figure 5.29.   Translation is an act of converting information from one communicative medium to another. In this example, spatial information is represented graphically. From that representation, a spatial and formal construct is generated. Moving from a graphic language to a three-dimensional language is an act of translation in the design process. STUDENT: BRITTANY SPRUILL—CRITIC: JIM SULLIVAN—INSTITUTION: LOUISIANA STATE UNIVERSITY

As a designer develops a project in one medium or format, he or she will be able to reconfigure it in another. This implies a transformative aspect of translation.

Different media present information differently; the process of translating from one to another forces the designer to consider previously unexplored information sets. That logic is also the foundation of translation as an evaluative tool. The different sets of information that each media type or format portrays provides a different understanding of the architectural intent. Having multiple media and representational formats will enable the designer to assess different sets of information. This will impact both a presentation and the process of making. For instance, decisions made in a section might not be completely understood for their ramifications on three-dimensional spatial composition.

This principle of transferring information might also be applied to the translation of spatial ideas presented in other artistic disciplines into an architectural medium or format. A painter, a musician, and an architect each are able to portray both experiential and structural ideas in a variety of media. Given that there are similarities in the experiential conditions being presented, one might also be able to translate some experiential notion from the medium of one discipline into another—from music to architecture, for example.

How is spatial or formal information identified in other artistic disciplines? How can it be re-represented as architectural space and form? Music has an organizational structure that is manifest in sequence, rhythm, and time. Form and space can also be structured using these principles, but they are manifest and experienced in different ways—perhaps through the repetition of elements or an ordering of spaces. Attributes can be found through many artistic devices that are common to architecture. Identifying spatial information inherent to the product of another discipline can generate architectural intent regarding experience, composition, or organization. In this way, translation becomes a catalyst for architectural conception or the inspiration for design thinking.

Figure 5.30.   In this example, translation occurs over the course of several iterations. With each, a new study is undertaken. The result is a translation of the graphic information into a model. STUDENT: ELIZABETH SYDNOR—CRITIC: MILAGROS ZINGONI—INSTITUTION: ARIZONA STATE UNIVERSITY

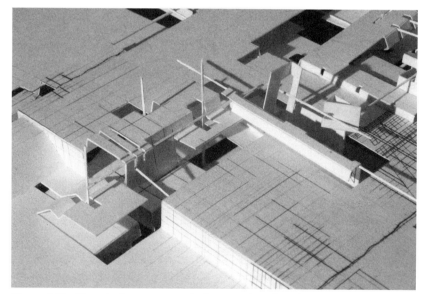

Figure 5.31.   Translation occurs as the image printed on the paper is used as a guide for the constructing space. STUDENT: ARI PESCOVITZ—CRITIC: JAMES ECKLER— INSTITUTION: UNIVERSITY OF CINCINNATI

Figure 5.32. This study began as a diagram of compositional elements derived from another source. From the diagram etched in acrylic, a constructed spatial system arises. The act of making the diagram uses interpretation to translate information from one format to another. The derivation of space from the diagram is also a translation from one medium to another. STUDENT: CARI WILLIAMS— CRITIC: JAMES ECKLER—INSTITUTION: MARYWOOD UNIVERSITY

BIBLIOGRAPHY

American Heritage, Inc. *The American Heritage College Dictionary*. 4th ed. Boston: Houghton Mifflin, 2007.

Bachelard, Gaston. *The Poetics of Space*. Boston: Beacon, 1994.

Barnhart, Robert K. *The Barnhart Concise Dictionary of Etymology: The Origins of American English Words*. New York: H. W. Wilson, 1995.

Ching, Francis D. K. *Architecture: Form, Space, and Order*. 3rd ed. Hoboken, NJ: John Wiley & Sons, 2007.

———. *A Visual Dictionary of Architecture*. New York: John Wiley & Sons, 1995.

Clark, Roger H., and Michael Pause. *Precedents in Architecture: Analytic Diagrams, Formative Ideas, and Partis*. Hoboken, NJ: John Wiley & Sons, 2005.

Cook, Peter. *Drawing: The Motive Force of Architecture*. Chichester, West Sussex, England: John Wiley & Sons, 2008.

Holl, Steven. "Idea, Phenomenon, and Material." In *The State of Architecture at the Beginning of the 21st Century*, edited by Bernard Tschumi and Irene Cheng, 26–27. New York: Monacelli, 2003.

Le Corbusier. *Towards a New Architecture*. Mineola, NY: Dover, 1986.

McCreight, Tim. *Design Language*. Cape Elizabeth, ME: Brynmorgen, 1997.

Pallasmaa, Juhani. *The Eyes of the Skin*. Chichester, West Sussex, England: John Wiley & Sons, 2005.

———. *The Thinking Hand: Existential and Embodied Wisdom in Architecture*. Chichester, West Sussex, England: John Wiley and Sons, 2009.

Peirce, Charles Sanders. *Peirce on Signs: Writings on Semiotic by Charles Sanders Peirce*. Edited by James Hoopes. Chapel Hill: The University of North Carolina Press, 1991.

Porter, Tom. *Archispeak*. New York: Spon, 2004.

Rasmussen, Steen Eiler. *Experiencing Architecture*. Cambridge, MA: MIT Press, 1962.

Semper, Gottfried. *The Four Elements of Architecture and Other Writings*. Translated by Harry Francis Malgrave and Wolfgang Hermann. Cambridge, England: Cambridge University Press, 2011

Unwin, Simon. *Analysing Architecture*. Milton Park, Abingdon, Oxfordshire, England: Routledge, 2009.

———. *Twenty Buildings Every Architect Should Understand*. New York: Routledge, 2010.

Zumthor, Peter. *Thinking Architecture*. Basel, Switzerland: Birkhauser, 2010.

INDEX